LALO ALCARAZ

GREAT COMICS ARTISTS SERIES
M. THOMAS INGE, GENERAL EDITOR

LALO ALCARAZ

Political Cartooning in the Latino Community

Héctor D. Fernández L'Hoeste

UNIVERSITY PRESS OF MISSISSIPPI / JACKSON

www.upress.state.ms.us

The University Press of Mississippi is a member of the
Association of American University Presses.

Copyright © 2017 by University Press of Mississippi
All rights reserved

First printing 2017
∞

Library of Congress Cataloging-in-Publication Data

Names: Fernández l'Hoeste, Héctor D., 1962– author.
Title: Lalo Alcaraz : political cartooning in the Latino community / Héctor
    D. Fernández L'Hoeste.
Description: Jackson : University Press of Mississippi, 2017. | Series: Great
    comics artists series | Includes bibliographical references and index.
Identifiers: LCCN 2016039776 (print) | LCCN 2016058383 (ebook) | ISBN
    9781496811370 (hardback) | ISBN 9781496811387 (epub single) | ISBN
    9781496811394 (epub institutional) | ISBN 9781496811400 (pdf single) |
    ISBN 9781496811417 (pdf institutional)
Subjects: LCSH: Alcaraz, Lalo—Criticism and interpretation. | Comic books,
    strips, etc.—United States—History and criticism. | American
    literature—Mexican American authors—History and criticism. | Political
    cartoons—United States—History—20th century. | BISAC: LITERARY
    CRITICISM / Comics & Graphic Novels. | SOCIAL SCIENCE / Popular Culture. |
    SOCIAL SCIENCE / Ethnic Studies / Hispanic American Studies.
Classification: LCC PN6727.A39 Z63 2017 (print) | LCC PN6727.A39 (ebook) |
    DDC 741.5/6973—dc23
LC record available at https://lccn.loc.gov/2016039776

British Library Cataloging-in-Publication Data available

To my sister, who has been waiting since 2004.

CONTENTS

Preface and Acknowledgments   IX

Introduction   3

CHAPTER 1   On Lalo Alcaraz and the Latino Community   11

CHAPTER 2   Lalo Alcaraz in the Context of Latino Comics   35

CHAPTER 3   *Migra Mouse*: Political Cartoons and the Immigration Debate   70

CHAPTER 4   *La Cucaracha*: An Alienated Bug's Struggle against a Hidden Norm   129

CHAPTER 5   A Q&A with Lalo Alcaraz   168

Conclusion   175

Notes   178

Works Cited   186

Index   190

PREFACE AND ACKNOWLEDGMENTS

THIS BOOK BECAME A REALITY OVER THE COURSE OF MANY YEARS, DURING WHICH I SLOWLY transformed my enthusiasm for a medium that I have always loved into a bit of an academic enterprise. It has been a meandering journey, as I had to educate myself on the ways of the US academe and the local comics industry, which is certainly different from what I used to consume back home in Latin America. The fact that I had an uncle who for a long time held the post of editorial cartoonist in my hometown newspaper must mean that, in one way or another, a certain affinity for the graphic arts runs in our family. As a child, I remember drawing proficiently. I even received lessons at the School of Fine Arts of the local public university. However, once I entered adolescence my interests drifted elsewhere, surely to my parents' relief, as one cartoonist in the family was thought enough. Yet, from a very early age, my father nourished this yearning for graphic narratives in a steady way. When I visited his downtown office, he would take time off to walk with me a few blocks south to the main branch of Librería Nacional, where I would enjoy a vanilla ice cream cup and a comic book. Usually, it was in English. My dad was very concerned about my practice of the language—he wanted to make sure his hefty investment at the local private bilingual school paid off—and, as an underhand strategy, he would con me into reading with some superhero issue (*Green Lantern*, in the Hal Jordan inception, used to be a favorite), *MAD Magazine*, or even the occasional copy of *Creepy* or *Vampirella*. This surely had a lot to do with my love of pop culture, which influenced deeply the way in which I came to conceive of the United States, as a sort of cultural playground with great rock bands, cool flicks, and comic books galore. Gradually—very slowly, I must admit—I came to terms with the fact that Latin America had its own brand of pop culture, in many cases as good or even better than the one produced and consumed by "gringos." By the time I moved to Stony Brook for graduate school, graphic novels were all the rage. I recall heading to the local Borders bookstore to browse the newest copies or venturing into the city in search of novelties, relishing the possibility of including some of them in my budding research. In time, all I managed to do was to incorporate some Quino

(Joaquín Salvador Lavado, a fixture of the Latin American comics scene) and (Roberto "El Negro") Fontanarrosa (whose production mesmerized me) into my first pieces of academic writing, no small feat in the academe of the late 1990s. Happily, I always found conferences with academics with common interests, which allowed me to travel to many places—DC, Connecticut, Florida, Illinois, Louisiana, Ohio, Oregon, Texas, Vermont, Brazil, Canada, Colombia, Mexico—to present on comics. My good fortune in meeting John Lent, who turned out to be the ideal role model for a young Latin American scholar bent on writing about graphic narratives, explains a great deal of my persistence and enthusiasm. Through it all, I even had the good luck to produce an edited volume on Latin/o American comics—an uncommon coup in the field of Latin/o American cultural studies—with my friend Juan Poblete, from the University of California, Santa Cruz, which allowed me to consider the possibility that academic endeavors based on graphic narratives were perhaps not as far-fetched as I once had deemed them. And to top things off, Georgia State University's Office of Undergraduate Studies assigned me a yearly Perspectives course that I love to teach, in which I discuss fifteen breakthrough graphic novels with a bunch of very astonished and hyperactive minds.

The fact that I landed a job in Atlanta, capital of the New South, certainly has a lot to do with my interest in immigration. California may be the beachhead in the immigration-reform wars, but the South is the region that has gained the most Latino immigrants in the past few decades and this change is very visible. As political allegiances shifted from Democratic to Republican, a wave of red covered the region and I got to witness the harsh exchange between both parties, bent on exploiting the situation to their benefit. In addition, the fact that I had to deal with a broken immigration system, having filed for my sister in 2004 and still awaiting a result (at present, although her application was approved years ago, her turn for a resident visa is scheduled for December 2017), might have contributed to my decision to cover Lalo Alcaraz's work, which I find very timely. When I met him in 2003, I thought the stars had aligned, as he categorically made his points come across loud and clear.

This text would never have come to fruition without the help of Rudyard Alcocer, my friend and colleague in my department at Georgia State, who, in due time, moved onto better horizons at the University of Tennessee at Knoxville. Rudy read my drafts patiently, corrected my English, and made helpful suggestions. I owe him a lot of gratitude. Some of the ideas in this volume resulted from a graduate course on Latin American graphic novels during the fall of 2012, so I am also thankful to the students who generously supported and tolerated my enthusiasm for comics, especially Tanja Bilakovic and Jana Ferguson, whose insightful comments stimulated my thinking and taught me new ways to see graphic narratives. Also, during the many years of participation at the International Comic Arts Festival (ICAF), I would like to thank colleagues José Alaniz, Bart Beaty, Charles Hatfield, and Ana Merino, among others, for all they have taught me through conversations and presentations. They are true masters of the art of comics research and champions of an academic practice that some folks still view as a pipe dream, regardless of how much money the comics industry continues to pour into the economy through published titles, motion pictures, TV shows, and paraphernalia. From my travels throughout Latin America, I would like to thank Óscar González Loyo, a man who showed me the amount of effort it takes to run a independent comics studio in the land of Montezuma; Ernesto Priego (whom I unsuccessfully tried to bring to the United States), the editor of *The Comics Grid* and the United Kingdom's gain, courtesy of the US State Department's inhospitality; Santiago Fernández (whom I unsuccessfully tried to bring to Georgia State), founder of the the aptly named *Cenizas*; Bernardo Rincón at the Universidad Nacional de Colombia, perhaps the leading authority in comics in my native country; Isabel Lustosa, from Fundação Casa de Rui Barbosa in beautiful Rio de Janeiro, who bears a historian's keen gaze on the practice of illustration; and, quite obviously, Waldomiro Vergueiro, at Universidade de São Paulo, who has managed to transform comics research in Latin America into the most successful endeavor with his wondrous yearly conference. Through my exchange with them, they have assisted me in thinking this manuscript through and through. At Georgia State University, I would like to thank the College of Arts and Sciences and especially Deans Lauren Adamson, William Long, and Carol Winkler, as they were instrumental in providing a sabbatical that was crucial to the culmination of this manuscript and for generous support for Lalo Alcaraz's visit to Atlanta. Vijay Shah at the University Press of Mississippi was quite graceful from the moment we met at the conference of the Popular Culture Association. His sensible opinions and practical approach added a lot to the quality of this volume. Lisa McMurtray and Valerie Jones were instrumental in the latter stages of manuscript preparation, and I'd also like to give special thanks to Anne Rogers for her wondrous copyediting. My son Sebastián has also borne the weight of this work, as on not a few occasions I have had to put things aside to persevere in my research and writing. Finally, I would like to thank Lalo Alcaraz for his patience with my many inquiries and his kindness and unflappability during his time in Atlanta.

LALO ALCARAZ

INTRODUCTION

THIS BOOK IS MOTIVATED BY A FAIRLY STRAIGHTFORWARD PREMISE. IN A TIME OF POLITICAL immoderation, when the words *compromise* and *negotiation* have been demonized and virtually banished from the political landscape, is it possible for a Latino cartoonist to play a relevant role in matters pertaining to immigration and naturalization reform, or to even play an influential role within mainstream culture? Can a cultural production relying on millennial sensibility influence the level of discourse pertinent to matters of Latino immigration to the point that it will signify an important contribution? In this text, I want to argue exactly this: that the work of California cartoonist Lalo Alcaraz may serve as a platform to test these queries and determine whether his cultural practice could play a part in molding views related to the aforementioned topics, at times, even with unintended results; that is, not entirely positive. In this sense, I contend that, as a committed cultural actor and community activist, Alcaraz is more symptomatic of the rise of Latinos within the US population than many other more recognizable cultural actors, as he happens to embody and express the degree of alienation experienced by a growing number of immigrants—sometimes not in the most politically correct fashion, admittedly.

A highly regarded colleague from a fellow public university once ventured the idea that comics and cartoons may sometimes operate in a cultural void. In my review of some of this colleague's work, I stated my difference of opinion openly, though in a very collegial fashion. As the appalling attack at the offices of *Charlie Hebdo* on January 6, 2015, has come to prove, comics and cartoons definitely do not exist in a vacuum. In due time, we agreed on this fact: as cultural artifacts, comics and cartoons are intimately linked to the current social, political, and ethnic circumstances of their production. The political times that followed have offered a suitable test for this theory. As many political analysts had predicted, the 2014 midterm elections were a significant blow to the Democratic establishment. Amid a very low turnout, Republicans took over control of Congress. Almost immediately afterward, President Obama issued a series of executive orders to protect five million undocumented immigrants. The centerpiece was a measure called the Deferred Action for Parents of Americans and Lawful Permanent Residents (DAPA). The initiative was hotly contested and Republicans threatened to block a number of presidential measures, including appointments to key positions in government, in retaliation for its implementation. To counteract such threats, outgoing Senate majority leader Harry Reid, during his final days of congressional leadership, managed to pass as many judicial appointments as possible, seeking to shape the legal landscape for some time to come. Ultimately, Obama's orders were never put into effect because they were obstructed by a federal judge in Texas. To make matters worse, on June 23, 2016, a deadlocked Supreme Court blocked Obama's efforts to protect undocumented immigrants. And so, the fact that the current immigration system is in dire need of reform remains unattended. This is the general political context of the work of Lalo Alcaraz, a cartoonist whose production is deeply influenced by the Mexican and Latino experience in Southern California—never mind the notion that, within the greater scale of things, his experience is becoming more and more representative of many Latinos throughout the entire country. In his work, be it through his editorial cartoons or his comic strips, Alcaraz advances some of the harshest critiques available in US media toward the ill treatment of Latinos, regardless of their immigration status. Hardly anything on the national cultural landscape comes even close in terms of acuity and critical nerve. In a country like the United States—such a cultural powerhouse—Alcaraz's singularity strikes as shocking, evincing penetratingly the degree of marginality of Latino cultural actors, usually unable to cross over into the mainstream.

There is a definite lack of US Latino cartoonists willing to engage the political and cultural landscape from a critical perspective. At one point, when a staff member of a museum at a nearby Southern city contacted me, hoping to locate examples of Latino cartoonists born and bred in the South producing imagery critical of societal and racial exclusion, I wondered who was more awestruck by this gap. Despite being a California native, Lalo Alcaraz's name immediately came to mind. However, precisely because of his West Coast origin, he did not qualify for inclusion in the exhibit on Latinos in the New South. Nevertheless, the inquiry motivated me to visit Chamblee and Doraville, two cities in the Atlanta metro area well known for their sizable Latino and immigrant population. In Atlanta, Latinos tend to live in small pockets, mixed in with immigrants of Asian and/or Eastern European descent. When I looked at copies of the local Latino press—*Mundo Hispánico*, *El Nuevo Georgia*, for example—as expected, I found Alcaraz's work, which had been picked up after the *Atlanta Journal-Constitution* dropped it from its comic strips page in 2003 as it tried to avoid backlash from its readers during the height of an economic crisis. In those days, Latinos, who used to be visible at any workplace in the South, were a cheap scapegoat. Sadly, beyond Alcaraz, there was not much else in these papers in terms of cartooning. Thus, the void in cultural production became evident. I really hope that in the coming years, as the population changes, younger and more talented Latinos will gain awareness of this absence and join the comics and cartoon community, a group of people not exactly known for its diversity—racially, socially, or genderwise. Latino presence is already palpable in the credits of many Marvel and DC products. It is only a matter of time before Latinos begin to assert their cultural relevance on their own terms.

Most recently, I made an inspiring discovery during a stay in Miami, which, to many Latinos, has become a glorified ghetto, with a low per capita income in comparison to other metro areas throughout the country—notwithstanding the glitz and gloss of Miami Beach. During a visit to the 2014 Miami Book Fair at Miami Dade College, one of the largest higher-education institutions in the country (with an enrollment of over 100,000), I had the opportunity to learn about the production of Creature Entertainment, a collective headed by John Ulloa and Julio Álvarez that includes the work of Anthony Dones, Juan Navarro, Ricardo Porven, Al Quesada, and José Varese, all Latino artists. At the fair, they were pitching their latest production: Zombie Years, a series that takes place in a zombie-infested Miami. It is findings like this that give me hope regarding the influence of Latinos on the comics industry. Additionally, a brief look at academic titles like Fred Aldama's *Your Brain on Latino Comics* (2009) does wonders for any enthusiast in terms of expectations for the near future. In due time, I believe cultural practitioners of this nature will begin to have an impact on mainstream US culture, as they will gain further validation from an evolving national population, more in tune with ethnic, social, and gender diversity.

Comics and cartoons are not the only segments of culture from which Latinos are missing. In spite of increasing achievements in US society, such as the first appointment of an associate justice for the US Supreme Court, Latinos are remarkably absent from the general cultural landscape. That Latinos are more visible on television does not detract from the token nature of their presence as a concession to hypothetical diversity rather than as an organic consequence of social and cultural ascent. On a general basis, television programs with Latino characters lack longevity—fellow Barranquillera Sofía Vergara's participation in *Modern Family* is the greatest exception to this rule. In cinema, Latino-based dramas or comedies fail to have the grasp on mainstream culture that African American narratives are beginning to exhibit. To many US nationals, the notion that, under current Census Bureau data, one of every six US citizens is Latino remains a mystery (by midcentury, it will be one out of three). Along the same lines, if someone were to remind people about how fifty thousand Latinos will turn eighteen every month during the next two decades, a concrete urgency would be apparent regarding the integration of this population into the US mainstream, both in terms of economic opportunity and political stature. Otherwise, the quest for the American dream will experience a massive failure and, amid growing disparity, a new, more inequitable age will dawn for the nation. As the growing imbalance between 1 percent of the population and the rest of the country is beginning to show, the conditions are ripe for the consolidation of an abysmal social gap.

It is against this contextual background that the figure of Eduardo López Alcaraz draws a stark contrast. His editorial cartoons and comic strips serve as testament for the predicaments and travails of Latinos at a time of challenge for new immigrants. They register the tensions resulting from a dramatic demographic shift. In the course of the past two decades, media outlets like FOX News and figures like Lou Dobbs or Rush Limbaugh contributed substantially to the polarization of the discourse pertaining to immigration. Rather than dispense constructive criticism, pundits like Pat Buchanan or Bill O'Reilly toyed irresponsibly with a subject that directly affects a sizable segment of the population, exhibiting a dearth of cultural sensibility and the occasional lack of information (as attested to in some of Alcaraz's production). To make matters worse, the economic downturn of 2008 brought about a backlash against immigrants, which was dutifully exploited by politicians seeking to benefit from public animosity. High unemployment and the overall malaise of the economy set the conditions for a clash between special-interest groups and the fastest-growing minority community in many states. In the South, where I live, the rate of increase in the numbers of Latinos has been simply flabbergasting during this period, given the need for cheap hand labor around the countryside and the urban service sector. In a way, from his California post, Alcaraz has chronicled and documented the development of this exchange, with political parties pitching blows at each other while families are being torn apart and separated by the federal administration.

This book is divided into five chapters. As readers will see, a great deal of its prose involves the stylistic evolution of Alcaraz as he tries to figure out a more appropriate manner for a critique of the normative cultural order, a process that has not taken place without backlash or drawbacks. The first chapter provides a general context for the comics industry and the immigration debate. It highlights the rise in popularity of graphic novels and the concurrent benefits for comics publishers in the ensuing film and television productions and an extensive popularity for superheroes. It also speaks about the Latino experience as an unappreciated workforce, excluded and exploited to the tune of millions of dollars. While the story of the comics industry is that of a vertiginous rise in sales and profile, the one of the Latino community is that of backbreaking work and societal inequity. It is an account of two very dissimilar stories. On the one hand, according to recent information provided by each label, Marvel and DC have announced they will release up to forty films in a period of six years (2015–2020).[1] Superheroes have become such an integral part of the cultural landscape that they even serve as an alternative for more sophisticated proposals, as in Mexican director Alejandro González Iñárritu's celebrated *Birdman* (2014), starring Michael Keaton. In whatever package or version, the superhero boom seems to have no end, fueling myriad expectations of growth for comics enthusiasts. On the other hand, the story of Latino immigrants in this country seems to be a never-ending tale of struggle, given the political unwillingness to seek an effective resolution for their impasse. From the time when the economy was buoyant, back in the 1990s, to the current economic crisis, which languishes dismally, little has been done to attend to the needs of people who contribute significantly to the national output in terms of services and manufactured goods. Thus, if matters seem rosy on one end of the spectrum—that is, the world of comics—on the other end—that is, the immigration debate—they are far from sorted out. In addition, within the greater context of racial politics in the United States, chapter 1 discusses how comics and graphic novels have made a name for themselves within the academe, achieving educational acceptance. Given their conjugation of words and imagery, at the present time, graphic narratives play an integral role in the education of today's youth, a generation accustomed to the power of illustration. During the fall of 2014, the place where I work and teach—Georgia State University, which has become the largest higher-education institution in the state—adopted Andrew Aydin and Nate Powell's account of the travails of John Lewis as one of the required books for the incoming class of freshmen. When was the last time a graphic narrative was espoused to fulfill a duty of this sort? Enter Lalo Alcaraz. His presence serves as a brash link between the two previously noted story lines: the burgeoning cultural practice, bent on making millions, and a segment of the population suffering from prejudice and intolerance, bent on achieving social acceptance and community recognition. Henceforward, the text notes Alcaraz's involvement in academic circles, hoping to popularize his production and to establish himself as a household name. It narrates the circumstances under which I met the artist and invited him for a short stint to present at Georgia State. Lastly, the chapter provides precious biographical information on Alcaraz, which should allow readers to contextualize his work and perhaps visualize from where many of his combative viewpoints emerge, regardless of the degree of agreement.

The second chapter situates Alcaraz's work and production in the context of the US comics industry. Before setting the context, the chapter posits a theory behind Alcaraz's worthiness as an object of study; that is, it contends that the cartoonist's work is befitting for analysis because of the way it chronicles the frictions and tensions emanating from a coming shift in the history of national demographics—the passing from a nation with a predominant ethnic majority to one in which many groups will coexist in plurality. The chapter traces the early influence of Latino cartoons, personified in the work of precursor Gustavo "Gus" Arriola and his comic strip *Gordo*. Arriola's work spans the 1940s to the 1980s, attesting to the general lack of visibility of Latino cultural production in the field of cartooning during those years. It then ventures into the 1980s with the seminal work by the Bros. Hernandez—Gilbert, Jaime, and Mario—who, thanks to their stories in *Love and Rockets*, awarded precious representation to a number of marginal collectivities, including, most obviously, Latinos from the southwestern part of the United States. The chapter next centers on the work of selected Latino cartoonists: animator and illustrator Frank Espinosa, comic-book artist Rafael Navarro, the creative duo of Héctor Cantú and Carlos Castellanos, and the Argentineans Eduardo Risso and Carlos Trillo, as well as on the way in which the career and/or work of each of these authors informs the evolution and thematic bent of the work by Alcaraz. In the case of Espinosa, his graphic novel *Rocketo* serves as an aesthetically driven, metaphorical approach to the topic of migration. Partly inspired in biographic details, *Rocketo* is one of the most inventive and arty proposals in the field of comics, Latino or otherwise. In *Sonambulo*, Navarro's *lucha*-noir comic book series, he employs the mechanisms from cultural production based on Mexican wrestlers, and is interested in upholding conventionality in a nation dealing with the embrace of modernity to deconstruct the hard-boiled genre and reveal how it is complicit in the articulation of an established monocultural norm within US culture. Cantú and Castellanos make a case for the integration of Latinos into the US population by way of acculturation and market-driven imperatives, riskily exchanging one set of stereotypes for another. Their comic strip *Baldo* comes across as the ultimate neoliberal assault, replacing sociological understanding of Latinos with data and/or research from theories of management and the field of advertising, which it is fair to admit that Alcaraz at times also considers, only with a less accommodating approach. Lastly, Risso and Trillo take a stab at the plight of Mexican American immigrants in New York City, only to substantiate the most clichéd of views on the migratory experience and to exhibit scant knowledge of US demographics.

The third chapter proposes a general critique of Alcaraz's first published volume, a compilation of editorial cartoons inspired by diverse aspects of the controversy surrounding Latino immigration, from the questioning of corporate attitudes to the appropriation of language as an excuse for harassment. In them, we can recognize the budding temperament of an individual willing to take a stance against opportunist politicians and law-enforcement abuse. In fact, Alcaraz's illustrations document the escalation of a confrontation in some parts of the country as immigration and the presence of Latinos become a surrogate way of addressing the need for acceptance and tolerance of greater cultural diversity. The text also chronicles the cartoonist's predicaments while developing a suitable vehicle for his assessments. Although effective at a local level, Alcaraz's responses are in many cases too reactive. That is to say, Alcaraz fails to embrace the opportunity to take the confrontation in a novel direction. As a result, his arguments occasionally appear as extreme as those embraced by conservative pundits and politicians, who, for the most part, play an oppositional role. It will take some time for him to find a way that is more suitable and effective. Between opposition and retorts, there is little space for constructive resolution, at least in terms of discourse. My analysis of Alcaraz shows how, despite being well intentioned, his responses sometimes do not advance the case for Latino immigration in the most practical manner and thus perpetuate a polarized atmosphere, which tends to affect immigrants' interests even further.

The fourth chapter discusses Alcaraz's production for his nationally syndicated comic strip *La Cucaracha*, which was also released in a compilation. In this case, my primary interest is to show how, by way of problematizing the barrio experience, Alcaraz hints at the implications of ethnocentrism and a hidden norm, which benefits particular sectors of the population. In other words, he finally arrives to a way that suits him in terms of a critical evaluation of the country. In the United States, the developed country with the highest level of increasing economic disparity, it is key that the general population gains awareness of how the mainstream cultural context tends to favor some groups above others. The mechanisms by which Alcaraz systematically undermines the dynamics of a hidden norm, which in our culture tends to favor mostly white, Anglo-Saxon, Protestant males, are a matter of wonder. One by one, the cartoonist discusses in detail the ways in which the politics of the market and culture privilege a few. However, the drawback of this strategy is that, by emulating these mechanisms in such a way that they occasionally favor Latinos—even if hypothetically—Alcaraz fails to deconstruct them, thus rendering explicit the structures of social, racial, and gender exclusion. In other words, through his mimicry, rather than putting forward an analysis of the inner workings of society that condone and support such disparity, Alcaraz simply identifies them and fails to move forward in a more productive fashion, eventually suggesting a nobler condition.

The final chapter includes a brief interview with Alcaraz in the hopes of offering a more nuanced approach to the cartoonist's personality. In it, the cartoonist's humor and irreverence come across clearly, at times shifting between irony and skepticism. More than anything else, the interview assists in the development of a more nuanced perception of Alcaraz as an individual and not just as a cartoonist or cultural actor. It is a brief, informative window into the sensibility and wit of a contradictory man who, if things work out in his favor, may play an increasingly pertinent role in the way Latinos are perceived and consumed as cultural participants.

Taken together, the hope is that this volume provides an accessible, comprehensive view into the work of a cartoonist who could enjoy greater recognition, not only because he happens to represent well the degree of injustice and inequity prevalent in our society, but also because, as a US citizen, he embodies simultaneously the possibility of success and the consequences of alienation—two characteristics that usually foretell achievement in our media. A recent study by Yale professors Amy Chua and Jed Rubenfeld, *The Triple Package: How Three Unlikely Traits Explain the Rise and Fall of Cultural Groups in America*, suggests that a superiority complex, latent insecurity, and strict self-discipline are traits that explain the rise and fall of cultural groups in the United States. In Lalo Alcaraz, it is possible to recognize, to a greater or lesser extent, some of these features. Nobody who graduates from Berkeley, authors a nationally syndicated comic strip, and serves as scriptwriter for a FOX animated series does so without a considerable amount of discipline, a sizable chip on his shoulder, and a substantial dose of ego. Alcaraz may be a flawed, paradoxical individual—hagiographic spirit does not inspire this text—but it is precisely his perplexing nature that renders him an intriguing subject for academic analysis. I trust the reader will enjoy meeting Lalo Alcaraz and learning about his work as much as I have.

CHAPTER 1

ON LALO ALCARAZ AND THE LATINO COMMUNITY

Race matters because of the slights, the snickers, the silent judgments that reinforce that most crippling of thoughts: "I do not belong here."
—Sonia Sotomayor, dissenting, *Schuette v. Bamn*, April 22, 2014[1]

IN THE LATE 1990S, A GROUP OF US SCHOLARS, MOSTLY INTERESTED IN THE EUROPEAN TRADItion of comics and cartoons, organized and started celebrating a yearly conference titled the International Comic Arts Festival (ICAF). The first version of this event was held in 1997 at Georgetown University in Washington, DC. The event was an incipient effort at opening the doors in the United States to an area of studies that has long held an esteemed position in Europe. Comics served as a reluctant area of study in the United States—San Diego's Comic-Con started only in 1970—yet as a scholarly subject recognized for its cultural value and economic contribution, they were far from established.

On the other side of the Atlantic, things were quite different. To the French or Belgians, for instance, comics are, first and foremost, objects of art. The authorial tradition in the field, epitomized by figures like René Goscinny (1926–77), Albert Uderzo (1927–), Hergé (1907–83), and André Franquin (1924–97), is very solid. A short walk through Brussels leads to many murals celebrating the best of Belgian comic strips. European comics exhibitions contrast patently with US comics shows, as the former tend to favor curated displays and a more regimented, class-oriented approach to the practice, given their view of the subject matter first and foremost as objets d'art. The latter tend to be an apotheosis of capitalism and marketing efforts. Admittedly, this difference is not entirely unanticipated, given the European penchant for social difference and the influence of a highbrow imaginary, so prevalent in the way many Western nations tend to practice and consume culture, despite notable exceptions. In the United States, conversely, comics conventions and shows are much more commercially driven, and fans participate with little reservations in terms of familiarity and proximity to their favorites, a likely outcome of our more mainstream middle-class imaginary, which, in the eyes of other nationalities that are more prone to high-context communication, may occasionally appear less formal.[2] Extraordinarily, ICAF was an effort to bridge both traditions, serving as a point of communication between cartoonists, scholars, and enthusiasts. A brief look at its programs can attest to this fact.[3] On the one hand, it would share related research, positing US-driven perspectives on many titles; on the other, it would add depth and a tad of contemplation to capitalist excess, apportioning international sensibility.

Subsequently, the conference gained a wider scope, opening itself—as intended—to comics and cartoon production from other places in the world, including Asia, Africa, and Latin America. By and large, my modest contribution as scholar pertained to this latter area. Through the years, the number of attendees increased and shifted in interests. In consequence, the topics covered varied widely as well, ranging from comics, nation-building, and political identity to caricature, social satire, and dissidence. Also, to acknowledge the conference's growing range of concerns, the name was modified slightly to International Comic Arts Forum. Eventually, aside from being held in association with the Small Press Expo (SPX) in Bethesda, Maryland, a site that made for many wonderful exchanges between scholars and cultural practitioners, ICAF's location shifted, moving to the Library of Congress in Washington, DC (working in close collaboration with George Washington University); the School of the Art Institute of Chicago; the White Stag Building of the University of Oregon in Portland; the Ohio State University (in association with the Billy Ireland Cartoon Library and Museum); and the University of South Carolina, among others. The ICAF crowd has been varied and changing, but a few of us have participated repeatedly, as it was obvious we enjoyed the camaraderie, rapport, and the opportunity to learn from well-versed individuals with common interests. Bart Beaty, Craig Fischer, Charles Hatfield, Gene Kannenberg Jr., Jeff Miller, Marc Singer, and, most significantly, John A. Lent were some of the habitual attendees. Although now retired from Temple University, John edits the *International Journal of Comic Art* (IJOCA), to which many of us contribute, and plays the role of father figure in this field of research, being the grand precursor of the study of comics in the US academe. For the first few conferences, among the many academics and enthusiasts participating, José Alaniz, Ana Merino, and I were the only Latinos in the group. Gradually, other Latino scholars interested in the subject started arriving, like Pedro Pérez del Solar and Enrique García, increasing the size and span of our reach within Latino/a and Latin American studies circles in the United States. In retrospect, our initial efforts must have come across as quaint, at the very least. Not only were we peripheral within the overall field of media studies—some people tend to forget comics are a medium—but, as Latinos, we were also peripheral within the field of comics studies itself (not to mention our marginality in the field of language studies, predominantly Anglophone).

Who would have thought comics were a matter worthy of research? Nowadays, happily, this sort of questioning is beyond the point. Comics have gained acceptance within academia and are now recognized for their noteworthy contribution within the cultural industry and to the overall economy. Comics have been great business in the United States since at least 1938, with the early arrival of superheroes. Increasingly, there is cognizance of the level of profit and utility apparent in this cultural practice. Comic book sales in the United States amount to between $30 and $40 million a month, but the indirect financial figures of this cultural production, particularly when you consider the close connection with other segments of the entertainment industry—Hollywood comes to mind immediately—are much higher. Movies like *Deadpool* (2016), *Ant-Man* (2015), or *The Avengers* (2012) can make millions over a weekend. As a matter of fact, three of the top ten highest-grossing films of all time are superhero films.[4] Clearly, comics are not child's play anymore. A sizable portion of what the motion picture industry and the TV networks have produced in the past forty years has been influenced by or adapted from comics. In recent years, to the public's general unawareness, the number of films based on graphic novels has increased at a steady clip. A peak at Wikipedia, that ever-growing source of information and news, confirms the large number of Hollywood productions based on comics in the past decades, not to mention the many films in French, Japanese, Cantonese, German, Italian, Spanish, and Turkish.[5] In the summer of 2014, a flop in terms of Hollywood's usual expectations, the motion picture *Guardians of the Galaxy*, based on the comic of the same name published by Marvel, was one of the few bright spots amid a season of commercial disappointments. At times, the jump in the other direction, from film or television to graphic adaptation, has added to the general public's lack of cognizance of the medium's grand contribution to mainstream culture. In plain terms, given the number of film or TV adaptations from comics—particularly superheroes—the mainstream public is beginning to lose track of when comics serve as inspiration or when it is the other way around. Nevertheless, conventions like San Diego's Comic-Con, a grand fest of popular culture, and highly rated sitcoms like *The Big Bang Theory* have highlighted the role of comics within the greater scenario of US culture. Along the way, graphic novelists, such as Alex Ross (*Kingdom Come*), Frank Miller (*Sin City*; *300*), and Art Spiegelman (*Maus*) have become renowned exemplars of US culture. Along the same lines, imprints like Dark Horse, Vertigo, First Second, Drawn and Quarterly, and Top Shelf are familiar to anyone remotely interested in the world of comics. The rise of the Internet also contributed to a greater awareness of the medium because the advent of web production greatly influenced the industry. In this sense, the turn of the twenty-first century will perhaps be recalled as the moment of a second effervescence for graphic narratives after the golden age of postwar comics.

Then again, comics are not just a matter of money. They play a key role in our cultural assessment of significant issues and predicaments. When it comes to documenting and processing key realities in the United States and throughout the world, the work of journalists/illustrators like Joe Sacco (*Palestine*; *Safe Area Goražde*), Marjane Satrapi (*Persepolis*; *Embroideries*), or Guy Delisle (*Shenzhen: A Travelogue from China*; *Pyongyang: A Journey in North Korea*) comes to mind. Graphic novels, especially popular at the beginning of the twenty-first century, have covered and analyzed the intricacies of conflicts all over the world, the rising tensions resulting from globalization and a changing culture, and the evolution and resolution of a number of controversial issues. Issues of migration, in particular, have been covered by much international production and, as we will see, by many US cartoonists, whether intentionally or not. In addition, comics are increasingly used in academic settings thanks to their appeal to millennial sensibilities. Because of the quality of their relationship with technology, today's students, bred on a regime of sensory incitement and immediate audiovisual gratification, find graphic narratives suitable for their tastes. For this reason, the way in which comics fuse language and image turns out to be an ideal vehicle for information in class. US academics (ICAF regulars chief among them) have used comics in multiple settings for well over two decades now and, if our students' response is proof of anything, it would seem that, as a tool for education and source of entertainment and knowledge, comics are here to stay, given their capability to reflect the harshest of matters in a package that, at first, appears harmless and, in even the worst of cases, turns out to be wonderfully instructive in spirit. For a generation raised on a diet of audiovisual overstimulation and used to processing information at a faster rate than any previous one—thanks to a never-ending relationship with video-game consoles, tablets, laptops, and cell phones—the complexity and possibilities of the interplay between image and words are more than obvious. Quite simply, millennials are affecting the nature and the quantity of our relationship with data. The days when interpreting comics as watered-down prose (the dated and insubstantial manner in which people used to view the medium) prevailed seem to be, happily, a thing of the past. These are the sort of matters addressed at ICAF, in which cartoonists and personalities from around the world present and discuss their work amid the dedicated attention and judicious observation of scholars and enthusiasts.

It was at the 2003 ICAF conference that I first met Lalo Alcaraz, who appealed to me because of his high visiblility within the US comics circuit. Latino cartoonists are not uncommon, but few reach national stature or gain name recognition beyond their state or region. For instance, at an event at Stanford University, I had the pleasure of meeting Cuban American cartoonist Frank Espinosa, best known as the author of *Rocketo*, a comic well regarded for its degree of artistic virtuosity. While Espinosa's record is impressive, he does not have the consistent national exposure that Alcaraz enjoys regularly thanks to *La Cucaracha*. National syndication has its advantages, regardless of the circulation of the corresponding newspapers. At the time when I met him, Alcaraz's *La Cucaracha* was one of the only two nationally syndicated Latino comic strips in the United States—Héctor Cantú and Carlos Castellanos's much milder *Baldo* being the other. In terms of content, it was, by far, more politically oriented than anything else in the Latino spectrum of US cultural production, which tends not to make waves, despite any impression to the contrary. *La Cucaracha* reminded me of the critical disposition of comic strips I consumed as a college student in Latin America, prior to my migration to the United States—Joaquín Salvador Lavado's (a.k.a. Quino) *Mafalda* or Roberto Fontanarrosa's *Boogie El Aceitoso*, to name an Argentine pair—only with a more acerbic, locally focused vein. Alcaraz, I discovered, focused like a laser beam on the travails of Latinos and migratory issues; furthermore, his intensity while discussing prejudice was contagious. Thus, I was enthralled by the discovery of this singular individual and even more by my personal realization of the politically charged nature of his production, which gave voice to the sort of criticism that I had imagined frequently but had encountered nowhere up to this point.

Latinos are habitually paraded around by the entertainment industry. Yet, aside from the music industry, in which they have managed to carve a niche of their own—a development I am not altogether comfortable with, given the resulting sense of isolationism, almost ghetto-driven, in the Latin Grammies—their visibility in other areas remains particularly limited, constricted by the need to make space for a sample of each ethnicity. In this sense, from my viewpoint, the dynamics of multiculturalism are not very organic. My recurrent problem with much of what is circulated by mainstream US media as *Latino* is that it smacks of tokenism—John Leguizamo's wonderful specials for HBO in the early 1990s are a sad example because, despite the comedian's unquestionable talent, the cable network failed to follow or establish continuity with more Latino comedians.[6] Thus, Leguizamo's work comes across more as a talented anomaly than as a rising, consecrated form of US identity. Later, other comedians (like Paul Rodriguez, George Lopez, and Cristela Alonzo) would land sitcoms or TV shows, though on a highly individualized basis. Aside from rendering Latinos in a particularly solitary or clichéd fashion, current Latino/a representation in mainstream media—think of shows like *Telenovela* (2015-)—tends to accomplish little in terms of demands for greater visibility or participation. Once again, Sofía Vergara seems to be the exception. Outstanding talents like Paul Rodriguez and George Lopez have faded into the cable channel netherland. Even police dramas set in places known for their largely Latino population—the Las Vegas–based *CSI: Crime Scene Investigation* (2000–2015) or *CSI: Miami* (2002–2012), for example—appear noticeably exempt of a generous Latino presence, so when more than a few Latino actors surface together, it appears almost anomalous. On the other hand, the thought of a police force of Latino underlings managed by Anglos in a city with a predominantly Latino population should give us pause for thought. Events in Ferguson (Missouri), Staten Island, Cleveland, Baltimore, and Chicago suggest doubts of this nature are well founded. In this respect, the US cultural industry sometimes coincides—intentionally or not—with the dynamics of Latin American television, which, when it comes to racial diversity, falls dramatically short. Viewed in context, what many Latin American TV programs reproduce is just the internalized mind-set of racial privilege of certain sectors of the population in the Western Hemisphere, as far as depicting which figures of power and authority are supposed to conform to certain ethnicities when it comes to physical appearance (obviously conflating considerations of race, class, and gender). Hence, although tokenism might seem to address some need for representation (think as far back as Edward James Olmos's role as squad chief in *Miami Vice* [1984–90]), the lack of consistency in the presence of Latinos in key roles—particularly in locations well known for a solid Latino population—continues to be troublesome.

In this respect, a brief review of the origin of the term *Latino* may prove handy. People are frequently confused by the terms *Hispanic* and *Latino*. In fact, throughout my academic career, I have been contacted frequently by media seeking to clarify the issue. *Hispanic* and *Latino* are not interchangeable, as some may think—even if the US Census Bureau pretends so. When they are used repeatedly, it is key that they are contextualized properly, particularly if one intends to discuss the work by a Mexican American cartoonist focused on migratory issues. Back in the day, when US citizens used to conflate anyone remotely connected to the Spanish-speaking world—as was the case with Desi Arnaz representing Cuban bandleader Ricky Ricardo in CBS's *I Love Lucy* (1951–57)—regardless of whether immigrants were of Spanish or Latin American origin, everyone was called *Spanish*. It was for this very reason, for purposes of accuracy and clarification—it was evident that all Spanish speakers did not belong to a single nationality—that, during the Nixon administration (1969–74), the US Census Bureau decided to embrace the identifier

Hispanic. The 1970 census was the first time the label was used for purposes of data collection. However, in the following years, the label proved inadequate and problematic. Many immigrants seemed to equate *Hispanic* with Iberian and/or European origin, given its etymological relation to the toponym *Hispania*, popularized in antiquity to describe the Iberian peninsula. Asked to identify themselves, Spanish speakers of Latin American extraction would consistently reject the label, arguing that it did not describe them properly. For this reason, the US government adopted the term *Latino* in 1997, effectively expanding and/or substituting the term *Hispanic*. However, although some government agencies, including the US Census Bureau, sometimes use the terms interchangeably, conventional wisdom has fallen along the lines of definition popularized by US cultural staples like *The American Heritage Dictionary*, according to which the term *Hispanic* encompasses people from both hemispheres, whereas *Latino* emphasizes an origin in the Americas.[7] Yet, the US Census Bureau defines *Latino* as "a person of Cuban, Mexican, Puerto Rican, South or Central American, or other Spanish culture or origin regardless of race."[8] Thus, contradictorily so, an actor like Antonio Banderas can be described as *Latino* even though he is a Spanish national. To make things even worse, while conventional wisdom identifies Brazilian Americans as Latinos, the US Census Bureau fails to do so, given their Lusophone heritage; in other words, the bureau distinguishes in terms of language. Clearly, the terms are construed in a different way by mainstream culture. To avoid the confusion, one must boil things down to basics. The necessary difference to keep in mind remains the same: one emphasizes European descent (*Hispanic*) while the other highlights Latin American origin (*Latino*). This is the commonly accepted use that I favor throughout this text. Personally, I tend to favor the label *Latino*, but, if I use *Hispanic* at any point, it will be because I am citing sources such as the US Census Bureau, which tends to use it frequently. It is also important to note that, at a very general academic level, *Hispanic* seems to be favored by East Coast higher-education institutions, whereas West Coast ones tend to side with *Latino*.

When it comes to demographics, regardless of the label embraced, data yield a more complex picture. According to 2010 data from the US Census Bureau, one out of every six inhabitants of the United States is Latino and, by 2020, this figure will rise to one in five. If current rates of national population hold, by 2035 Latinos will be the largest "minority" in a country in which non-Hispanic whites will be outnumbered; by 2044, Euro-American whites will be a minority.[9] On the whole, it seems as though a sizable percentage of the country—never mind the political system—continues to be oblivious to these facts. Nonetheless, if the United States is to thrive as a country during this century, it is of the essence that further opportunities are made available for Latinos in terms of education and work so that the country continues to grow exhibiting social inclusion rather than disparity. It is logical to expect that, by 2035, media representation will have adjusted to new realities. As a result, when one finds Latinos like Lalo Alcaraz, who share this yearning for visibility and acknowledgment of Latinos' contributions to the cultural, social, and economic landscape of the United States, there is a tendency to feel validated—a complacent response in itself, since it runs the risk of involving a less critical approach to their production. And when these two characteristics are accompanied by a healthy sense of self-deprecation and the ability to not take yourself too seriously, it is possible to feel even more legitimated, especially if one shares the belief that there is no need to be pompous or righteous to share information of this nature—that is, the fact that, unknown to the general public, Latinos already occupy relevant positions in key sectors of society—and have it contribute to an enhanced appreciation of the collective role of the community in everyday life. This is why, in part, it is important to have an early balance of the work by Alcaraz, so that reception of his cartoons and comic strips does not go unchecked from a Latino perspective.

Alcaraz's personality, imbued with a sort of defiant, confrontational demeanor—the likely result of having "paid his dues" as a young Mexican American in the California of the 1970s and 1980s, it is valid to speculate—probably has much to do with this pressing need for legitimation. After all, the cartoonist has labored indefatigably to get to where he is. If truth be told, after witnessing his participation in ICAF, I was so eager to share my curiosity for his work and examine his efforts that, shortly thereafter, I invited him to lecture at Georgia State University, an institution in the middle of its own growing pains, due in part to its politically charged location at the heart of a major US metropolitan area, Atlanta, led by progressive administrations yet enclosed by a state population with conservative leanings. A healthy dose of chutzpah and disposition for grievance would do students well, I surmised.

Lalo's 2003 presentation in Atlanta, I recall, was not very well attended (roughly, a crowd of twenty-five students, mostly undergrads)—at least, not in terms of the potential public that the affiliate faculty of the Center for Latin American and Latino/a Studies at Georgia State was hoping to attract, considering the nature and quality of Alcaraz's production. During that time, the *Atlanta Journal-Constitution* was publishing *La Cucaracha*, his comic strip about an anthropomorphized cockroach, so we assumed there would be a good turnout. (Amid the immigration-reform backlash, some newspapers—including the *Journal-Constitution*—have since dropped the comic strip; nevertheless, it has managed to survive in enough of them to maintain its nationwide status.) Judging from the general response (letters to the *Journal-Constitution*'s editor, comments among the Georgia State faculty and student body, and so on), the comic strip had struck a nerve in the heart of a booming municipal area in the South—this was prior to the Great Recession—a place where Latinos were ubiquitous as manual laborers at many construction sites and in the food industry. However, at a campus smack in the middle of a large urban area—actually, one of the few to be so centrally located in the nation—it is not easy to guarantee attendance. Many activities take place on a daily basis and the pace of things can sometimes get very hectic. Students are easily distracted and their day is packed with multiple obligations. So, Lalo's audience, though solid, was not as large as we would have hoped, eager to witness responses by the public. In my opinion, this aspect also highlights the fact that, even if a nationally recognized Latino cartoonist manages to make it to the local press, this does not guarantee immediate recognition among the younger crowd, accustomed to receiving the news via other means (Reddit, the *Huffington Post*, blogs, etc.). As I have suggested elsewhere, millennials are widely known for their lack of appreciation of conventional means of information. Given the typical attendance for the center's events, which usually fluctuated between sixty to eighty participants per occasion, we were hoping for a much larger response. Nevertheless, Alcaraz managed to confirm my inklings. His presentation was not a mere rehash of the one he gave at ICAF; he cleverly contemplated a difference in the audience, and the range of his material allowed him to tweak things accordingly. Thanks to his readiness and informality, the few students in the audience left with a better measure of the work of a cartoonist and what it entails, and what it means to have your viewpoint circulated and heard, especially if it does not happen to agree with the mainstream view on a variety of topics. In this sense, Alcaraz's presentation and its corresponding response embodied a significant exercise in the US tradition of dissent.

Inevitably, the event was tinged by the spirit of the times, when, in the course of the George W. Bush administration (2001–9), the unquestionable presence of an increasing population of undocumented Latinos was gaining notoriety in the media and being exploited by politicians across the nation to sow political division and gain benefit, even to the slightest degree. In those days of booming construction in Atlanta—little did anyone know the debacle that would follow after 2008—when building cranes were everywhere (as in Miami and other thriving cities, people would jokingly suggest the crane as the official state bird), a strip like *La Cucaracha* was too hot to handle. Just as in the kitchens of the city's many restaurants and on the lawns of its endless subdivisions, construction sites were jammed with Latinos, many of whom labored under questionable legal status. Like a drug, the US economy was/is addicted to a cheap workforce. The *Atlanta Journal-Constitution* published *La Cucaracha* for a short while, only to drop it amid the most caustic of backlashes. As a news reader, I managed to witness its brief inclusion. Despite the metro area's progressive stance, Georgia was well on its way to becoming a deeply red state, the Democrats would lose the South for more than a generation (far exceeding LBJ's renowned prophecy upon signing the Civil Rights Act of 1964), and people would take nothing from a Latino comic strip bent on demanding greater Latino visibility. Atlanta was in the middle of an accelerated demographic shift, in which more than half of its population moved in from other states, but the local middle class (including one of the most prosperous African American bourgeoisies in the nation) lacked and still falls short of an adequate sense of social or cultural proximity to Latinos.

In the early 2000s, the demographic shift involving Latinos was still too recent. Most middle-class Atlantans—Anglos or otherwise—had never even met or socialized consistently with a middle-class Latino/a, a cultural habit that figures as a timeworn norm in places like California, New York, or Texas, regardless of the degree of racial harmony. In terms of social difference, Latino/a identity in Atlanta tended to be perceived almost exclusively as a working-class construct, given the preponderance of Latinos in a wide array of positions associated with this class status. Overall, this perception might even have been the correct one, but it left little space for the acknowledgment of social mobility among Latinos. In some other corners of the country bent on cultural homogeneity—where prevailing demographics sometimes condoned a particular degree of isolation—this perception did not even register. The absence of Latinos ratified the lack of a corresponding social construct, working-class or otherwise. Such a response was and is appalling in the city of Martin Luther King Jr., where I have lived for most of my time in the United States, and it indicates the degree to which the local culture will have to strive in its hope to achieve the as-yet unattainable title of cosmopolitan enclave in a more socially traditional South, characterized by a pervasive sense of conformity in terms of race, class, and gender. In the past years, the place has made great strides, but it still falls well short of the degree of integration evident in other large metro areas of the country, like Los Angeles, San Antonio, or New York, where Latinos already occupy important political positions. And, even if Latinos make up 45 percent of the population of Los Angeles, that does not necessarily mean that a Latino should have made it to the mayor's office. That it has happened only reiterates a certain faith in upward mobility and ethnic representation. Recent research coverage in the *New York Times* indicates that, precisely when it comes to upward mobility, the Atlanta metro area lags far behind many others.[10] Along these lines, I must reiterate, my measure of integration is that a particular ethnicity is able to reach the higher echelons of government and contribute to its administration. And Lalo Alcaraz's politics tend to operate with this situation in mind.

Then again, like much of the country at the beginning of the twenty-first century, the Atlanta private sector (and the local city/state government) turned a blind eye to the severe implications of a clear double standard. As long as the economy throttled along, went the saying, why care about immigration papers? That is to say, the Latino workforce (including its emerging pockets of affluence, comprised of corporate employees or professionals) was acceptable as long as it kept its head down and remained invisible from the higher levels of private and public administration. After all, for a very long time, the Atlanta political scene has involved two main players: whites and African Americans. In more ways than one, such a predicament was not only exclusive to the city. Amid the hypothetical economic boom of the early 2000s, most of US society paid little heed to the fact that, without the many illegal workers (mainly of Latino descent), the degree of general comfort in the United States would have been plainly unattainable in a number of areas (think about produce or beef products in our supermarkets, to quote a tangible example). As in other latitudes—the case of Africans and Arabs in France, Romanians and Albanians in Italy, South Americans in Spain, Turks in Germany, Indians in the Middle East, Bolivians and Paraguayans in Argentina, Peruvians in Chile, Nicaraguans in Costa Rica, Dominicans in Puerto Rico, Vietnamese and Filipinos in Korea, and so on—the US style of life is predicated on the ready availability of an underclass. The food offered in many of our supermarkets; the building and cleaning of many of our residences, condominiums, and office buildings; the cooking of varied cuisines (from fancy restaurants to fast-food joints); and even the care of our offspring went (and goes) through the hands of immigrants. For practical purposes, the contribution of the illegal labor force was (and is) akin to a heavy subsidy (over ten million people strong) for the US economy, as many of these workers (in constructions sites, commercial establishments, office buildings, and at home) labored and continue to toil under salaries and conditions simply unacceptable to the rest of the population. A case in point: in 2005, Mexican president Vicente Fox got into trouble when he suggested that Mexican immigrants in the United States took jobs "that not even blacks wanted."[11] In the early 2000s, with such low labor costs and an apparent real-estate expansion, the US economy chugged along swimmingly until the market crashed. Even today, in times of higher unemployment, this situation persists. Statistics being what they are, as of this writing (2016), the official unemployment rate has gone from 6 percent to 4.9 percent, and decreasing, although this number is only made possible by the number of people who have given up on finding a job.[12] The dark side of it all, nonetheless, is the widespread hypocrisy in certain political circles, which tend to cloak themselves in the flag. While boasting of patriotism and nationalism, they fail to consider or even to contemplate the enormous influence of these workers on the general economy and society. As long as the politics of division prevail, it always seems to be more beneficial and appropriate to blame another group for the failings of the system. In terms of immigration, this has been the usual case in US history, as it was with, for example, Dutch, German, Scandinavian, Irish, Italian, Chinese, and Japanese immigration, each in its own time and location. Such are the societal dynamics in a place built on a tradition of hosting newcomers, so each group can labor—and be exploited—and contribute its share to the greater well-being of those who arrived earlier. Hence, it seems that it is now the turn of Latinos (and Muslims) to face this age-old opposition to the inflow of immigrants.

This is the general context in which I faced the work of Lalo Alcaraz and in which he produced the early part of his oeuvre. His intense personality and the strain resulting from his shared awareness of the persistently marginal nature of Latinos, despite having attained a critical mass and accomplished substantial progress in terms of income, also add to the controversial proclivity of his work. Thus, this tension tinges much of his production. For this reason, my main argument with respect to this initial portion of his cultural production as cartoonist, activist, and public figure is that it serves and will continue to act throughout the years as a vital testimony of a particularly sad chapter in the history of the nation, when the country not only turned its back on its proud tradition of immigration to a far greater degree than conventional wisdom would dictate and according to which it must serve as a place of refuge for outcasts from throughout the world, but also failed to acknowledge how its very own demographics had shifted. This pronounced failure to admit the changing face of the United States throughout the late 1990s and early 2000s, more evident in certain corners of the country than in others, brings the risk of squandering precious human capital, which is what has allowed this nation to reach its potential until now. Most sadly, this peril is apparent when current demographic trends forecast a radical shift in the composition of the population, with the demise of the traditional ethnic majority and the rise of a moment of plurality. Throughout its short history, the United States has repeatedly figured out that, for it to move on successfully as a whole, as a nation capable of moving on around the globe, it needs to be inclusive and supportive, so that each of its collectivities feels empowered to contribute and thrive. Not on few occasions, this inclusion has involved massive exploitation of human resources. Along the way, many groups have slowly but surely ascended the social ladder. This process has been far from smooth, for sure, but, nevertheless, it has taken place at a much steadier rate than in other corners of the world. As I have stated earlier, the usual rate of progress has generally dictated that an initial group suffers so that the next generation ranks far better within the overall US social arrangement. When the country has failed to realize this fact, economic reality has usually beckoned, as in the case of impoverished immigrants of various nationalities, women, African Americans, and the gay community, which were eventually able to gain widespread acceptance—or at least are well on their way to attaining it.

Regrettably, in the course of the past thirty years, this has not been the outcome in the case of undocumented Latinos. According to different estimates (e.g., the Pew Research Center Hispanic Trends Project, the Border Patrol), the current number of illegal immigrants in the nation (mostly Latinos) fluctuates between twelve and twenty million, notwithstanding the fact that President Obama's actions may have chipped away at this number by five million. It is no secret that the Obama administration, headed by a man whose rise to power was thoroughly substantiated by the cry of *sí se puede* (yes, we can) and intimately linked to the hope of revamping the national immigration system, has deported more people than the administration of George W. Bush, which acted with duplicity and unkindliness toward Latinos—witness many of the initiatives implemented by a Justice Department led by Attorney General John Ashcroft (2001–5)—fed by the rampant paranoia nurtured by the events of September 11, 2001. One would think that it would be in everyone's best interest for this population's migratory status to be resolved, so it could contribute more effectively to the nation's well being, including its security. However, when we look at the work of Lalo Alcaraz, it becomes blatantly clear that not only has this not happened, but also that even many of those who live legally in the country remain, for all practical purposes, functionally invisible. When it comes to a portion of the population largely responsible for the survival of the Social Security system and the success of the Affordable Health Care Act—the Latino population has more young people than any other group in the United States and, theoretically, could contribute enormously to the preservation of Social Security—the country is unfortunately lagging. This is one of the main reasons that the implementation of the health care bill has suffered because, despite its many efforts, the US government does not know how to reach out to Latinos, traditionally forsaken when it comes to greater social mobility, in a clear and operative manner. Dismissive of the importance of cultural codes along the practice of social and political engagement, many offices of the government simply lack the dexterity to engage Latino audiences in a fruitful fashion. It is no coincidence that, according to the US Census Bureau, some of the major metropolitan areas in the country with a higher proportion of Latino inhabitants are also, statistically speaking, the ones with the lowest per capita income within their corresponding groups (only surpassed by Puerto Rico)—like the Miami–Fort Lauderdale conurbation, one of the major urban areas with lowest per capita income in the country, or the metropolitan statistical areas along the US-Mexico border (packed with *colonias*, the name for the unincorporated, improvised neighborhoods lacking services from Texas to California, echoing the term for residential vicinities in Mexico)—thus tending to isolate Latinos along parallel realities in comparison with the rest of US territory. In a way, it is as though it were possible to see, before our very eyes, the partition of the United States into various separate—and highly unequal—communities. If anything, Lalo Alcaraz's work is proof that comics do not take place in a void, as I have stated previously. In fact, this is—unashamedly speaking—one of the aspects I tend to enjoy the most about his work: how it places social disparity and exclusion in a different light and brings these matters to the forefront. Thus, taking into consideration the previously described context, it is clear that graphic narratives must be dealt with in an appropriate manner, seeking to dissect their many peculiarities and the ways in which, as cultural products, they reflect the countless contradictions of the day. This is the critical objective of this volume.

Emma Lazarus may have alluded to "your tired, your poor, your huddled masses yearning to breathe free, the wretched refuse of your teeming shore" when it came to immigrants, but, throughout early twenty-first-century US society—more than one hundred years after thirty million Europeans migrated into the country, reaching a peak in 1907, when almost 1.3 million people arrived—many politicians, so absorbed in their self-interest, continue ignoring the importance of addressing key disparities in our population, chiefly among which figures the effect of a dysfunctional immigration system.[13] For the most part, Alcaraz's work qualifies as an earnest reminder and testimony that habitually generates a very heterogeneous response across the country. In not few cases, as we will see, hatred and bigotry surface easily—not unlike the primary elections of 2016—demonstrating the degree of animosity against Latinos promoted by certain media outlets and political affiliations. The politics of otherness can be a mean-spirited tool in the hands of irresponsible and ill-informed individuals, both in and outside government. In this way, the role of scapegoat of the day is blatantly clear. With this context in mind, Alcaraz's work acquires many tones of vibrancy. The early part of his production documents and chronicles how two Republican administrations—those of Pete Wilson and Arnold Schwarzenegger—and the right-wing political establishments of two states—Arizona and California—acted during this time, exploiting the issue of illegal immigration with scant constructive criticism. In the strips and editorial cartoons compiled in the texts discussed in this volume, Alcaraz's response goes from sarcastic to bitter as the level of alienation turns visible. The inflammatory rhetoric might have resulted from the powerful imagination—or lack thereof—of political leaders, but it certainly did little to assuage growing tensions between Anglos and minorities in the southwestern corner of the country, of all places. In light of these developments, more contemporary outrages, like the Arizona bill condoning discrimination of sexual orientation on the basis of religious freedom (SB 1062), seem almost predictable. As a consequence, except for a few groups with a long-lasting Republican tradition—for example, the case of south Florida Cubans, largely of Caucasian descent and benefiting from the immediate clarification of their migratory status upon arrival to the United States—Latinos have tended to side more and more with the Democratic Party, effectively suggesting the possibility of a Democratic monopoly on the White House for years to come. That such a polarization renders a disservice to the nation escapes very few because, when the two main political bodies of the country stand at opposite ends and fail to negotiate differences, few options remain available for any group in need of more definite, pragmatic representation. In other words, when a single party becomes the only possibility for the efficacious resolution of barriers, the mechanics of democracy render a disservice to any group with a concrete political interest at play—the case of any community or interest group closely identified with a single political affiliation, and thus more liable to extensive partisan manipulation, be it through the National Rifle Association or the Tea Party. Democracy is about options, yet the only seemingly available one in much of Lalo Alcaraz's art seems to be sheer outcry and objection before the prevailing inequalities in present-day USA, given the indifference of a morally bankrupt—and almost autistic, when it comes to matters dealing with immigration reform—political system. Amid this standoff, people tend to lose patience with the US government, engendering extremes like the Tea Party or Occupy Wall Street movement. Cultural practitioners like Lalo Alcaraz should know better. They ought to realize the value of our system and understand that, although sometimes impractical or elephantine, it is far superior to many of the existing ones around the world. In such a case, the only reasonable response is to proceed with the healthy exercise of dissent, hoping the system will get the message sooner rather than later.

LALO ALCARAZ: A BRIEF BIOGRAPHY

Lalo Alcaraz (born Eduardo López Alcaraz) is perhaps one of the most prolific Chicano cartoonists/artists in the nation. For more than twenty-five years he has chronicled the political and societal materialization of Latinos in the United States and, through his art, has pushed the boundaries of Chicano activism in the middle of an era that is largely post-Chicano in spirit. Unlike what many of his detractors claim so furiously—some have gone as far as suggesting his deportation—he was indeed born on US soil: in San Diego in 1964 to Mexican parents (his dad, a gardener, is from Jerez, Zacatecas). In fact, as is the case with many other immigrant parents, their travel to the United States was with the hope of seeking a better future for their child, an objective Alcaraz seems to have achieved not without lots of hard work, ample networking, and a very combative (almost in-your-face) spirit. As a San Diego native, he grew up in the vicinity of Lemon Grove, close to the US-Mexico border, which contributed significantly to his biculturalism and bilingualism. Nonetheless, in Alcaraz, aside from being an asset, biculturalism also operates as a lack, as when one is never Mexican enough to please distant relatives, nor Anglo enough to appease acquaintances or readers in the United States. The precious liminality of being *pocho* (Americanized, especially in the case of Mexicans) comes to life. Though culturally advantageous, viewed from Alcaraz's perennially critical perspective, biculturalism comes with heavy duties and responsibilities; thus his evolution as a cartoonist with a very profound critical voice. As a child, aside from being an avid reader of *MAD Magazine* and *Gordo*, the classic comic strip by Latino pioneer Gus Arriola, Alcaraz watched his mother clean the houses of middle-class white families whose economic status contrasted sharply with his own. Most likely as the result of these recollections, he tends to be very outspoken about how badly many people treated his parents.[14] Artistic ability seems to have run in his mother's family: his grandfather, though illiterate, could draw architectural plans easily and then build matching structures, revealing a great grasp of size, density, and volume. During his high school years, Alcaraz was chosen for a vocational program for graphic arts and soon mastered offset printing and poster making. During this time, his art instructor, Ms. Nichols, recognized the value of the young illustrator's doodles, influenced him, and encouraged him to follow a career based on art. She would share with Alcaraz information on prestigious private art schools of the region, like the Otis College of Art and Design, where Alcaraz served as a faculty member until 2013, much to his satisfaction. He left to work for FOX as writer for the TV show *Bordertown*, released in early 2016. About this, it is important to make a distinction between the FOX network and FOX News. Although tied in revenue, the former holds a rewarding tradition of irreverent animated TV series, like Matt Groening's *The Simpsons* and Seth MacFarlane's *American Dad!* and *Family Guy*, which make fun of conservatives and progressives alike. One could interpret Alcaraz's career move as mercenary, given financial connections and considerations. In the end, it is a matter of making a living and providing for a family, of making ends meet. Still, Alcaraz maintains that teaching college kids is infinitely more stimulating than teaching youth at the high school level, as he used to do, given the astounding level of their skills. In addition to his art teacher, Alcaraz claims that a counselor named Edge also motivated him to get ready for college.[15]

Aside from being one of the few kids from his class to enter college, he alleges his first published drawing was an angel for the school Christmas program.

In the 1980s, he attended San Diego State University, where he befriended political artist David Avalos, cofounder of the Border Art Workshop, and painter/muralist Víctor Ochoa, one of the pioneers of San Diego's Chicano art movement, eventually receiving a bachelor's degree in art and environmental design. While at San Diego State, he also joined MEChA (Movimiento Estudiantil Chicano de Aztlán), a student group promoting Chicano activism and education, and started illustrating single-panel editorial cartoons for the university's newspaper, which resulted in his first encounters with criticism: racist scribbles on a bathroom wall.[16] In terms of artistic influence, it was during his college years that he developed a taste for Garry Trudeau's *Doonesbury* and Berkeley Breathed's *Bloom County*. By then, Alcaraz was already playing hooky and making time to attend the Association of American Editorial Cartoonists (AAEC) convention, spelling out his interest in a career as a cultural actor.

Later, Alcaraz moved north and attended the flagship campus of the University of California system, Berkeley, where he graduated with a master's degree in architecture in 1991 (and roomed with state assembly speaker John A. Pérez). During graduate school, Alcaraz cofounded the political satire comedy group Chicano Secret Service and met Esteban Zul (part of the rap group Aztlan Nation), with whom he would tour and eventually work on the radio. After graduate school and together with Zul, Alcaraz launched a Spanglish-themed zine called *POCHO*, reclaiming a term that was originally a slur, used pejoratively by many Mexicans to describe a preference for US culture. Nowadays, the term's meaning has evolved and it even holds bragging rights. In due course, the zine matured into a successful website by the same name, ratifying how Alcaraz had anticipated the semantic shift. Once his wife found work at a school district in Los Angeles, Alcaraz moved back to Southern California, only to witness police brutality during the 1992 LA riots. A few months later, having shared some of his work with staff writer Rubén Martínez, Alcaraz started working for the tabloid-sized alternative publication *LA Weekly* (a sort of West Coast equivalent of the *Village Voice*), where he produced editorial cartoons from 1992 to 2010. Once he was officially employed as cartoonist, Alcaraz joined the AAEC and began publicizing his work with "L.A. Cucaracha" (as his character was known when it was published in editorial format).

In 1994, together with Zul and sickened by the Proposition 187 ballot initiative, which aimed to prohibit illegal immigrants from using state-run hospitals and schools in California, he created one of his most celebrated characters: the militant, right-wing, self-deportationist Daniel D. Portado (in Spanish, it reads like "deported": *de-portado*), a sort of *avant la lettre* version of a Latino Stephen Colbert. Through this enactment, Alcaraz proved to be ahead of the times. Together with Zul, he cofounded Hispanics Against Liberal Takeover (HALTO; the pronounced acronym, *halto*, is Spanish for "stop") and produced a mock radio ad in which Portado expressed his support for Governor Wilson's "self-deportation message." Their ploy proved to be highly successful. In November 1994, unaware of the ruse, a Telemundo show interviewed Alcaraz, still in character as the conservative activist ranting against illegals, with Zul at his side, playing the part of an extremely uneasy bodyguard. It is ironic that the term *self-deportation* showed up again many years later, during the 2012 presidential campaign, when Republican candidate Mitt Romney suggested it as a measure for the return of undocumented workers to "their countries of origin."[17] Time and time again, Alcaraz's endeavors have prompted sad cases of life imitating art.

In 1998, the Universal Press Syndicate (now called Universal Uclick), the same respected outfit in charge of strips like *Doonesbury* and Aaron McGruder's *The Boondocks*, started syndication of Alcaraz's editorial cartoons. In 2002, adapting his character to the comic strip format, he created *La Cucaracha* (thus removing the periods from the title), the first nationally syndicated, politically themed Latino daily comic strip, based on the travails of Cuco Rocha, an anthropomorphized cockroach (a way of reclaiming a negative view of Latinos), which, amazingly, was picked up by thirty-eight newspapers from its very first day of publication. After all, the term is widely known, be it through the well-known song "La Cucaracha," a popular tune of Mexican folklore that is quite familiar to the US population (most recently discernible in the horn of Michael Peña's Ford Econoline van in the 2015 film *Ant-Man*), or clichés like Al Pacino's mispronunciation of the term in Brian De Palma's 1983 gangster classic *Scarface*, a bristling critique of Latino alienation in the late 1970s; either way, the word *cockroach* is closely linked to a Spanish-speaking context. Moreover, the term *cockroach people*, occasionally used to designate Latinos, goes back to the early 1970s, when Hunter Thompson's pal, Oscar Zeta Acosta, published *The Revolt of the Cockroach People* (1973), a semiautobiographical account of a Chicano protest against the Vietnam War. Along with Cuco Rocha, the main character of the series, we have his pal Eddy López, a laid-back blue-collar Mexican American (Alcaraz's alter ego), his iron-willed girlfriend Vero (modeled on Alcaraz's wife), and Eddy's little brother Neto, the most Americanized of the group, fan of the Internet and rock *en español*. Initially, Alcaraz signed a ten-year contract with Universal. Today, despite setbacks characteristic of circulation adjustment—like when he was temporarily dropped by the *Los Angeles Times* for thirty-six hours and the audience (and some *Times* columnists) came to his rescue—*La Cucaracha* is published in over sixty US newspapers nationwide, including the *Houston Chronicle*, *Chicago Tribune*, and *Chicago*

Sun-Times, all of which appeal to readerships with a large Latino component (preferentially of Mexican origin).[18] Nevertheless, initial reception of his work brought him to the sad conclusion that many middle-aged Latinos lack a sense of irony. Early criticism was founded mostly on the failure to realize how stereotypes and clichés can be embraced as a form of cultural resistance. The amount of feedback confirming a strong disposition to read things literally on the part of the audience was simply baffling. In addition, the amount of race-driven hate mail, another occupational hazard of his profession, contributed to his degree of motivation, as he concluded that he must have done something well to generate such a level of response.

The balance of Alcaraz's production is wide-ranging. His books include a volume illustrated for US scholar Ilan Stavans, titled *Latino USA: A Cartoon History* (2000); a short anthology of some of his editorial cartoons, titled *Migra Mouse: Political Cartoons on Immigration* (2004); and a collection of his daily production from *La Cucaracha*, his syndicated comic strip (2004). In 2014, he produced another volume with Stavans, titled *A Most Imperfect Union*, in which the pair delivers a humor-driven, critical reading of US history in a bit of a call-and-response mode, with Stavans serving as the guide for the journey and Alcaraz providing the punch lines.

Throughout the years, aside from his opinionated inventiveness, Alcaraz has proved uncannily resourceful at promoting his art. As a result, his work has appeared in a number of venues, including the *New York Times*, the *Village Voice*, the *Los Angeles Times*, *Variety*, *Hispanic Magazine*, *Latina Magazine*, Mexico's *La Jornada*, and Germany's *BUNTE*. It has also been featured in a variety of media, like CNN, the *CBS Evening News*, ABC, NBC, Univision (where he has been interviewed at length by Jorge Ramos), Telemundo, PBS, Al Jazeera TV, NPR, and Spain's Radio Nacional de España. Alcaraz has been named Best Latino Cartoonist in Los Angeles by *Mi Ciudad* magazine, an honor not to be taken lightly in a city so linked to the US entertainment industry, and has been featured by *Rolling Stone*, *Los Angeles Magazine*, *Editor and Publisher*, and the Associated Press, and profiled extensively in the prominent *Comics Journal*, which covers the US comics industry from a more critical, academically driven perspective.

A core element of Alcaraz's reputation is founded on his connections to the Latino community. Like few artists of his field, he tends to combine his work as a cartoonist with community outreach and grassroots efforts. This might be because, traditionally, he views himself as part of a larger disenfranchised body. Alcaraz habitually volunteers in local Los Angeles–area schools, demonstrating his cartooning work and teaching cartoon workshops. Moreover, together with Esteban Zul, Patrick Perez, Jeff Keller, and D.J. Boxy Dee, he has served as cohost of KPFK's popular satirical talk show *The Pocho Hour of Power*, which includes discussions and interviews on a variety of topics related to the Latino community. As a result of his efforts, multiple small and large community organizations have honored Alcaraz for his work in political cartooning and advocacy for the Latino and immigrant population. His close ties to the Latino community have even resulted in official recognition by a number of government entities in Southern California. Through this process, he has received four Southern California Journalism Awards for Best Cartoon in Weekly Papers, as well as numerous other awards and honors, including the Latino Spirit Award from the California legislature and the office of the governor and honors from the Los Angeles City Council, the California Chicano News Media Association, the UC Berkeley Chicano Latino Alumni Association, the United Farm Workers of America, the Los Angeles County Federation of Labor, the Center for the Study of Political Graphics, the Los Angeles Interfaith Justice Center, and the Rockefeller Foundation. According to his official biography,[19] Alcaraz lives in Whittier, California, in an area he calls the Greater Eastside (excluding the vicinities of Silver Lake or Echo Park, he clarifies), with his wife, a hardworking public schoolteacher, and their three children, who are described as "extremely artistic."

Within the greater context of Alcaraz's circumstances, it is of key importance that, in terms of an immigrant experience, the arc of his story seems to follow well the outline of success in US society. The son of humble immigrants, Alcaraz graduated from the crown jewel of California's public-education system, an event that, from most perspectives, should not only underscore the fact that he's fully operational in Anglo society and fluent in its language and cultural codes—thus symbolizing the required level of acculturation, having embraced the cultural traits of the dominant group—but also signal his rise into prominence within a certain view of the entertainment world—at least in terms of symbolic capital, if not economic—granting him access to the greater tradition of Americana in the cultural industry. The fact that FOX hired him as writer for *Bordertown*, the adult animated sitcom created by Seth MacFarlane, of *Family Guy* fame, certainly seems to ratify this reading. In other words, while much of Alcaraz's work is predicated on the need for greater visibility of Latinos, his work in itself has risen to a critical level, in which, within a specific set of constraints, it does not suffer from an extreme lack of visibility and is in the process of being accepted—and celebrated—as an additional, acceptable form of US identity. This set of constraints includes, as I have pointed out earlier, considerations like location of publishing (for the time being, Alcaraz's work tends to be more available in urban areas with large Latino populations) and local cultural politics, which tend to influence the degree of openness to discourses conventionally identified as marginal or peripheral and ethnically driven.

Now, within the context of this biographical information, when it comes to analyzing the work of Alcaraz, a crucial consideration is his open admission of an "attitude," which is not necessarily a good or bad thing, although it implies a healthy dose of irreverence and sporadic disagreements with analysts and authorities. As a cultural actor, Lalo Alcaraz is critical of the status quo and skeptical of the printed word. That is why, I believe, he prefers to rely on the power of the image. For better or worse, his work chronicles a crucial time in the modern history of our country because it documents the longest span of time without substantial reform to the national immigration system as well as the increased polarization of the political landscape, evinced in the emergence and popularity of media outlets like FOX News and MSNBC and the rise of movements like the Tea Party and Occupy Wall Street. It also manages, for the first time ever, to voice the concerns of the Latino community from a socially committed perspective, fully aware of its tangential role within the mainstream of US culture.

As in any competent text willing to do justice to its subject, rather than a rushed job of glorification or idealization, the true purpose of this volume is to provide a critical assessment of Alcaraz's cultural production and an understanding of the intricacies of its context. Hence, it is imperative to represent him as what he claims to be: a flawed subject, with the limitations and shortcomings proper of a cultural practice in an environment fraught with pressures and antagonisms. Quite clearly, his life as an opinionated Latino cartoonist has brought about its share of clashes. Being Lalo Alcaraz seems to be no bed of roses. Among many other alternatives, heated discussion is the potential outcome of freedom of expression. Such is the price for the healthy exercise of dissent. On the other hand, this does not mean that Alcaraz is a bitter recluse bent on controversy. He travels widely promoting his work and, at every possible opportunity, cranks out jokes and fiercely imaginative comments. But, when your daily work deals with topics that are volatile and culturally sensitive, some backlash is to be expected. The cartoonist has been quite explicit about the fact that he responds passionately to injustice, hatred, and discrimination. Correspondingly, the politics of confrontation sporadically ensue. Then again, it is, after all, Alcaraz's view of injustice, hatred, and discrimination that, by and large, refers to swipes at Latinos across the country, with notable exceptions (like the Trayvon Martin case, in which the cartoonist immediately sided with the child's family; "Wrong is wrong," he stated).[20] Some of the work discussed in this volume shows the breadth of his production and his wide span of interests, at many points exceeding the limitations of Latino boundaries.

For the most part, the convergence of art and politics in his work is the upshot of what he admits to be a chip on his shoulder, the likely outcome of his critical view of the difficult working and living conditions among Latinos (as far as one could tell, including his childhood memories).[21] Alcaraz even defines the title of his website POCHO as "pissed off Chicano outcast," revealing his sense of alienation as a cultural actor.[22] At times, he even reiterates that his object is to generate anger in his readers, hoping to inspire them to condemn discrimination and change the world. Alcaraz is also very critical of the fact that Latino artists are viewed as insular when they focus on Latino matters, countering that no one else will if Latino authors don't do it. In fact, he signals the lack of diversity in the portrayal of Latinos as a fundamental problem in the perception of general identity in the Americas, given the projected growth of Latinos in the United States. As represented in his art, the true test of a melting pot is not the assimilation of people sharing a common racial background (i.e., Caucasians of various nationalities arriving from Europe during the past two centuries), but the successful inclusion and incorporation of cultural groups embodying a varying degree of racial mixture, as in the case of Latinos—particularly when race is a society's main paradigm of identity, as in the case of the United States. For that matter, the failure to understand the existence of Latinos of all races—African, Asian, mestizo, mulatto, Caucasian, and so on—further complicates the degree of invisibility of the community. Moreover, as long as Latinos are not accepted as playing a wider variety of roles within US society—thus attaining class diversity in the eyes of the public—it matters very little whether they are included as a measure of media appeasement.

In this sense, the cartoonist is unabashedly unapologetic of his political postures, condemning figures like George W. Bush, Arnold Schwarzenegger, Pete Wilson, Patrick Buchanan, and Bill O'Reilly, given the Republican Party's reticence and continued opposition to developments on the subject of immigration. For better or worse, given its inflexibility and anger at any policy shift suggesting an overhaul of immigration policy—not to mention the possibility of an amnesty, an inadmissible consideration for the Far Right—the Republican Party has become the preferred target of Lalo Alcaraz's criticism. (Which is not to say he doesn't sometimes criticize Democrats—or Dumbocraps, as he calls them.) The lack of social and racial diversity apparent in the ranks of Republicans—notwithstanding the improvised attempts to simulate diversity during presidential conventions—does not help. To this extent, it is lamentable that the Republican Party managed to come up with not one, but two white Latino candidates for the 2016 primaries—both of Cuban descent. Politicians and their cohorts are just too easy a target and, in the hands of Alcaraz, it's so much fun to laugh at their blunders. How *not* to make fun of business executive Herman Cain, who, during a visit to Miami in the 2012 presidential campaign, asked, "How do you say 'delicious' in Cuban?" Or when former speaker of the house Newt Gingrich described "bilingual education" as teaching "the language of living in a ghetto" (i.e., Spanish)?[23] It is at moments like these that a lack of exposure to difference (in terms of race, class, sexual orientation, and so on) becomes evident in US politicians. Suddenly, their true colors show and it becomes clear that being born with a silver spoon in their mouths insulates them from everyday life—cloistered privilege does have its drawbacks—and reveals its disadvantages. Take, for example, the story about George Bush Sr.'s astonishment at electronic-scanner technology during the National Grocers Association convention in Orlando in 1992, much maligned by the conservative media.[24] And it is then that Alcaraz performs at his best, refusing to give up an inch to the politicians' clumsiness.

To achieve this objective, in the course of his long career as cartoonist and satirist extraordinaire, Alcaraz has resorted to all kinds of means. In the beginning, he would promote his work with photocopied flyers. In the 1990s, he would fax copies of his fake anti-immigrant Latino organization to various news outlets.[25] The arrival of the Internet was a boon because he could circulate his production directly and reach out to his fans and detractors. Ultimately, by way of Apple computers, he embraced social media, espousing all available means to advance his art and political activism. During the 2012 elections, Alcaraz created an uproar when he surfaced as Mitt Romney's alter ego in Twitter, calling himself "Mexican Mitt Romney" and tweeting things like "My goal is to knock my tax rate down below Juan percent" as soon as it became public that Mitt Romney's father was born south of the border. This is not, many readers may recall, the first time Alcaraz has used the Spanish name "Juan" as a source of humor. In *La Cucaracha*, Alcaraz repeatedly mocks the efforts of the US Armed Forces to target minority kids, labeling its contingent an "army of Juan," hinting at the disproportionate number of Latinos in the institution's ranks, many of whom do not even figure statistically because they are legal aliens (green-card holders) enrolled in the various branches of the armed forces in pursuit of expedited naturalization.

That said, with time, Alcaraz claims he has learned to self-censor for the sake of preserving communication with the public. He distinguishes markedly between topics suitable for editorial cartoons and those relevant to the comic strip. Serious matters like pedophilia in the Catholic Church or in collegiate athletic circles are acceptable for the editorial medium, but not for the comic strip, he makes clear. The nature of the subject matter and the wide range of cultural sensibilities in various regions of the country play a big role in this consideration. During the George W. Bush administration, Alcaraz published a cartoon criticizing the president's response to a shooting at an Indian reservation, which followed the shooting at Columbine. Basically, Alcaraz argued that the response to the shooting at the reservation was muted in comparison to the uproar generated by the events at Columbine, an aspect that is very telling of the level of importance of certain populations at the political level and the diminished role they may play within the national imaginary. A newspaper in Minnesota flagged the cartoon and warned its readership about the potentially sensitive nature of its content. Within a month, it stopped carrying Alcaraz's work. Given experiences of this kind, the cartoonist has become increasingly conscious of the importance of preserving channels of communication with his readers, moderating the straightforwardness of his material in sensitive instances.[26] Nonetheless, within the boundaries set by considerations of this caliber, he remains as irreverent and intellectually inquisitive as possible.

The next few years will be crucial. They could signal his arrival to the national media scene in a big way. His second book with Stavans, *A Most Imperfect Union: A Contrarian History of the United States*, was released in July 2014 and garnered great reviews from the *New York Times* and *Washington Post*. In addition, together with Gustavo Arellano, author of the *OC Weekly*'s "Ask a Mexican" column, he debuted as writer for FOX's *Bordertown*, an animated show that satirizes the Mexicanization of the United States through the lens of a border town. It premiered in early 2016 and is already generating controversy. The presence of Alcaraz on a TV channel whose news shows have habitually pandered to the whims of the Right is a sight to behold. Yet, the fact that Seth MacFarlane underwrites the show speaks to the level of flexibility that FOX has when it comes to generating good ratings numbers (and cash flow, the ultimate goal). According to Felix Sánchez, chairman of the National Hispanic Foundation for the Arts, the show represents an opportunity, since Alcaraz "has the ability to further educate and bring a new level of consciousness as it relates to the Latino community."[27] Only time will tell. If Lalo Alcaraz's previous cultural production is proof of anything, it is that the cartoonist is dexterous enough to recalculate and reposition himself amid a changing audience. The public may change, but Alcaraz will most likely continue to be provocative, committed, and unapologetic when it comes to attesting to the vicissitudes of the Latino community.

CHAPTER 2

LALO ALCARAZ IN THE CONTEXT OF LATINO COMICS

Whenever you find yourself on the side of the majority, it is time to reform (or pause and reflect).
—Mark Twain

IT IS CRITICAL TO SITUATE THE WORK OF LALO ALCARAZ WITHIN THE GREATER CONTEXT OF Latino comics so that it can be consumed with a better degree of appreciation. To do so, it is helpful to contemplate the elements behind his art as well as the context affecting its production. Yet, as we trace the evolution of Latino comics to provide some context, it is also possible to see how the politics of immigration are represented in and affect Latino comics. With these aspects in mind, the importance of Alcaraz and the fact that his production is worthy of study become easier to comprehend. In this light, once the bearing and context of his art have been elucidated, his efforts acquire prescient meanings, providing a window not only into the recent past, documenting excesses and injustice, but also into the future, to a country in which the largest so-called minority embraces its responsibility to play a greater role in the resolution of national matters.

First impressions matter. Artistically speaking—that is, the professional quality of his imagery—Alcaraz's style may first come across as effortlessly unassuming. Formal elements in Alcaraz's art are rather straightforward given that, aside from the clarity and ease of consumption, his art is not particularly idiosyncratic. His style of illustration, for instance, fits in well within the US tradition of Latino comics authors. The outline of his characters is not especially complex and features tend to be anatomically discrete, even when it involves exaggeration, for the sake of humor. Honoring a graphics tradition for an art that at first appears easy and unsophisticated but subsequently attains gravity and zing—think Garry Trudeau or Aaron McGruder—Alcaraz's characters look better up close. Honoring Mexico's lengthy tradition of black-and-white graphics, his art is not given to great strides in terms of color and focuses instead on the practicality of its pictures, trying to make the most of simple scenarios, conflating illustration and language, à la Rius (a.k.a. Mexican cartoonist Eduardo del Río, a great elder of Mexican graphic narratives). At the same time, his no-nonsense brushstrokes always seem to me reminiscent of works like *Maus* or *Persepolis*, in which the style of drawing serves as sensible support to a narrative interest yet does not detract from communication as a methodological distraction. It is, for the most part, effective, well-composed illustration, intended to operate without a hitch. This is a crucial characteristic of his art; it becomes apparent that Alcaraz's imagery plays a characteristically supportive role to ideas and words—unlike Frank Espinosa's, in which the role of art is primordial, to make a radical distinction. In Alcaraz's work, art plays the role of second fiddle, if you will—a really good fiddle, albeit secondary. In plain terms, Alcaraz's images do not overpower the language or message, yet play a wonderfully supportive role. At times, when he takes images from other places, like highway signs, Alcaraz resembles a cultural collector, capable of capturing and tweaking images to his benefit. His knack therefore resides in generating a new context for them, allowing readers into new possibilities. Perhaps this is a big reason for his success. His use of realia, his ability to partake in objects or settings that appear familiar to many readers, grants a recognizable, friendly air to his production. In this way, most of his political messaging comes across as unpretentious and accessible. Despite being proficient in the art of illustration, the main thrust behind his work is usually the story or plotline rather than its shape or style. This certainly does not mean that his art is not competent. For all the power of its message, it would most definitely not work well without the proper packaging. Witness, if you will, the ease with which the cartoonist can imitate the style of other illustrators—Disney, Hank Ketcham, Charles M. Schulz, or Bill Watterson—as long as it contributes to his humor.

Alcaraz's humor and art are as idiosyncratic as other ethnic graphic and/or humor traditions with particular contexts and backgrounds—Jewish, African American, or Asian American. They are deeply representative of the Latin/o American tradition, which tends to be more confrontational and irreverent, yet usually ends on a light note. While Jewish graphic art is ingenious enough to dwell on a tradition of self-deprecation or disparagement (to the extreme that some decry it as prejudice), stylistically speaking, it embraces a wide variety of styles (as produced by Will Eisner, Jack Kirby, Joe Shuster, and Jerry Siegel, to name a few). Yet, for a very long time, Jewish graphic humor, given its precursor role, has been the benchmark in terms of critical spirit and the implementation of strategies to undermine an established cultural norm. From the embracing of superpowers to galvanize the neighborhood weakling to the animalization of conflict, Jewish cartooning has devised a wide variety of options to settle accounts and deal with issues of power. African American cartooning, initially born within the margins of what was culturally acceptable (including the work of Barbara Brandon-Croft, E. Simms Campbell, Jerry Craft, Charlos Gary, Aaron McGruder, Jackie Ormes, and Morrie Turner) has evolved to be subversive and prone to de-emphasize and/or reject tropes favored by the Euro-American tradition, although it comes in a variety of types as well. Stylistically, the art of early African American cartoonists resembled that of Euro-American cartoonists. Lately, as its position has progressed as the result of social advances, it seems to have grown more independent and conscious of its choices, both graphically and thematically. The design of McGruder's characters, for instance, appears more influenced by the economy and restraint of the design of manga than by other US cartoonists. The identity of his family of suburbanites, the Freemans, relies more on traits like color, stature, or hairstyle than on conventional facial features to convey a sense of differentiation, shunning Euro-American approaches to the depiction of African descent. At first, Asian American graphic creators (Thi Bui, Ellen Jo, Derek Kirk Kim, Laura Park, Lark Pien, Jason Shiga, Adrian Tomine, Jen Wang, and Gene Yang, among others) appear to be light and almost whimsical, particularly because their style seems to favor fine lines and low contrast, even when it involves edgier coloring. What most of them share in common is the desire to speak up and develop alternatives for transgression, visual and thematic, even if along a subtler, more reflective path.

To some extent, Alcaraz has benefited from all of these ethnic graphic/humor styles, integrating cues from other traditions while remaining distinctively Mexican American and Latino. Perhaps that is also why, even as Latino, he has managed to attain a recognizable profile within the national comics landscape in such a short period of time, given the easily digestible nature of his work. And he is more than a novelty; I contend that his increased presence in media is the likely result of an organic process: the eventual integration of Mexican Americans and Latinos in general into the US cultural mainstream, starting by way of California. This now brings us to context, or the conditions under which most of Alcaraz's production has taken place. Clearly, Alcaraz's work does not operate within a void. It is the result of a variety of events that have taken place before and during his lifetime. This is no mere concoction of mine. The way in which ethnicities interact is dictated by a timely reality as well as by geographical setting, by time and space. Race relations today are far from race relations fifty years ago, thankfully. And so, just as the achievements of Jewish, African American, and Asian American cartoonists set the ground for his work, the previous generations of Latino cartoonists also add a touch.

The politics of migration also contribute. A recent map by *TIME Labs* highlights how certain states of the nation—California standing notably among them—are more representative of the nation of the future than others, in view of demographic growth.[1] In it, the current racial and ethnic makeup of California, New Mexico, and Texas resembles what the entire country is expected to look like in 2060. On the other hand, states like Iowa and New Hampshire resemble the national demographic makeup of 1930, validating common criticism on their precedence during elections. Midwestern enclaves like Minnesota, Missouri, Indiana, and Ohio resemble the United States of the 1970s. My home state, Georgia, comes slightly ahead, resembling the way the country will be like in 2018, shortly into the future. From this perspective, the fact that a cultural actor like Alcaraz is so vocal about matters of immigration speaks volumes about our current transition from a nation of the present to the nation of the future, in which Latinos will represent a sizable portion of the population. The United States stands among the most dynamic societies and cultures of the world, so one could argue that this type of change has always been taking place, in one way or another. However, what most concerns Alcaraz is the documenting of a remarkable moment during which a major shift will take place, as our society's primary paradigm of identity—race—begins to evolve rapidly, perhaps more so than at any other previous moment, resulting in the end of a dominant group and in the existence of plurality rather than in absolute majority. For the first time in modern history, the prevailing ethnic majority (Anglo-Caucasians or Euro-Americans) will need to contemplate a sharing of presence and responsibility—culturally, socially, politically, economically—with other growing ethnicities (African Americans, Asian Americans, Latinos, etc.) to achieve systemic national progress, at least as long as we suppose there is a faint pretense of fairness and/or inclusion in a viable national project. With demographic change, it is granted that the illusion of an unquestioned cultural norm, representative of the preferences of a majority, will deteriorate to an evident magnitude. The lack of a dominant demographic guarantees the end of the possible substantiation of a single cultural standard working for the mainstream. Taking everything into account, what Alcaraz is interested in is in the travails and consequences of the so-called browning of the country and, at least from a Latino perspective, debunking the cultural norm imposed by Euro-Americans. In his art, it is possible to see the nature of topics that will become increasingly germane for the definition of national identity under these circumstances. And this is precisely what makes his work so pertinent and deserving of analysis: because it provides precious clues into the frictions and vulnerabilities of a major paradigmatic shift for the identity of our nation.

However, to see Alcaraz's work as part of a greater picture, it is key that we posit a diachronic view, in which various Latino cartoonists figure as part of a continuous narrative of social achievement. Because Alcaraz is one of the few Latino syndicated cartoonists nationwide, for purposes of context, it seems more practical to situate his work in a map influenced by more Latino practitioners engaged in topics of migration, some of whom are not comic strip artists, in the conventional sense of the term—like the Bros. Hernandez, Rafael Navarro, or even Carlos Trillo and Eduardo Risso, who, although published and celebrated extensively in the United States, have never lived here. While they may belong more to the realm of comic books and graphic novels, their production figures highly among the names with broad recognition in the culture and, therefore, plays a significant role in the contextualization of most Latino cartoonists, particularly if one is dealing with someone involved in the politics of immigration. Within this picture, we can contemplate forerunners like Gus Arriola, as well as the work of the Bros. Hernandez, and eventually advancing toward that of more present-day cartoonists, like Frank Espinosa, Navarro, and Héctor Cantú and Carlos Castellanos, who tend to be more representative of the current state of affairs in the comics industry. Each of these cartoonists incarnates a separate wave of migration. Arriola exemplifies the early travails of acculturation, with little possibility of dissent. The Hernandezes embody peripheral discord, resulting from an acculturation that questions disparity from the fringe. Finally, Alcaraz and most of his contemporaries personify an acculturation that, having gone mainstream, seeks to redefine the conditions of culture, speaking up and questioning the established order directly.

It is also convenient to acknowledge that, by and large, the greater proportion of Latino cartoonists has been of Mexican descent, paying tribute to the tradition of graphic narratives in the greater context of culture south of the border and replicating the overall momentum of Latino immigration into the country over the past decades. After all, according to the 2013 census numbers, Mexican Americans comprise 64 percent of the Latino population and, just on their own, slightly over 11 percent of the entire US population. It is incontrovertible that Mexico's graphic tradition plays a significant role in terms of Latino representation. From pre-Columbian times, the widespread use of imagery has been evident in Mexican culture, perhaps to a slightly larger degree than in other corners of the Americas. Think of pictographs from New World pyramids and other structures, which included phonograms and ideograms used by Mesoamericans to record calendar information, administrative data, and genealogies. Considering the extent to which Amerindian culture has survived in Mexico despite three hundred years of colonial rule and two hundred years of nationally validated discrimination, it is only sensible that an autochthonous graphic tradition prevails, nourished by Western influence and Mesoamerican endurance. Thus, it is only logical that Latino cartoonists of Mexican descent rank higher in visibility and presence than other nationalities.

Still, it is through the imperfections in Alcaraz's work, through his manifest alienation, that we may recognize what it takes to become an integral part of the national cultural landscape, especially at a time when immigration debates energize antagonisms and the lack of political reform for a broken system only adds fuel to the fire. Amid this context, it is easy to recognize that it is not an accident that immigration is so tightly woven into the thematic fabric of his production—just as it surfaced, consciously or not, in his forebears. Earlier Latino cartoonists might have faced more daunting circumstances, yet it is hard to imagine Alcaraz's career as Latino cartoonist as carefree. Given the pressure to conform—never mind (in)visibility—early Latino cultural actors had limited options. Lacking a threshold of conspicuousness, it was more difficult to attain the overall level of recognition granted to Alcaraz. Without a doubt, parts of US society were and are still not prepared to acknowledge certain brands of difference and/or even to admit them as their own. Alcaraz steps in at the peak of the moment, when the immigration-reform debate is particularly charged, providing a rich context for a critical questioning of the dynamics of US culture. What are the factors that will determine a successful integration of Latinos into the US mainstream? How will emerging tensions be resolved? How will the prevailing cultural norm respond to increased presence of alternative cultural norms? How will it negotiate differences? In this sense, it is possible to suggest that Alcaraz's success as a cartoonist is the result of a process long in the making, passing from key figures of Latino comics—Arriola and the Bros. Hernandez play significant roles, I insist—to the rise of people like Cantú, Castellanos, and even Peter Ramirez (author of the comic strip *Raising Hector*), with whom Alcaraz shares the dubious honor of authoring the few syndicated Latino comic strips available in the country.

An additional note: Within our national tradition of graphic narratives, this process crops up in many ways. It is not just by way of editorial cartooning or comic strips in the funnies. It is also tinged by the growing presence of villains and superheroes of Latino origin, which has gradually accustomed the public to the consumption of narratives founded on experiences related to circumstances south of the border.[2] In other words, in the very presence of villains and/or superheroes of Latino descent, it is feasible to recognize the consequences of migration and eventual integration of new groups into the US cultural landscape. In the world of superheroes, so pertinent to the analysis and definition of US identity during the late twentieth and early twenty-first centuries, a time focused on the valuation of transformation and alternate identities—thus an ongoing examination of difference—this is no small accomplishment. Behold the current boom of superhero films, with Marvel expected to release nineteen movies between now and 2019, and DC considering ten or eleven by the summer of 2020, according to varying reports in the entertainment industry. So, just as individual cartoonists like Navarro or Risso inform the work of Alcaraz, it is also helpful to contemplate the contribution of superhero narratives, which, after all, represent a substantial portion of the comic book industry. In fact, superhero narratives seem to be ahead of the curve, since they do incorporate Latinos into the creative process in a more generalized fashion (both abroad, as cheap labor, and at home, as well-established authors, illustrators, pencillers, inkers, and so on). Also, their effect on the marketplace is undeniable, having taken over much of the shelf space at many comic book stores. Comics are about representation, and this promotes inclusion, even if in a narrow, initially limited way, as superhero comics have managed to do. All told, during the past decades, there has been a steady stream of Latinos in the field of comics, in many shapes and sizes, and it is important to take them into consideration because they influence and contextualize the world represented by Lalo Alcaraz.

First and foremost, I cover Arriola and the Hernandezes, since I believe they are seminal figures in this field. As I have stated previously, they embody successive waves of immigration and the desire to engage the cultural mainstream according to their own possibilities. Each in their own way, Arriola and the Hernandezes have emerged as the expected result of being Latino under specific circumstances in US cultural history, and they also speak about what it means to be an immigrant or the son of immigrants in a world completely defined by an alternative cultural norm. Through a discussion of their work, we may recognize the context of the politics of immigration in the work of Alcaraz. In the case of the Hernandezes in particular, the established cultural norm begins to show signs of fraying. Arriola, however, dealt with a world far less open to difference than the Hernandezes. Arriola is a Mexican immigrant at a time when Mexican identity was merely making inroads—thus engendering initial backlash—and people were expected to renounce their previous culture and adopt new ways and a new language, without questioning. His were the times of the US melting pot, when outright acculturation was customary. A brief review of his life sheds light on some of these aspects.

In the world of US comics, the most evident forerunner to what nowadays is a very healthy vein of illustrated narrative production of Latino extraction is Arizona native Gustavo "Gus" Arriola (1917–2008).[3] Arriola is widely considered to be the established precursor of Latino cartoonists. At the time of his birth, Arizona had only enjoyed statehood for five years, so Arriola would often joke that he was from "northern Mexico." At the age of eight, his family moved to Los Angeles, where he studied at the Manual Arts High School. Most of his early career involved working for the motion-picture industry in California—with a small interlude in Arizona—and eventually for national media through his syndicated cartoon strip, ratifying in terms of geopolitical commonality the sense of regional context in Alcaraz's work. Like many initial Mexican Americans—including those who became US citizens because of changing borders—Arriola lived most of his life in the West and Southwest, remaining in states that harbored the first waves of Spanish-speaking immigrants. During the latter part of his life, Arriola lived in the city of Carmel-by-the-Sea on the Monterey Peninsula in the company of his wife and friends, consolidating an artistic, almost bohemian social circle. There, he blended in as an English-speaking, almost fully acculturated Latino.

Arriola became a renowned cartoonist after working at the Mintz Studio and MGM, among other places, at a time when Latino presence was but a blip on the radar of identity politics in the mainstream of US culture. After working there as an animator, he decided to pursue his dreams and traveled briefly to New York City to pitch his idea for a comic strip, where his project for a novel character—arguably the first Latino-authored protagonist—was accepted. Despite its crucial role in the admission of difference, when it came to the Latino population, even with its long-standing history of migration, New York was no match for what was happening at the other end of the country. Perhaps precisely because it narrates the travails of a Mexican bean farmer called Perfecto "Gordo" Salazar López—talk about a clichéd perception, yet it was one of the few relatively positive ways of imagining *latinidad* back then—*Gordo* was heavily influenced (at least at the outset) by the motion-picture industry, embracing many stereotypes. In particular, Arriola admitted to have based Gordo's preliminary persona on Pancho, the Cisco Kid's sidekick as portrayed by Latino actor Leopoldo Carrillo in the popular 1950s TV series (1950–56, although the radio series ran from 1942 to 1955). This is an aspect that Arriola at first incorporated with some reticence, given the ease of connection it fostered with an audience that was so unaware of further complexities, and ultimately regretted, conscious of its limitations for the Latino community. It seems he tried to outgrow it as soon as possible. Initially, the first run of his comic strip was rather short-lived, as the Second World War started and Arriola enlisted to work at an animation unit that made training films for the Army Air Corps, hoping to remain linked to his interests amid troubled times. Like Alcaraz, who also covers the role of the armed forces in the lives of immigrants, Arriola had to acknowledge military service as a way to prove allegiance to a country that yet did not accept his cultural background on its own terms. The war also provided opportunities to verify his patriotism in his work, as when Gordo and his friends blow up a Japanese submarine-refueling station they discovered in the Gulf of Mexico.

Subsequently, the cartoonist figured out that he could revive his creation as a Sunday strip, despite his full-time employment at the military facility. This period entailed complex logistics and the generous assistance of his wife, Mary Frances, who would eventually inspire a character in the comic strip; without her cooperation, one could easily suggest that Arriola's career might have floundered. The daughter of immigrants of French and British descent (her mother's maiden name was Ellis), Mary Frances Sevier Arriola (1914–2008) was born in Deming, New Mexico; unlike him, she was Euro-American and, by way of her charming Southern accent, facilitated his integration into the melting pot. Through these years, even the naming of their son, Carlin, born in 1946, evidenced a certain willingness to blend in. In the 1940s and 1950s (the comic strip established itself as a staple during this time, although it lasted much longer), thanks to his status as a pioneer, Arriola had to deal with a number of issues involving the education of his audience. The intricacies of Mexican culture were still unknown across the country, so Arriola had to endure what most first immigrants of any nationality must: getting locals acquainted with alternative customs and habits. For instance, during Christmas, Arriola acquainted his readers with customs like *Las Posadas* (the nine-day celebration preceding the holidays) and the piñata. By the end of the war, when *Gordo* returned to its daily schedule, the strip had also evolved stylistically, with a more mature drawing style. The line work is pristine and settings become realistic, fostering a clean, crisp look, which added to Arriola's reputation as talented illustrator. Eventually, as it matured and managed the sure-footedness to establish its own prerogatives, *Gordo* served as an introduction to Mexican culture for many US readers. In fact, it can be argued that many commonplace expressions and phrases in Spanish entered the US mainstream by way of Arriola's work in *Gordo* because the cartoonist frequently interspersed the strip's dialogue with Spanish terms. Language is key in his production, as his early strips embraced a cheeky dialect—a phonetic transcription of broken English—eventually migrating toward a more generic register. Despite the fact that, up to this point, most of his information on Mexican identity had come from books, it is possible to recognize the linguistic and cultural negotiation inherent to immigration in this period of his work.

In the 1960s, Arriola transformed his character into a tour guide, allowing himself the opportunity to play an even more didactic role. In this way, while the character played this part in the strip's narrative, it also led many readers to increased acquaintance with less commodified Mexican culture, free from Hollywood stereotypes. Arriola first traveled to Mexico in 1961, hoping to steer this shift with some of his firsthand experience across the border. For a few years, the Arriolas went there on an annual basis, infatuated with Oaxaca's colorful culture. From 1961 to 1964, the couple opened a Mexican import shop; thanks to it, they learned a lot about Mexican culture. Without a doubt, this evolution was also the result of Arriola's awareness that, back in the day, his work was one of the few venues to portray Mexicans in a positive light. In the end, the comic strip ran successfully from 1941 to 1985, a lengthy streak by any standards, and a crucial time in the integration of Latino culture into the national consciousness, considering the well-documented struggles of figures like Cesar Chavez and Dolores Huerta. One can surmise that Arriola's career as a Latino cartoonist in a time exempt of greater appreciation for difference must have had the occasional brush with prejudice, even though he landed at a privileged location like Carmel. Nonetheless, his work was widely respected for its colorfulness and art, setting a high standard in the comics industry. Charles Schulz is said to have praised *Gordo* for its color and the quality of its images.[4] It is quite telling that his final strip, in 1985, a time in which migration debates were already heating up and fostering anti-Latino feelings within certain circles—what with the Reagan administration's implementation of the Simpson-Rodino Act, among other things—alludes to "the nature of current rising tides." In a sense, Arriola and *Gordo* represent the best possible venue for the introduction of Latino presence in the comics industry, given the way the history of the Latino community has evolved, from braceros to the largest "minority" in the country.

It was around this time, during the course of the 1980s and about when *Gordo* was discontinued, that a changing of the guard took place. Many other Latinos were trickling slowly into the national comics scene, but few managed the splash and repercussion of the Hernandez brothers. The 1980s represent, without a doubt, a time of cultural transition. The Vietnam War was over and the Cold War was about to end. Thanks in part to the first oil crisis and the exhaustion of an economic model founded on an inflexible view of the welfare state, the postwar economy reached bottom in the 1970s, giving rise to the adoption of new conservative policies, with dire consequences for the US middle class. Economists like Robert Reich have argued repeatedly that it is precisely thanks to the embrace of these measures that the average US middle-class income has not risen since this time (when adjusted for inflation).[5] Amid this turbulence, the number of Latino immigrants skyrocketed. Despite so many challenges—hovering inflation, rising crime rates, a growing drug market, and so on—there was an awareness that US culture prevailed. Disco was a respite from these bad times, and punk and new wave promptly furnished an outlet for working- and middle-class anxieties. And graphic novels began surfacing, offering another outlet for new sensibilities. *A Contract with God* (1978), *Maus* (1980–91), *The Dark Knight Returns* (1986), and *Watchmen* (1986–87) all date to this time. The cultural outpouring had an impact all across the Western Hemisphere. In 1981, Gilbert, Jaime (sometimes spelled "Xaime"), and Mario Hernandez, better known as Los Bros. Hernández or the Hernandez brothers, a team of Mexican American cartoonists from Oxnard, California, self-published the first issue of an alternative comic book series titled *Love and Rockets*. In a sense, Gilbert, Jaime, and Mario are the logical follow-up to Gus Arriola: they are fully acculturated Mexican Americans willing to settle accounts with mainstream culture on their own terms. They are the sensible next step in what happens when you bring people to a new country, teach them the culture, and tell them they have to make a place for themselves: they seek to redefine the cultural order and suggest a new set of rules. Because their culture has not yet gone mainstream, they do so from the margins. In their work, they depict a new, more peripheral world, a reality in which Latinos are featured noticeably along an extended parade of recluses and outcasts; especially, the presence of strong Latina characters is rather conspicuous. This is an alternative view of US society, one in which, for a change, outsiders figure prominently. They are not just the main characters; they also actively chip away at the norm. Suddenly, California is not just a place of sunny beaches, perfect bodies, and fabulous vehicles, but rather a more divergent enclave that is more representative of the fallacies and limitations of the American way of life than of a world of fantasy and escapism. The Hernandezes do not engage in autobiographical dalliances; instead, they portray a world besieged by marginal identities, among which Latinos stand uncontested when it comes to difference. Thanks to language, which the Hernandezes manage dexterously in their comics, enclosing quotes in parentheses to denote the use of Spanish, Latinos embody the ultimate form of alterity. Compared to *Gordo*, this is a world in acute disarray, in open defiance of the Anglophone world's cultural norm. In it, aside from depicting the act of migration itself—the series oscillates between the United States and the Mesoamerican enclave of Palomar, with characters going in either direction—readers get to witness what it feels like to be an illegal immigrant. In the words of Ana Merino, "Their comics are stories that question race, gender, and ideology, and look for ends within these discourses to address readers and force them to acknowledge spaces with contradictory realities, which, in many cases, have previously stood ignored."[6] Merino also points out the naturalness with which sex is addressed in the narrative and the way in which Anglo culture is brought closer to the Latino/a experience, exempt from prejudice or inferiority complexes, as two of the leading traits of the series. In 1982, *Love and Rockets* was picked up by Fantagraphics Books (then based in

Los Angeles; in 1989, it would relocate to Seattle) and became a regular staple in shops around the country. Amid a decade marked by greed, a boom in the stock market, and the rise of conservative political agendas—fueled by the Reagan and Thatcher administrations—the series gained household status, even spanning a rock band by its name in the United Kingdom. It lasted until 1996 and was later revived in 2001, although the Bros. have been engaged in separate projects for some time.

Based partially on the underground scene of Los Angeles, with its effervescent punk-rock culture, *Love and Rockets* depicts a world in which (to the amusement of the readership, who are generally unacquainted with such candid representation) strong female leads preside over much of the action. The series is complex and imaginative, and includes occasional segues into science fiction and magical realism as well as a dizzyingly broad array of characters (à la Faulkner or García Márquez). Initial episodes include rocket ships and prehistoric beasts, conflating the past and present into one, adding a contemporary equivalent to the interpretation of alternate versions of reality from the perspective of US Latino immigrants. One of its most important traits is the fact that the narratives stand independently, although the affinity of art and subject matter is palpable. In due time, Gilbert and Jaime emerged as the mainstays of the family cartooning tradition. Although the Hernandezes have repeatedly denied the influence of Nobel Prize–winner Gabriel García Márquez (they have read him only recently, they assure critics who insist on the closeness), their work bears the imprint of magical realism—this is a point in common with Alcaraz, though from an entirely different point of view. Giving a more Latin American feel to their production, Gilbert constructs yarns around the fictional town of Palomar, where women rule with an iron fist—Luba, the matriarch and mayor, is a central character. He also manages to incorporate migratory tensions into his yarns, with race-based conflict and hostility emanating from the exploitation of illegal workers. Maricela and Riri, two women from Palomar, migrate to the United States hoping to live their relationship more openly; in turn, Steve, a California kid who has visited the place looking for the perfect wave, washes ashore after a car accident in the United States and is adopted by the locals.[7] People go back and forth across the border, underscoring its pertinence to their identity. Gilbert's stories are usually subsumed under the heading "Heartbreak Soup." In contrast, Jaime's stories are more US-centric (using the Los Angeles metro area and the local enclave of Huerta, known in the story as Hoppers, as the setting), depicting in detail an underground culture and centering on the relationship between two Latinas: Margarita Luisa "Maggie" Chascarrillo (a great mechanic, with a tendency toward obesity) and Esperanza Leticia "Hopey" Glass (born in California, she's of Colombian Scottish descent). These stories are subsumed under the heading "Locas" (Crazy women) or "Hoppers," which is how Jaime has chosen to include Oxnard—by way of Huerta—in his work. As a depiction of an immigrant subculture in Southern California, it rules uncontested. In addition, two main features of Jaime's art are the import of an alternative music scene—bisexuality and biculturalism—persistently debunking the notion of a monocultural, established norm.

Another remarkable characteristic of *Love and Rockets* is that, unlike most illustrated narratives of this period, its characters change in physical appearance over time; that is, women age and gain weight, an aspect that contributes to the realistic nature of plots, despite the occasional flights of the imagination into science fiction or prehistory (particularly at the beginning of the series). Maggie Chascarrillo's struggles with increasing weight are renowned, and Luba, the bosomy mayor of Palomar, ages through the years, remaining a fervent and dissolute leader. It is logical to conjecture that the Hernandezes' penchant for strong female characters likely resulted from a household with a strong female presence. Their mother, a native Texan, certainly vindicated all things Mexican, instilling in the brothers a pride for their *raíces mexicanas* (Mexican roots). And a Mexican-influenced perspective on life most certainly fails to include the US culture's infatuation with youth. Nevertheless, the contrast is striking in a medium so well known for its degree of testosterone and the diminished presence of female contributors and critics. (It is not lost on me that this text itself suffers from an absence of Latina cartoonists but, for the most part, this is a consequence of the market.) In their own novel way, the Hernandezes precede Alcaraz's condition as outsider, although with a twist. Unlike Arriola, who seemed content educating the audience, the Hernandezes seek legitimacy for their peripheral norm, without any excuses. In the interview by Neil Gaiman that Merino quotes in her work, both brothers speak candidly about how all media and public facets of US society remind them constantly about not being white, because being white seems to be the norm: "You are constantly reminded that you are not white in this country—by the system or whatever. I'm not saying by individuals, but in television and advertising, that sort of thing. Whites are normal and then there is everybody else."[8] This quote speaks volumes about the same established cultural norm that Alcaraz works so hard to question and destabilize. The Hernandezes, however, aren't interested in growing demographics and the cultural crossover. And so, aside from being peripheral as alternative cartoonists, their new-fangled version of Latino identity sneaks into mainstream culture through the cracks. This is not the comic strip of an Anglicized Latino ("Gordo") coerced to conform to the cultural norms of a melting pot. This is a nation in which the fissures and fragmentation proper of a more multicultural order are beginning to surface. It is through punks, gays, lesbians, undocumented immigrants, and marginal characters (like the members of the *lucha* circuit) that the Hernandezes begin to posit a new understanding of Latino/a identity that is as of yet unaccustomed to its heightened visibility and higher profile. They seem to claim, "We embody difference and it is OK." Siding with outsiders and misfits, the Hernandezes begin to challenge the cultural norm and empower new sectors of society that appear concealed under the Anglo standard. This is a side that, most probably, must have appealed greatly to Lalo Alcaraz as he matured in the context of California's educational system, developed his skills as an artist, and gained awareness of his shortcomings as a politicized Latino cultural actor.

Still, presently there are other Latino cartoonists, more or less the same age as Alcaraz, who have managed to carve a niche for their production within the comics industry, such as Cuban-born, New York–based Frank Espinosa, the author of *Rocketo*; Mexican-born Rafael Navarro, author of *Sonambulo* (a very different type of hero: a wrestler in a noir setting); and the team composed of Texan Héctor Cantú and Cuban-born Carlos Castellanos, who have enjoyed relative success with their comic strip *Baldo*. Just like Alcaraz, all their narratives pertain to or reflect on the politics of immigration in one way or another. Perhaps this is a natural consequence of being a Latino cartoonist in the United States in the early twenty-first century. Nevertheless, as fully acculturated immigrants (or sons of immigrants) in a country in which Latino culture has crossed over and joined the mainstream, each one does it on his own terms from a more conventional location, unlike Arriola or the Hernandezes: Espinosa prioritizes aesthetics to engage issues of migration; Navarro favors a more theoretical line of attack, simulating a genre to question its culture; and Cantú and Castellanos utilize a down-to-earth, pragmatic manner that is based on economic imperatives. Each one is representative of a different approach to the practice of comics; yet, as a group, they personify the wide range of possibilities, well along the spirit in which Alcaraz's work has evolved. Together, they show that the degree of inclusiveness for Latinos and their graphic work is increasing. And it is allowing for greater experimentation and more freedom of expression—ideally, for a vocal, politically minded production such as Alcaraz's. Taken as a whole, these cartoonists provide a context and framework for a graphic narrative critical of the politics of immigration. While Espinosa made a mark thanks to an innovative comic book series, Navarro established himself through a more convoluted formula, and Cantú and Castellanos managed to gain syndication in a very open, commercially driven manner. However, as a collective representative of the various possibilities for a Latino cartoonist in the US cultural industry, they all inform Alcaraz's experience and attend to issues of immigration. Comics scholar Frederick Aldama has managed to compile a list with a formidable array of Latino/a cartoonists, evocative of the present and most upcoming generations, making it clear that, to a certain extent, Latino/a comics have come of age.⁹ These four authors are included in his compendium, among many others. Nonetheless, the point I want to make with these cartoonists as examples is the degree to which an organic integration of Latino cartoonists has taken place (or not) within the US comics industry. These are authors who have managed to make the leap from critical recognition to successful publication, but have chosen a different path from Alcaraz, evincing the perils and predicaments of the cultural industry. And, by doing so, by complementing the Latino comics scene, they have, to a fair extent, shed light on the work by Alcaraz. To sum up, his production is better viewed when considered alongside that of other successful Latinos in the field.

As I said, I had the fortune to get to know Frank Espinosa personally at an event at Stanford University in 2011. He came across as an amazingly approachable, down-to-earth guy, eager to share his love of all things visual with others. A graduate of the School of Visual Arts in New York, Espinosa is best known for *Rocketo*, his gorgeously illustrated comic book series (initially released through Speakeasy Comics, later through Image Comics, and eventually as two separate volumes in the graphic novel format by Image) about the travels of disgraced navigator Rocketo Garrison, a world-famous mapmaker and explorer in a postapocalyptic Earth. In Rocketo's world, a monster called an *ull* destroys Earth. Amid a style of illustration that plays a fundamental role in the story, Rocketo fights to protect a utopian colony—where many virtuous ancestors and characters have sought refuge—from the machinations of his evil nemesis Scarletto and the powerful nation Lucerne. Aside from autobiographical overtones—for example, Rocketo is born on the island of Kova (akin to Espinosa's birth in Cuba)—it is easy to see that *Rocketo*'s narrative has a mythological bent, with postcolonial implications; in a way, its epic feels almost cyber-Greek. Technology, for instance, displays a quasi-biological nature in the story, very much along the lines of ancient narratives. In his interview with Aldama, Espinosa cites Homer, Joseph Conrad, and the myth of Orpheus as influences, all rather obvious given the hero's encounters with harpies and alien creatures (birdmen, tigermen, dogmen) in worlds that stand in for lands unknown.¹⁰ In the story, Earth's magnetic field has been distorted and the only people able to navigate it are the Mappers, a group of genetically engineered humans to which the protagonist and his main nemesis, Scarletto, both belong, problematizing the notion of difference. Skepticism among land dwellers for these chosen few is explicit throughout the story. In a way, thanks to his navigational ability, Rocketo is the quintessential migrant, going from one place to another trying to make sense of the world, exploring and hoping to find the best for those he cares about. Migration is not always the prevalent topic, but the inclination for exploration and crisscrossing the world from one end to another is especially clear.

At the end of the first volume, Espinosa hints at the fact that the essence of *Rocketo* is found in Espinosa's arrival to New York from Cuba—he arrived in the Big Apple at the age of seven—when he went from a world frozen in the late 1950s to a place hooked on modernity. Even if the place was going through rough economic times, next to Cuba and its time warp, the New York of the 1970s definitely felt cutting edge. Espinosa also includes a picture of his family and a few lines about his parents' valor as explorers, which granted him the opportunity of a life in a new world. My reading—that Rocketo's peripatetic ways speak to a world in which national boundaries are to be questioned—is substantiated by Espinosa's concession. Immigration may not always be the central topic in *Rocketo*, but it does play a key role in the narrative. I did not choose to discuss the cartoonist because his work informed directly the issue of migration; that would be akin to saying that, just because he is Latino, he is obliged to attend the issue of immigration and the breakdown of the country's Citizenship and Immigration Services in some form or fashion through his work. Clearly, this is not his thing; at least not the main one. In fact, I chose Espinosa precisely for the opposite reason: because he is a great example of a Latino cartoonist who has managed to succeed with other prerogatives, mostly aesthetically driven, as his guide; because the main premise behind his art is his love of motion and how it can be portrayed accurately (*Rocketo* feels very lively to the eye); because he exemplifies how, although evidently Latino, his imagination searches and creates worlds beyond, and is not limited to the daily context of a humdrum experience in the United States; because, within the present group of Latino cartoonists, his drawing style best exemplifies the understanding of comics as art, with scrupulous attention to detail. As Alcaraz reminds us, we may be Latinos, but our interests are and are not amazingly mainstream at the very same time.

In Espinosa's lavish imagery, nothing is accidental. Every single brushstroke of shade or texture is there for a reason. In plain terms, Espinosa's style of illustration is, by far, the most sophisticated one I have encountered among the current generation of Latino cartoonists. It is extremely kinetic, bold, and loose, with tons of negative space—very seldom have I seen a comic with so much usage and reliance on the concept—and spare use of color (embracing a mostly two-tone hue: one as background and another one for contrast). In *Rocketo*, Espinosa has single-handedly done away with the black line, borders, gutters—anything that suggests restraint. And it looks beautiful, making great art. More than comics as art, it feels like a story that has emerged from—as a by-product of—the art, which attains foundational nature. Out of the entire crop of current cartoonists, his style comes the closest to deserving the designation *avant-garde*, which awards a demanding quality to his production. Readers seeking gratification from sensory stimulation through imagery usually enjoy Espinosa's work best, aside from the fanciful temperament of his stories. Yet, despite the superb quality of his work, like most Latino/a cartoonists, Espinosa's trajectory has been eclectic: he worked for both Disney and Warner Brothers, taught at MIT, lectured at Ohio State, developed a comic book series for Princeton and a graphic novel for Salvatore Ferragamo, and reached acclaim with *Rocketo* and his work in Glen Brunswick's *Killing Girl* for Image Comics, only to set up shop with Zum Zum Books in Italy. Raised in New York, Espinosa is very much an East Coast product, typifying the sort of journey undertaken by a Latino cartoonist more interested in the idea of beauty; that is, paying special attention to form rather than function. In this sense, his work stands in sharp contrast to Alcaraz's, who, though caring about form, is far more focused on message.

Although I am positive Espinosa is no stranger to what it means to have grown up Latino/a in the New York metro area, the fact that he is Cuban (actually, he is Afro-Cuban, which makes for a very different take from most well-known cultural actors of Cuban descent) does manage to inform his approach to comics. Traditionally speaking, Cubans have fared better than most Latinos when it comes to immigration, given the special policies in place to facilitate their migration into the country. Unlike most Latinos, the legal status of Cubans is clarified at a relatively quick pace, easing the weight of their burden as undocumented aliens. In this sense, I am positive Espinosa did not have to deal with the threat of illegality as do many other immigrants of different nationalities, tied up as they are in the backlog of the system (instead, he had to deal with life in Hudson Heights). This does not mean that Espinosa is unaware of the dilemma of many fellow Latinos, but it is clear that an open assault on the failure to reform the immigration system does not figure as a priority within his story lines—even if metaphorically, as I have just suggested, *Rocketo* comes across as the narrative of the ultimate migrant. This explains, for the most part, Espinosa's aesthetically driven, imaginative approach to the experience of migration; although it involves challenges, it also includes an element of wonder—not fear, as for many others—given the assurance of the resolution of the legal situation. In the United States, perhaps because of the country's history as a destination for immigrants, aside from a few experiences exploited mediatically—the case of the Sudanese, for instance—precious few people contemplate heartbreak or fear as the primary corollary of the act of migration; in the national imaginary, it is coded as an experience of hope, as an opportunity to remake one's self. While it is fairly certain that at some point Espinosa faced prejudice—given his Afro-Cuban, peripheral context—in terms of documentation, he was most likely spared the inherent anxiety of lack of legal definition. It is hard to assess how this failure to experience distress from naturalization uncertainty could have affected Espinosa and his work in a direct manner, but it surely makes for a very different perspective from those of other nationalities, whose story usually includes this aspect within their family circle. Thus, it colors to some extent the cartoonist's proclivity for demanding aesthetics rather than the power of the story line. Espinosa is an aesthete; this much is clear. And though his yarn can be read as a take on migratory issues, it is refreshing to contemplate the possibility of a successful Latino cartoonist with an affinity for aesthetics who is capable of succeeding with an oeuvre that stands out for the power of its graphic virtues, with only emblematic allusion to its creator's origin.

The case of Rafael Navarro is somewhat different, as Navarro is, like Alcaraz, a product of the West Coast. Like Espinosa, Navarro was born elsewhere—in Nogales, Sonora, right across the border—but landed in the United States (in Bell Gardens, California) at a very early age (two, in his case). Just like Espinosa, he grew up reading comics and cites Jack Kirby, Frank Robbins, and Jim Steranko as influences.[11] Navarro is best known for his comic book series *Sonambulo* (Nightwalker), in which the influence of an American cultural tradition is plainer, given the overall context of hard-boiled narratives, so fixed in the world of the postwar economic boom and the unprecedented rise of a middle class (thus far only surpassed in numbers by China's formidable monetary ascent). His story line is best described as *lucha*-noir, a combination of Mexican wrestler comic book tradition and Californian noir. It is important to note that in 1996, when Navarro started publishing his character, he was the first cartoonist to explore the genre; later on, Marvel, DC, and Dark Horse all followed with analogous creations. Mexican elements are most conspicuous in the main character's origin and recurrent references—in circumstantial or concrete fashion—to the land south of the border, where Navarro spent most of his vacation time as a child, nurturing a powerful bond. *Sonambulo* narrates the story of Salomon "Sonambulo" Lopez, a wrestler who is shot and left for dead after refusing to work for the mob. As a result, he falls into a deep sleep that lasts decades (a tip of the hat to Raymond Chandler's *The Big Sleep*) and wakes up with the power to read people's dreams, as well as with the inability to fall asleep again. As a character, he is given to constant ruminations on Mexican idiosyncrasy or history, not a small thing for a nationality so bent on revisionism. In fact, this aspect of the comic allows Navarro to give the story a very Mexican temperament. However, this persistent attachment to aspects of Mexican culture heightens the contrast with the surrounding world, extracted from the postwar era, with reminiscent architecture and automobiles, and echoing the noir setting of early Hollywood examples of the genre. And so, as a cultural product, it is hard to find another comic that combines so ingeniously the cultural codes from both countries, speaking not so much about bilingualism, but more about biculturalism, an auspicious by-product of migration. In addition, ever faithful to the genre's conventions, Navarro has even created a young, always dutiful secretary for his detective, much like Sam Spade's Effie or Mike Hammer's Velda. In this instance it is a jovial Latina named Xochil, hinting at Amerindian descent (in Nahuatl, the name means *flower* or *song*, given Aztec penchant for diphrasism), as is the case for the vast majority of Mexican Americans. That is to say, Navarro translates into Mexican culture the narrative conventions of a genre indicative of postwar US society. On more than one occasion, Xochil contributes efficiently to the resolution of the plot.

As in Espinosa's case, only in a different way, visuals are highly relevant to the story in *Sonambulo*. Although it is set in the present, its imagery emphasizes designs highly compatible with the 1930s, 1940s, or 1950s, establishing a tangible bond with the world of pulp fiction and film noir. Sonambulo's first ride evokes the lines of postwar classics, like Hudsons or Packards. It is soon replaced by recognizable, curvilinear Ford or Saab convertibles, vehicles that, while perhaps not mechanically impressive, certainly make a design statement. Art deco is the preponderant architectural style in several stories. The fact that Navarro attended the Art Center College of Design in Pasadena might have something to do with this attention to detail. Furthermore, the story's images are in black and white, favoring a style vaguely evocative of Mexico's golden age of comic books, significantly less reliant on color than its US version. In all, *Sonambulo* seems the type of comic that well deserves recognition for the inventiveness of its art, combining two cultural traditions with great skill. It is, without question, a testament to Navarro's biculturalism; in a way, he practices bi-aesthetics, favoring graphic cues valued by each culture. In 1996, in recognition of the comic's great promise, the Xeric Foundation awarded him a grant to publish *Sonambulo: Sleep of the Just*, the opening series.

Present-day analysis of Chicano/a detective fiction endorses the notion that contemporary detective-genre authors use crime fiction to subvert the underlying value system of the dominant ethos of US culture.[12] That is to say, in the majority of cases, noir narratives are about the weak—usually personified by an underdog, endorsing a peripheral view of events—devising a way to subvert the system and level the playing field; in a nutshell, a struggle by the powerless to bypass the schemes of the all-powerful. There are obvious affinities with the work of Alcaraz; in a world of humans, a cockroach reigns supreme. Under usual circumstances, this kind of criticism alludes to the intricacies of different belief systems, be it folk stories or superstition—as dramatically portrayed in *Sonambulo*, with habitual encounters with cults, demons, and various sorts of esoteric figures. This interplay not only alludes to the Mexican propensity for folk stories, but also to California's weakness for the bizarre. So, even in this manner, *Sonambulo* addresses biculturalism. Nonetheless, my primary contention for this comic is that its object is to contest and counter customary assertions about the ways of Mexican identity in the US context. From this perspective, Navarro rewrites detective fiction by parodying the hard-boiled genre. *Sonambulo* is a harsh remake of an archetypical noir text, and it tries to criticize the makings of a society by deconstructing a genre that, in itself, was developed as a critical assault on the US middle class. In other words, while noir emerged initially from the desire to assess what lurked beneath the middle class's gleaming prosperity, thus validating the critical disposition of the Anglo order, in *Sonambulo*'s case, conformity is enacted by way of rectitude, very much along the spirit of things Mexican, though hinting at the manner in which other groups exclude Mexican Americans. The integrity that is customarily used to preserve a bourgeois order in the Latin American context is turned upside down and employed to sustain the US order that excludes Latinos, so it materializes and may be criticized. In this manner, *Sonambulo* speaks to what it means to be an immigrant, a Mexican American.

Superficially speaking, the concern for the ways in which Mexicans are treated does not seem to be a priority for *Sonambulo*. For one, the comic accentuates the mythical dimension of Mexican identity, elaborating convoluted plots in which the hero must deal with deranged Satanic cults, à la Charles Manson; must contend with pre-Columbian deities bent on avenging the misfortune of its people and legitimating the recovery of Aztlán, the ancestral homeland of the Aztecs, now identified as California; and encounters regional legends like La Llorona (the wailing woman), the mythical figure who roams endlessly lamenting the loss of her loved ones. Such characters clearly fall out of step with customary evildoers in conventional hard-boiled narratives, typically rich entrepreneurs with incestuous inklings or political barons with nymphomaniac daughters so immersed in the seemingly risk-free environment of US middle-class subsistence. In addition to these encounters, thanks to his decades-long sleep, which partially explains the aesthetic anachronism, *Sonambulo* reproduces the gentlemanlike interests and behaviors of *luchadores* during the golden age of Mexican comics. Back then, wrestler stories were a regular component of the publishing landscape, with *luchadores* playing the roles of detectives. Mexican media used to churn out millions of these comics on a monthly basis, usually favoring black-and-white photography. The historian Anne Rubenstein has commented on this aspect, tracing the career of El Santo, the most popular of Mexican wrestling icons.[13] In fact, Navarro concedes that, from its very inception, *Sonambulo* was created with

El Santo in mind, which is not hard to imagine as his figure looms large in the universe of Mexican wrestling. In turn, Rubenstein's critique highlights El Santo's personification of the virtuous Mexican man as opposed to the stereotypical macho man. In the process of acting out the role of the counter-macho—and this is her main contention—El Santo validates a conservative, exploitative order that is no less oppressive than the one sponsored by Mexican machos. In short, the virtuous Mexican is the flip side of the same coin: the righteous gentleman who, with the excuse of values and honor, severely curtails female individualism.

Alas, Rubenstein goes no further. To identify the rationale behind this assertion and its context within the intricate maze of Mexican history, one must recall renowned media scholar Jesús Martín-Barbero's assertions on the influence of media in the formation of a national culture in Mexico in the middle of the twentieth century. To this respect, he suggests, "The struggle against injustice was transformed from a fight for an ideal into a fight motivated by loyalty to the leader."[14] In the context of Mexican cultural production, this means that, after the 1930s, with the arrival of the Lázaro Cárdenas administration (1934–40) and the institutionalization of nationalist populism, the discourse of the Mexican Revolution was stripped of meaning. By the time the ranchero, that most informal version of the Mexican cowboy, appeared onscreen and in illustrations and popular music, machismo, articulated as an unaffected rendition of nationalist expression, had already become folklore. In other words, as reproduced by the national cultural industry, machismo—be it as Mexican cowboy or gentleman—did not embody a way to confront class conflict, but was "a compensatory mechanism for social inferiority."[15] For this reason, as an attempt to integrate elements of Mexican identity to the tradition of hard-boiled narratives, *Sonambulo* ends up championing a context that stands in sharp contradiction with the objects delineated by the masters of this Anglo-American cultural practice. The object is not just to expose the fallacies of the middle class, as this would in turn validate the critical disposition of an order that excludes Latinos, but also to get to the root cause and expose an established monocultural norm. In the Mexican case, the priority of El Santo's virtue is the preservation of the status quo, to the detriment of women; in *Sonambulo*'s US context, it shows how Anglos benefit from white privilege. In a way, this is indicative of the interaction between two or more cultures, like in Spiegelman's *Maus* or Satrapi's *Persepolis*, in which the means to question or support a norm is to contextualize it in another culture. When all is said and done, *Sonambulo* is more about sustaining the conventional order of things, about legitimating a world in which the hero appears pure and unblemished, untouched by the degree of social disintegration surrounding him—a notion quite alien to Raymond Chandler, Dashiell Hammett, or

Mickey Spillane, who eagerly embraced flaws in their main characters—than about revealing the corruption and intrigue beneath a seemingly harmless collective façade. By doing so, it exposes the established order more than in the traditional hard-boiled way. In the 1940s, 1950s, and 1960s, the boom time for Mexican comics, the national cultural establishment was not interested in questioning the trappings of conventional order like the hard-boiled masters of the United States. On the contrary, by way of cultural hegemony—through comics, cinema, or music—the hope was to convince the population that Mexico's society and economy were at the door of the industrialized world, thanks to the ever-expanding role of the state. Hence, by siding with a Mexican tradition and its corresponding configuration of gender, Navarro ends up tinkering with a North American one. The cultural mechanisms that contributed to sustaining the Mexican status quo become the tools with which *Sonambulo* manages to deconstruct an Anglo cultural practice and bring to light a double standard; in a world that allows for the perversions of Anglo hoodlums, scant space is left for upright Latinos. That is why, in *Sonambulo*, things are not just Anglo, but also Mexican: to render explicit the monocultural order once it is forced to share space. What is highlighted is not the Mexican contribution, but the Anglo way of things, which, left standing alone, would pass as natural and would thus go unnoticed. In the end, *Sonambulo* comprises a merely cosmetic questioning of the existing state of affairs, failing to build on Anglo prerogatives. True to the Aztec wrestling tradition—the *luchador* as a prude, a man of honor—this work is very conservative in nature. It highlights how a cultural norm comes to be.

The case of the following pair of cartoonists that I am using to contextualize the evolution of the work of Lalo Alcaraz is, without a doubt, one of the most successful examples of integration of a cultural practice and business imperatives, which has a lot to do with the way in which many ethnicities have managed to make a mark on US society. Alcaraz himself has been no slouch in contemplating commercial value, but the way in which these notions are addressed by this pair of cultural actors sets a benchmark for the incorporation of Latino identity into the cultural market. Their example is key because, in particular, it speaks to the potential drawbacks of viewing immigration almost exclusively through an economic lens. Written by Héctor Cantú and illustrated by Carlos Castellanos, *Baldo* is a lighthearted comic strip that narrates the travails of Baldomero Bermúdez, a Latino adolescent of Mexican descent. It is important to note that, while Cantú and Castellanos have tried their best to integrate all sorts of Latino-specific hints and nods in the narrative, trying to establish some kind of pan-Latino context for the story, the crux of the content points to Mexico. Nonetheless, I must admit this construction is mine. The authors would never admit to this fact because their hope is to be commercially all-embracing, conveniently producing a strip that is equally at home in Chicago, Los Angeles, Miami, or New York; they have been quite explicit about *Baldo* supposedly lacking a specific national origin. Regardless, it is a comic strip deeply committed to capitalism, arguing that the path to mainstream integration is by way of the market.

In terms of structure, *Baldo* is much more conventional than anything produced by Alcaraz. In the story, the character belongs to a family (his dad, a widower; scatterbrained great-aunt Carmen, who fails to fit into US culture; and his sister Gracie, an intelligent and willful child) that, to a certain extent, suggests an archetype for the quintessential Latino household exposed to the constant bombardment of the US advertising sector and general media that is determined to conquer Latinos as the fastest-growing portion of the national market. In terms of migration, this is a comic strip that, as a premise, takes Latino integration into US society for granted. The key here is not to make waves, so despite the fact that *Baldo* includes a single-parent household, the presence of three generations is a guarantee for the authenticity of representation. As a result, *Baldo* feels a tad complicit in the promotion of stereotypes, something of a Latino *Leave It to Beaver* (1957–63). In their interviews with Fred Aldama, both authors allude to related aspects: the fact that, while they do not rely on stereotypes as heavily as Arriola, they still base their work on them because they serve as reliable ground for parody. Yet, although they do not think *Baldo* has attained a certain degree of success just because it is perceived as a token, they cannot negate that their work has arrived at the right time, on account of an increased interest for all things Latino.[16] In other words, critical mass in the population plays a significant role. In this sense, the comic strip denotes an initial stab at representing the process of acculturation and assimilation of new generations of Latinos into US society and culture. And this portrayal is critical for the effectiveness of the questioning of an established cultural norm, as intended by Alcaraz. To question this norm, readers must be able to discern its inner workings. Thus, within the overall context of capitalism, it is possible to argue that *Baldo*'s interaction with US identity takes place chiefly by way of its negotiation with economic imperatives, dutifully mediated by the advertising industry, rather than with strictly cultural ones, born out of folklore and ethnic or social tradition, as in *Sonambulo*, or through artistic ones, as in Espinosa's work. In fact, in *Baldo*'s world, economy and culture merge into one, very much along the lines once suggested by other countries—the French position on the economic implications of the cultural industry would be an obvious example—in their quest to defend national culture from the assault of global media. *Baldo* is an outstanding example of how extranational imperatives combine with the local to redefine the national, an altogether common event in an increasingly globalized world. While the overall contexts may differ, the actual combination of variables describes a similar process. Amid this setup, Latino identity represents one more demographic that must be engaged, co-opted, and hegemonized by the US economy and society, as a cultural machine, just as it manages to engage, co-opt, and hegemonize cultures from other countries within an international context. At the end of the day, the US economy and society achieve this goal by validating its norm as the viable and meritorious one, as is customary of a hegemon.

Then again, just as Alcaraz thrives on politics, *Baldo* reveals well the business acumen of its authors. The fact that Cantú, the scriptwriter, is someone with a background in the Latino business community—for a time, he worked as managing editor for *Hispanic Business*—plays a meaningful role in this operation. Also, upon returning to south Florida after a stint at the Art Center College of Design (just like Navarro), Castellanos started freelancing for some of the top advertising agencies in the region, an experience that informs his art at length. Accordingly, many of the story lines in the comic strip depict the negotiation of identity between the main character and members of his family and the US market—in harmony with the notion that market and culture overlap frequently. (This notion is also widespread in Alcaraz's work.) In the story lines, the US market comes across as a setting willing to engage and embrace identities as long as, in accordance with its prerogatives, they appear to bear economic potential. In this respect, many of the circumstances covered in *Baldo* mimic the history of the integration of previous groups into the US mainstream: women, Italian Americans, African Americans, homosexuals, and so on. In simple terms, economic leverage is construed as progress. Cantú and Castellanos develop their narratives based on the premise that economic integration into the US marketplace will precede social and cultural acceptance—to this extent, both authors operate as full-blown advocates of capitalism and wholly acculturated Latinos. As a result, it is vital to prove that Latino identity conforms and corresponds to the theoretical dictates of the US marketing and advertising industry, which will, in due time, facilitate its inclusion into the national mainstream, perhaps resulting in a redefinition of domestic identity, thus achieving transculturation or the full-fledged convergence of cultures. To say things have not operated in this manner in the past would be a tad naive. Typically, interest groups have managed to achieve social progress only after they have attained a certain degree of economic presence. For an ethnic/social group to be fully accepted and integrated into US society and culture—both authors seem to ascertain—it must first learn to flex its economic muscle. Being a pragmatist, I cannot allege to be in full disagreement with this contention.

In spite of this, my main claim when it comes to *Baldo* is that, in the process of proposing a cultural product that models and discusses the various stages of acculturation and assimilation as part of the immigration process, and suggesting as champion of its story line an individual with an apparently complete case of acculturation (Baldo, the character, is fully functional in English and very seldom utters expressions in Spanish, seems extremely comfortable and familiar with US culture, and performs like the average suburban teenager), thus validating the successful inclusion of Latinos into the cultural mainstream, Cantú and Castellanos end up passing from one stereotype to another, though not in the artful fashion they have hinted at when interviewed by Aldama. To be precise, instead of relying on what is considered to be the stereotypical Latino perception—basically, that of a group that has refused to relinquish its culture and blend into the mainstream in a fashion as concessive as previous communities—this pair of cultural actors ends up reinforcing certain biases with respect to the way Latinos will eventually integrate into US culture. This is not to say that they sustain conventionality in the way *Sonambulo* sustains an order, trying to highlight the inner workings behind what appears to be "natural." The way in which they portray acculturation is, to say the least, a bit problematic because, just as prevailing stereotypes fail to contemplate the Latino community in all its complexity, with a variety of races, national origins, class contexts, and sexual and religious preferences, this version by Cantú and Castellanos contains multiple normative, reductive, and homogenizing denominators. In the process of pursuing an audience, they have delineated a version of reality that conforms to prevailing notions in the world of marketing for what a fully acculturated Latino/a might be like, albeit in the course of negotiating her or his cultural viability with the advertising sector. While *Baldo* contends that, yes, Latinos will eventually assimilate and become a very functional component of US identity, it fails to acknowledge that Latinos are a heterogeneous group. The degree of acculturation and negotiation of identity, particularly in an age influenced by instantaneous access to information and communication across the globe, will vary significantly from one individual to another.[17] Following Cantú and Castellanos, within this difference, there is a denial of difference. Instead, *Baldo* portrays the process of acculturation in a staged, quasi-deterministic fashion. It fails to suggest that the process of assimilation of Latinos will be unlike that of previous groups because, at the moment of its occurrence, it involves a far greater number of variables that, unlike previous migratory experiences, have fluctuated significantly. Quite simply, it entails a migratory process in an age marked by an increased flow of information.

In this sense, Alcaraz's work tends to be more accommodating, constantly presenting new issues that add complexity to the immigrant condition in the United States. For Alcaraz, there is never an end to the ways in which negotiation of identity can gain complexity, closely replicating actual circumstances.

Migration has seldom been as homogenizing as conventional culture tends to portray it—be it the case of Latinos or previous collectivities—but this homogenizing mind-set, embraced by individuals seemingly influenced by theories emanating from the marketing sector, is indicative of an industry willing to deal with difference in the most coercive, normative manner available, regardless of its actual level of effectiveness. For Alcaraz, an author bent on the cultural challenge that Latinos pose to the melting pot, this sort of strategy, which replaces political imperatives with economic guidelines, must sound preposterous. In truth, what *Baldo*'s process of construction stands for is the implementation of a fully blown neoliberal assault. When identity stops being the outcome of a complex process involving social, cultural, political, and economic forces and is downgraded to a mere brand that is the product of market research and statistics trying to equate a group's preferences with the lowest possible common denominator, things begin to get sketchy—most fundamentally because turfs for the configuration of identity, culture, and society are being replaced by the market.

Statistics are always open to manipulation, but obviously this does not mean we should discount their relevance. In fact, just as statistics pose a risk in the hands of marketing experts, they may also embody a group's advantage, thanks to the US Census Bureau, when it comes to civil and political participation. For this reason, it is important to clarify the role of Latinos within the US market. In the twenty-first century, Latinos have become one of the most sought-after segments of the population within the US economy. Shortly before the Great Recession, 2007 marked the first year in which Latinos had more disposable personal income than any other "minority" group. The financial crisis altered these numbers, as certain ethnicities were more affected than others, but the trend continues and is clear. For this very reason, advertising companies are paying close attention to this portion of the population and analyzing it in detail, willing to develop more effective approaches toward the interpretation of its behaviors in terms of likes and dislikes. During the past decades, the US marketing sector has developed a number of theories with respect to Latinos, many of which are supported by quantitative research of varying quality; some of it is well documented, some of it is far from exhaustive. Hastily digested, this latter research may result in potentially reductive proclivities. Early psychographics for Latinos (or Hispanics, as the group was labeled in the past) emphasized the following: they were extremely proud people with strong family and cultural ties; they were willing to perpetuate their traditions through future generations (particularly through the use of language and conventional religious beliefs); they professed a growing sense of distinctiveness and unity, engendering a feeling of being Latinos first, Americans second (a new construct of nation, itself rooted in a new culture, having not superseded the preeminence of the previous culture); they subscribed to the notion that Latinos are more family-oriented than non-Latinos (amid the rigidity of familial constructs); and, finally, regardless of the actual level of linguistic dexterity, they valued highly the sharing of a common tongue (enabled by technology).[18] In terms of purchase patterns, marketing research was not much more elaborate in its findings. According to studies promoted by the tobacco industry, Latinos tended to believe that the biggest, most popular brands were best (coming from less selective and independently minded economies); selected name-brand goods over house brands (because the name brands were the familiar ones in the countries of origin); favored small neighborhood stores (because those were the ones available in most working-class districts); reacted favorably to Spanish-oriented advertising, as long as it was executed properly (thanks to the notion of linguistic dexterity as a class marker); and were more concerned with getting value (quality for the price) than US citizens as a whole (considering purchases were few and expected to last longer). Needless to say, with the passing of time, many of these notions were revised or complexified, especially those directly affected by judgments related to a degree of acceptance and interaction with Anglophone culture. Likewise, a need for further revision or complexification is what stands immediately apparent in some of Cantú and Castellanos's work. As a more protracted understanding of Anglo culture matured, it was only sensible that a mirror effect would take place. The more complicated a view you hold of yourself, the more complicated view you will hold of others. In general, Latino/a consumers were described as sociable (sharing and enjoying pleasure with others was an important factor), emotional (affectively inclined), pleasure-seeking (allegedly, devoting considerable time and energy to the pursuit of pleasure), polite (negative advertising figured as a definite turnoff), respectful (of others and authorities), and macho (thus essentializing maleness).[19] At the same time, independent of the depth of the assessment promoted by research, Latinos shared cultural values that were found to consistently influence consumer behavior. Irrespective of their tangible applicability within a wide spectrum of migratory experiences—that is, failing to consider how these aspects shifted within a variety of contexts (after all, migration is a highly individualized experience, affected by nationality, class, race, gender, and so on)—*respeto* (respect for authority, familiar or societal), *familismo* (family orientation), *simpatía* (harmonious social relationships), and *fatalismo* (resignation) were found to be important predictors of consumer behavior among Latinos.

Within this framework, cultural concepts such as acculturation and assimilation became the axioms of the day. They were said to play a key role in the definition of marketing models. According to *Merriam-Webster's*, *acculturation* is the "cultural modification of an individual, group, or people by adapting to or borrowing traits from another culture" or "a merging of cultures as a result of prolonged contact."[20] As understood by the advertising industry, acculturation involves abandoning one's original cultural background and measures the integration of one individual to another culture, two key considerations for anyone willing to influence consumer habits. Following Boas, a more traditional authority, all people acculturate to some measure since we are all influenced, in one or another way, by a foreign culture.[21] However, each individual develops her or his own style and pace of acculturation; just like migration, it entails an exceedingly personalized process. As acculturation happens, a selective progression of embracing the host country's culture takes place. Acculturation is a multifaceted procedure and it takes root in a different way in each person; it is affected by an individual's willingness to embrace the local culture while keeping some of her or his own culture. It is exceptionally hard to determine in what order or according to what logic it will take place. This much did not escape the grasp of the advertising and market industries. However, research does not seem to have focused on effective ways to assess this degree of variability. Instead, a variety of taxonomies surfaced that tried to explain acculturation in a less pliable, more categorical fashion. According to one, acculturation may be conceived as unidimensional—that is, taking place individually when an immigrant travels alone and lacks a context with which to resist the local culture and economy—or multidimensional, in which individuals embrace aspects of the host culture while preserving some of their own (such as language).[22] The degree of dependability of an essentially binary outlook remains dubious. Still, current research supports the notion that most Latinos are acculturating into US society according to the latter model, selecting from the culture what they find appealing—like choosing from a menu—because daily existence in a globally interconnected world renders the former impractical.[23] Then again, acculturation also allows for a segmentation of the market into more empirical categories, such as the unacculturated (at 25 percent, it comprises those who speak Spanish almost exclusively and use English reluctantly), the bicultural (at roughly 66 percent, it comprises those who live in and adapt comfortably to both worlds and languages), and the acculturated (at 9 percent, they are English-dominant and consume primarily English media).[24] In theory, there are also four distinct mind-sets that reflect the varying levels of acculturation among Latinos (although these descriptions are concrete, their nature is not exact): (1) the cultural loyalist, who is a foreign-born, Spanish-dependent, recent arrival who has been in the country for less than five years; (2) the cultural embracer, who, although foreign-born and bilingual, has become a resident and prefers Spanish; (3) the cross-culturer, who is usually first-generation US-born, bilingual, and bicultural and is equally comfortable in the Latino/a and Anglo worlds; and (4) the culturally integrated, who is a fully acculturated, US-born Latino/a, usually belonging to a second, third, or fourth generation—English-dependent, she or he may not speak Spanish or speak it well.[25] While practical for the handling of identities through a collective approach, this set of categories apparently fails to contemplate an expanded, more diffuse array of information—for instance, the fact that, as their migratory experience has matured, a large number of foreign-born Latinos have become equally comfortable with the Latino/a and Anglo worlds, effectively bridging the second and third categories. In all, what there seems to be is an ample assortment of taxonomies that, in one way or another, try to frame and render manageable behaviors or purchasing decisions that initially stand beyond the comprehension of interested parties, usually multinational consumer-products companies and/or global food and beverage emporiums.

Assimilation, on the other hand, refers to the process by which an individual's or a group's language and/or culture come to resemble those of another group. From a marketing perspective, this entails an ethnic group's almost complete acquisition of the values and behaviors of a national culture by shedding its own. (Think of the enormous potential in terms of consumerism. There is one key difference, though: in the case of acculturation, the minority culture may remain intact; in the case of assimilation, it changes.) Given its extreme nature, assimilation stands as one of the possible outcomes of acculturation, the others being integration, rejection, and marginalization. As a rule, assimilation tends to have a more definitive and all-encompassing connotation, describing the traditional way in which groups blended into the "melting pot" in the past, through coercion and social/cultural/economic pressure, discarding their language and many of their traditions or habits (something less likely in the age of the Internet). In other words, when it comes to marketing (and not sociology or anthropology, both of which tend to be more considerate), the difference between full acculturation and assimilation echoes more a matter of kind than quantity. As I have mentioned previously, this tendency to summarize and rationalize behaviors according to consumer attitudes fits well with the dictates of neoliberal economics, which generally substitute understanding from the social sciences with research from management and related fields.

It is not uncommon to find marketing research suggesting relationships between the degree of acculturation of an individual and the exercise of brand loyalty.[26] A relatively common viewpoint seems to support the idea that brand loyalty is inversely proportional to the degree of acculturation; that is, successfully acculturated individuals are, for the most part, more adventurous in their exploration of new brands, whereas recent arrivals tend to stick with established brands—US or otherwise—from their home country.[27] To me, this sounds like hasty elucubration. (In truth, I would suggest that in most groups, through the migratory experience, consumerism is largely dictated by economic imperatives.) In plain language, this is akin to claiming that, once Latinos have acculturated to a high degree or allowed themselves to be deeply influenced by US culture, they become more individually minded and therefore exhibit less brand loyalty, a transformation that in itself says a lot about the partial way in which Latino/a culture is imagined vis-à-vis US culture. Thus comes into play the concept of advertising "in culture" (rather than "in language"); that is, Latinos of various acculturation levels are exposed to advertising in both languages, as this particular variable no longer seems to play a defining role in the outcome of the purchasing experience. As long as Latinos identify with the execution, advertising in English is not out of the question. Mass communication also partakes in this exercise: TV is more effective at reaching unacculturated individuals and printed media are more effective among acculturated Latinos. (This would imply a boon for Latino/a cartoonists.) Therefore, with these audiences in mind, TV may be in Spanish but the press will tend to favor English (and even this seems to be at play: witness Univision and ABC News' joint media venture, Fusion, a fully bilingual TV network, and the number of newspaper editions in Spanish, starting with Miami's *El Nuevo Herald*). Even so, the press in Spanish might abound but the ultimate goal is to advertise in English, contributing to the imposition and acceptance of a monocultural norm. Accordingly, in *Baldo*, the power of the media is always acknowledged; for the most part, mass media are portrayed in English, just like the comic strip (despite a translated version). In addition, making things even more arresting, research by advertising powerhouses such as BBDO indicates the acculturated segment of the Latino population is the largest and fastest-growing portion of the community, increasing at an annual rate of 12 percent.[28] In just 2010 alone, the number of isolated Latinos—namely, those who prefer to cling exclusively to Latino/a culture—allegedly dropped from 32 percent to 25 percent.[29]

An eminent conclusion on the relationship between the work of Cantú and Castellanos and that of Alcaraz is that, quite obviously, Latino/a identity is not confined to just language and acculturation. In truth, these factors, though important, only play a supporting role in the overall experience of the Latino/a community within US society and culture. Demographic and marketing studies point to the continued importance of Spanish-language print and electronic media as expanding in market share because of patterns of acculturation that do not conform to earlier rates and vectors of adaptation into US culture. In this respect, Latino/a immigration proposes a novelty. At the same time, cultural consumption patterns that are common to both younger and older generations of Latinos regardless of levels of acculturation remain equally relevant, influencing market share. In this sense, Latino/a portrayal in *Baldo* is flawed and shortsighted. For all the noise they seem to create, language and acculturation are not true markers of Latino/a identity. National extraction, for instance, is just as critical. This much is evident from Alcaraz's work. To make matters even more puzzling, current research shows that people identify as Latinos well past the point of being unable to perform effectively in Spanish, just like any other ethnicity void of a language tradition.[30] Ultimately, while certain aspects of Latino/a identity might be familiar to the advertising industry—the case of collectivism, *familismo*, or *simpatía*—what truly stands out as significant is the degree of interconnectedness between these aspects. In other words, rather than awarding prevalence to these few notions, what must be prioritized is the relationship among them, which makes for a wonderfully complex mix for understanding how Latinos will gradually settle into the US mainstream. Within this scope, the eventual acceptance of English or the number of generations that have lived in the United States plays a lesser role. Instead, at the heart of Latino/a identity we may have more relational and broadly defined constructs, such as interpersonal orientation (how Latinos relate to other people), perception of time and space (potentially influenced by constructs of weather and social relations; public versus private), degree of spirituality (the multiple forms of being a believer/the multiple forms of being a nonbeliever), and discernment of gender (straight, gay, bisexual, trans-/intergender, and so on).[31] In this way, what becomes increasingly evident is the question that marketing companies are so desperately trying to understand—What is it that makes a Latino/a different?—will remain a continually evolving conundrum until the possibilities for definition are exhausted. While *Baldo* exploits all this material in the creation of a narrative proposal for Latinos, it also provides a precious contrast to the work of Alcaraz, who, although he occasionally dwells on criticism of similar topics, does so from an almost opposite perspective, trying to tint the harsh reality of economics with more humane considerations, born from the desire to heighten the visibility of the community and to complexify its makeup.

Beyond this succession of cartoonists, whose work is related in many ways to the treatment of the Latino experience, covering migration and eventual incorporation to US society, there is one final case I would like to discuss: that of *Chicanos*, a graphic novel series by a pair of Argentineans, cartoonist Eduardo Risso (b. 1959) and scriptwriter Carlos Trillo (1943–2011). Both authors are well known in the US comics industry. Trillo's writing has received many accolades in Europe, and Risso has won four Eisner Awards. Just from its title, it is easy to see why this piece of work might be germane to this chapter. *Chicanos* narrates the travails of a Mexican American detective named

Alejandrina Yolanda Jalisco, a modern-day "invisible" woman—I use the term in an Ellisonian manner—who, thanks to her humble appearance, is able to resolve situations involving gangsters and delinquency amid a degraded New York. The reason I deem this work relevant is simple: both authors have never been—in the case of Trillo, he never was—US residents nor, to my knowledge, have they ever expressed any interest in migrating to this country, yet they are willing to make a graphic novel series indicting the treatment of Mexican Americans and other Latinos in the United States, substantiating a prejudiced view of the experience of immigration from a Latin American perspective The US version of *Chicanos* circulated well, enough to distort things even further. In plain terms, the pair was willing to create a narrative critical of an immigration experience they seem to know little about because, as most people familiar with the Big Apple tend to realize, Mexican Americans do not yet play a preponderant role in New York culture and society, unlike what is immediately evident in places like Los Angeles. Chicanos are, by and large, a West Coast cultural group, not an East Coast sociological event. Even if Mexican Americans are increasingly showing up in locations like New York, North Carolina, or Georgia, their circumstances differ widely from the militant nature of the Chicano movement. And so, aside from the humor, the object of this series seems to be the claim that Latin Americans are better off suffering at home than venturing to the North, ratifying a sort of chauvinist nationalism intrinsic to Latin American sectors unwilling to recognize the achievements of Latinos awarded a better opportunity away from their place of origin. For this very reason, given their lack of firsthand acquaintance with the immigrant experiences of Mexican Americans or, for that matter, any Latinos in the New York metro area, this account tends to be problematic.

Mexican presence is a relatively recent arrival to the Big Apple.[32] Felipe Galindo, known as Feggo, a Mexican cartoonist who has contributed occasionally to the *New Yorker*, jokes about coining the term *Manhatitlan* in the 1980s, when Mexicans were blatantly absent in the New York area. All the same, in the early fall of 2008, Feggo celebrated an exhibition of his Manhatitlan Codex, an ongoing art series created over a twenty-year span. Inspired by the intertwining of Mexican and US cultures, the codex emulates pre-Columbian illustrations, discussing issues of nationality, migration, and globalization. It suggests that Mexican nationals, while not yet established in New York as firmly as in other parts of the country, are beginning to gain visibility. Nevertheless, they are still far from achieving the degree of presence attained elsewhere. Thus, it is slightly out of place that two Argentineans, when developing a narrative based in New York City, chose as their title a label that best describes a politically militant tradition of the Mexican American population at the opposite end of the nation; in particular, people linked with experiences like the clash between *pachucos* (zoot suiters) and soldiers, sailors, and civilians in the Zoot Suit Riots of 1943; the bracero program; and with Cesar Chavez and the United Farm Workers movement during the 1960s and 1970s. Generally speaking, the term *Chicano* is not as prevalent nowadays; for the most part, it describes academic departments and other interests reflecting the achievements of these movements. When appropriated, it is usually on a conscious basis, as in the case of Alcaraz, keenly aware of its militant connotation. These days, Mexican Americans embrace a number of labels and *Chicano*, strongly associated with earlier struggles, is not among the most circulated ones; they opt instead for a more general *Latino* or the more nationally oriented *Mexican*. Thus, the choice of title by Risso and Trillo evinces the degree of their ignorance of ethnic matters in Gotham—and, in fact, the entire country.

In terms of New York City's population, until the late 1970s, Puerto Ricans clearly prevailed, as evidenced by the rise of cultural expressions like salsa music. To this day, the Puerto Rican Day Parade, held annually on the second Sunday of June, is a celebration of *latinidad* in the Big Apple. Then came the Dominicans, with a growing presence in Washington Heights and the corresponding boom of merengue melodies in the 1980s. Their visibility peaked in the following decade, with eventual displacement to other vicinities. Even the music in *Chicanos* betrays the fact that both of these nationalities are substantially more visible in New York than Mexican Americans, yet the authors opted for the more controversial label. For instance, during a party at the local diner, characters celebrate to the beat of "La Bilirrubina," the 1990 smash hit by Dominican merengue star Juan Luis Guerra. This much could be circumstantial. Then, in a later work, Jalisco cleans her diminutive apartment while a boom box blasts "Pedro Navaja" in the background. This song, recorded by salsa virtuosos Rubén Blades and Willie Colón for their 1978 *Siembra* album, marks the peak of Puerto Rican salsa music. In this case, the inclusion of "Pedro Navaja" is a no-brainer because its narrative is fixed in the urban context of New York City—anyone even minimally acquainted with the genre will know this because *Siembra* was, for more than a decade, the best-selling salsa album in history. In contrast, Mexican music, so conspicuously present wherever its followers tend to group, is dramatically absent. (In fact, the only instance that Jalisco sings a Mexican tune, an emblematic ode to tequila, she does so in English.) What's more, *Chicanos* cleverly omits any mention of the fact that the main character's name, A. Y. Jalisco, alludes to a much-acclaimed verse of a song immortalized by *charro* icon Jorge Negrete, as in "Ay, Jalisco, ¡no te rajes!" (roughly translated: Oh, Jalisco, don't chicken out!). This is pertinent because, first, Negrete epitomizes the singing Mexican cowboy, a true archetype of machismo with his all-encompassing, intolerant view of gender, and, second, because he sings to the state of Jalisco, one of the most conservative places in the Mexican union and the heart of all things über-Mexican, from tequila to mariachi music to *charrería* (Mexican rodeo). Jalisco is where the most quintessentially stereotypical incarnations of nationality emerge, something akin to a Mexican Texas. Nowadays, though, Mexicans migrating north do not tend to come just from Jalisco. Instead, they come from any of the states affected by drug-related violence, like Guerrero or Michoacán, desperate to find safety. The ones who started arriving en masse to the state of New York through the 1990s, mainly from Puebla, were mostly economic refugees. At the time of the initial publishing of *Chicanos* in Italy and France in 1997, Mexicans were beginning to pop up around the city, mostly linked to the farming industry on Long Island and rural sectors of industry in upstate New York. Even today, as in other pockets of our nation, they are largely invisible and lead parallel lives, seldom intersecting with the Anglo every day. This circumstance makes even more awkward the fact that Risso and Trillo chose to use the emblematic *Chicanos* as the title, as though their story pertained to a saga of La Raza activists. If their intent is to add conspicuousness to this group, it is hard to do so at the expense of actual demographic and chronological accuracy. And, if their intent is to criticize US society, the sheer misguidedness of their effort is appalling.

To complicate things even further, the allusions to Jalisco and Negrete immediately summon images of machismo centering on loosely triggered weapons, cantina brawls, and heavy womanizing in the minds of most well-informed readers—not just Mexicans or Latin Americans. Such is the import of the Mexican cultural industry in hemispheric terms. It can be argued that this choice was intended to heighten the subversion of conventional gender in the narrative. What better namesake for a female advocate than the most celebrated line from the repertoire of an archetype of Mexican masculinity? Doesn't this hint at a parodic attempt to address issues of gender? Though *Chicanos* habitually plays heavily on gender, race, and class in its narratives, those who end up on the winning side of things are physically well endowed, like Jalisco's best friend Marita, who picks up guys like a magnet, and even the occasional New York City female detective; or Guadalupe, her flamboyantly gay brother, who, despite his homosexuality, continually manages to reconstruct his life and embrace new opportunities, whether with Italian mobsters or Mexican truckers. This aspect openly contradicts the notion that Jalisco's homely appearance—Risso underlines this—is a tool for paradigmatic subversion, projected for cultural resistance. If *Chicanos* represents an intent to trump the conventional way of life according to prejudiced views of gender, race, and class, it only does so by heavily relying on substantiation of prejudice. And this is not a matter of cynicism, parody, or irony. Subversion of the established order is, from this viewpoint, only a superficial first impression. Within this narrative, there's no mobility, regardless of status. Latinos remain poor and downtrodden, blacks are entrenched in the ghetto, and whites, legally or not, enjoy the good life. This is a static world, largely out of touch with the dynamics of US reality. While the end result is a text confirming the injustice emanating from a cultural double standard, it also denotes the authors' ignorance with respect to Latino/a experiences in the most populated city in the nation. And so, even a graphic novel that lacks accuracy—and despite its flaws—builds up momentum for the work by Alcaraz, who is eager to address the topic from a more judicious angle.

Together, the cartoonists in this chapter inform and provide a context for any Latino/a cartoonist in the country, yet they do not zero in as markedly on the forthcoming changes in our population nor embrace attitudes as combative (and sometimes extreme) as does Alcaraz. It is for this reason that, despite all its shortcomings, Alcaraz's production plays an influential role documenting the advances and difficulties experienced by Latinos. From Arriola to the Hernandezes, as well as Espinosa, Navarro, Cantú and Castellanos, and even a pair of Argentineans who have never lived in this country, the work of other Latino/a cartoonists has paved the way for a more outspoken form of expression and criticism, specifically when it comes to the politics of immigration. Not many Latinos have risen to the challenge as prominently as has Alcaraz, chastising politicians and general society for their incongruities and moral ambivalence, failing to admit how the presence of a growing immigrant population puts society's monocultural norm to the test. The following chapters shed some light on these aspects.

CHAPTER 3

MIGRA MOUSE
Political Cartoons and the Immigration Debate

> Preservation of one's own culture does not require contempt or disrespect for other cultures.
> —Cesar Chavez

EVERY NOW AND THEN, HISTORY PROVIDES A VIVID CONTEXT FOR CONTEMPORARY POLITICAL battles. The name *California* dates back to the Spanish tradition of *novelas de caballerías*, the chivalric romance novels discussed by Miguel de Cervantes Saavedra's classic *Don Quixote*, in which an elderly gentleman has consumed so many of these books that he goes mad and fails to distinguish between an imaginary world, full of damsels in distress, and reality. Perhaps the best-known title among books of this kind is *Amadís de Gaula*, of unclear origins, although there is a conclusive edition authored by Spaniard Garci Rodríguez de Montalvo in 1508. In its introduction, Montalvo admits editing the first three volumes from a previous edition and adding a fourth one. Given the edition's popularity, Montalvo's name gained renown among followers of the genre. *Las sergas de Esplandián* (The heroic feats of Esplandián), the sixteenth-century romance novel by the same Spanish author, narrates the many adventures of its eponymous hero—the word *serga* is an archaism for *feats* or *heroic deeds*. In particular, the book narrates Esplandián's battle against King Armato, whose armies include a contingent of fierce dark women (similar to the mythological Amazons), originally from an island called California. The island, described as having *escarpados farallones* (steep sea stacks or cliffs) and *pétreas costas* (rocky shores), must have fired the imagination of Spanish conquistadors. According to Colombian historian Germán Arciniegas, upon traveling around western Mexico, Spanish conquistadors like Cristóbal de Olid were reminded of the descriptions in *Las sergas de Esplandián*, so it was only natural that cartographic interpretation concurred with literary imagination.[1] In 1539, commissioned by Hernán Cortés, Francisco de Ulloa explored the area, concluding that Baja California was a peninsula; his reports, however, were used to reinforce the idea of an island. That is to say, despite concrete evidence that it was a peninsula, the Spanish establishment clung wistfully to the idea of California as an island. A year later, Hernando de Alarcón confirmed Ulloa's findings. Eventually, explorers like Juan Rodríguez Cabrillo and Bartolomé Ferrer ventured farther north and west from New Spain (modern Mexico), possibly navigating as far as coastal Oregon, but it took a while for the deeply rooted notion of the existence of an island to be dispelled. For this reason, well into the eighteenth century, maps of the region portrayed California as detached from the mainland, in accordance with ancient accounts of archipelagos east of Cipango (Japan). In the vivid imagination of the Spaniards, California must have figured as a precursor to the Orient.

In addition, however, there exist other, multiple theories behind the origin of the name *California*. According to some, the word comes from the Spanish *califa*, of Arab origin, meaning the head of a caliphate, a political division of the Moorish empire, which ruled Spain from the initial invasion in 711 until their final expulsion in 1492. This particular etymological theory is founded on the close proximity between the Spanish language and words and phrases of Arabic origin that resulted from the long centuries of Moorish occupation. Modern Spanish is still sprinkled with many words attesting to this lengthy relationship. Throughout the years, conventional wisdom has suggested the word comes from Catalan, the language of the autonomous region between northeastern Spain and southwestern France. In this version of the name's origin, the word means *lime kiln*, from the words *calç* (lime) and *forn* (furnace). In any case, it is ironic that a place with such a historically contested name serves today as the primary battleground for much-needed immigration reform in the United States, considering the rise in the state's Latino/a population. This effectively highlights the fact that California has become the second state (following New Mexico) where whites are not the majority and Latinos incarnate the plurality (the largest group, but not more than half of the population).[2] Then again, the contrast between New Mexico, a state with a low per capita income, high poverty levels, and a low ranking in terms of population, and California, the most populous state in the nation, with an economy that could rank well among the world's top ten richest countries, is rather obvious. Surely, neither California's original inhabitants nor its Spanish conquerors ever imagined that, many years later, their descendants would have to struggle against the descendants of their traditional enemies—in the case of US Native Americans, the Anglos who carried out the conquest of the West, coming from faraway lands to the east (the Spanish conquest was not as extensive and conclusive as integration of these lands to the United States); in the case of Spaniards, their long-standing enemies, the inheritors of the rivaling Elizabethan empire—to establish their right to live in these lands. The work of Lalo Alcaraz, which combines all of these heritages, embraces California as the setting for its musings. In essence, his work is a reflection on what it means to be a US citizen and partake in the country's cultural context, including discrimination as a Latino/a in Southern California.

MIGRA MOUSE IN CONTEXT: SOME CONSIDERATIONS ON IMMIGRATION

Migra Mouse: Political Cartoons on Immigration is the first volume of cartoons published by Lalo Alcaraz. It was released in 2004 and, to a fair extent, serves as a balance of the cartoonist's early production on the subject of immigration, so intimately linked to the Latino/a condition since the 1980s, amid the controversy started by Ronald Reagan with the Immigration Reform and Control Act of 1986, better known as the Simpson-Rodino or Simpson-Mazzoli Act.[3] Back then, this piece of legislation was lauded as the first sincere effort to deal with the matter of illegal immigration in the context of an outmoded federal apparatus. In truth, Reagan's stab at solving the immigration bottleneck was much more problematic than people tend to think. For one, it did not embody an actual amnesty, in the sense of a pardon in exchange for a sensible list of requisites. Traditionally, amnesty was viewed as a direct vehicle toward the legalization of aliens, involving the admission of transgression and the payment of a fine in exchange for eventual acceptance; nonetheless, in a politically charged environment, many legislators in Congress were unwilling to risk voters' animosity and come across as weak in terms of law enforcement. Such a conflictive climate generated dismal results for undocumented immigrants. People were not offered anything close to a "free ride" (as it was construed by many opponents), as many Latin Americans began to realize. Second, it contributed to the tension between immigrants and legislators, an aspect that has hindered real possibilities of progress in immigration reform during the following administrations, despite efforts by presidents Bill Clinton and George W. Bush. It is a testament to the sad state of affairs in this area that, more than ten years after the publication of *Migra Mouse*, and given the absence of any reform in the field of immigration policy, Alcaraz's work is as relevant as ever.

Until 1965, when the Hart-Cellar Act came into effect, US immigration policy favored a quota system that was proportional to the population of each country of origin, although, in truth, the system was largely biased in favor of immigrants from northwestern Europe, an aspect readily evident in the overall makeup of the US population at the time. In cultural terms, the melting pot brought in assimilation—as long as your descent was northern

European. If anything, until the 1960s, US immigration policy progressed very slowly, gradually conferring the right of citizenship to disenfranchised groups: honorably discharged army veterans from various previous wars in 1862 (for a young nation, the armed forces recruited with less attention paid to birthplace), African Americans in 1870, Asians (Chinese Americans, actually, as people made little distinction at the time) in 1898, Native Americans in 1924, and so on. The story of US immigration policy has long been one of a delayed and protracted admission of injustice, since it was only in 1952 that racial and gender discrimination were forbidden in terms of the naturalization process. In a way, since the country's inception, it is as though the system has been consistently playing catch-up with the general dynamics of demographic growth and social representation and its purported charter of values, established in documents like the Declaration of Independence and the US Constitution. After Hart-Cellar, origin supposedly mattered less and special skills—as well as other conditions, like international politics and economic interests—started to figure as the basis for a preference system.

In any event, Simpson-Rodino or Simpson-Mazzoli (both names are used) allegedly offered an amnesty, though with a catch: candidates were required to prove that they were in the country prior to January 1, 1982—that is, an entire population that even back then tried to maintain a low profile, hoping not to incur persecution by authorities, was suddenly requested to submit proof of residence in the United States before a certain date. For practical purposes, a population that spent a good amount of time and effort trying to eliminate any trace of its presence—effectively hiding or concealing any proof of residence—was told, in the course of a few days, that they had to document their long-lasting participation in US society. Behold a genuine contradiction. However, this was not the only problematic aspect of this law. In the case of employers, the law gave everyone a deadline to verify that workers were either citizens or undocumented immigrants. Beyond the deadline, the Immigration and Naturalization Service (INS) would check business records to verify citizenship and infringement would be penalized with fines of up to $10,000. Since then, signs started showing up at workplaces all over the nation distinguishing between legal and undocumented workers, putting in place a two-tier system that, in every practical sense, endorses the existence of an underclass. In other words, if Latinos worked and served in the shadows before Simpson-Rodino, after its implementation, this double standard became the norm, with all of the might and power of the federal government behind it. Much attention was awarded to lip service, but, for practical purposes, businesses continued employing thousands of undocumented workers. In addition, the very fact that Simpson-Rodino was associated with the word *amnesty* led to the demonization of the term. Empowered by the rise of the

Far Right (launched in full vigor by Reagan), conservative groups zeroed in on the word as a sign of leniency in the war against poverty and widespread governmental apathy. On the other hand, the disputed popularity of "trickle-down" economics (championed by the Republican administration) and the questionable morality of the 1980s (greed is good, à la Gordon Gecko), with its get-rich-quick zeitgeist, generated substantial acrimony against these contingents.

To make matters worse, in 1990 and 1996, the federal government stiffened the laws for immigration. Most relevantly, the Orwellian-sounding Illegal Immigration Reform and Immigrant Responsibility Act of 1996 (IIRIRA) was passed, stating that immigrants unlawfully present in the United States between 180 and 365 days should remain outside the country for three years unless they obtained a pardon. In many cases, the affected parties involved undocumented parents of children born in the United States. In this way, the trauma of separation was not only implemented but augmented as well, given the time period of wait imposed by the law. In the case of immigrants in the country for more than 365 days, to be eligible for a legal status, they were to stay out of the country for ten years unless they obtained a waiver. Needless to say, after a wait of ten years, all sorts of links and connections to a community in the United States were severed, rendering the individual nonfunctional in the place where she or he had once operated successfully and contributed effectively to society. Also, if the affected parties returned to the country without the pardon, they would not be able to apply for a waiver for a period of ten years, for practical purposes shutting them off from access to the United States. On top of that, under IIRIRA, individuals caught for minor offenses, like shoplifting, were eligible for deportation. It was a measure of this nature that triggered a rise in the number of naturalizations, given the fear of a witch hunt among legal residents. In large part, this consideration might be the primary reason that so many individuals have been deported at a record pace during the Obama administration, as a *New York Times* analysis of internal government records attested later, concluding that two-thirds of the nearly two million deportation cases involved people who had committed minor infractions, including traffic violations, or had no criminal record at all.[4] Upon the IIRIRA bill's passing, it was also applied retroactively to individuals convicted of deportable offenses, dramatically increasing the number of deportations. All of this took place under the guise of a supposedly progressive and Latino/a-friendly Democratic administration—Clinton's—just as in the case of the Obama administration.

With Obama, there has been very little progress in this area. Having promised immigration reform during his campaign, Obama chose instead to spend political capital in support of initiatives like health-care reform. During his first term and the earlier part of his second one, as a down payment for eventual support from Republicans on the topic of immigration, he strengthened security at the border and enacted widespread deportation. Later, given the Democrats' loss of Congress and with few options remaining, he opted for a series of executive actions, which were halted almost immediately by Andrew Hanen, a Brownsville, Texas, federal judge appointed by George W. Bush in 2002. By delaying his actions until after the 2014 midterm elections, Obama effectively undermined any progress on immigration.[5] It was a clear-cut case of "too little, too late." And so, since the 1980s, for all intents and purposes, thanks mostly to Reagan's "leadership" in this area, Latinos have been caught between a rock and a hard place. The fact that our existence leads a mostly invisible path, overlooked by many Anglos in a number of settings, is not an accident. This sort of twisted parallel reality, in which the legal status of Latinos becomes a disputable concern, belongs among the failures of the institutionalized order in most of the nation, thanks to a misguided, ill-conceived approach by the government.

The work of Lalo Alcaraz provides meaningful clues for understanding how this paradox came to be. In a way, his production can be read as a manual of the relationship between immigrants and the federal, state, and local governments' efforts to contain them, despite their shortcomings in a variety of aspects. On its cover, *Migra Mouse* sports one of Alcaraz's most popular images, that of Mickey Mouse dressed as an INS border guard, alluding to the Walt Disney Company's support of California governor Pete Wilson, who exploited the illegal immigration issue as a way to drive a wedge through the electorate. Alcaraz saw this character as a way to connect Disney with the spirit of Proposition 187, the xenophobic state-ballot initiative spearheaded by Wilson. The image became so popular that posters were circulated in Mexico and adopted by French protesters for the frequent picketing at Disney's amusement park in Paris. For many decades, the Disney character, with his constantly cheerful demeanor and high-pitched voice, was the epitome of Americana. Entire generations were bred on a diet of Mouseketeers, from Annette Funicello and Keri Russell, to Britney Spears and Christina Aguilera, and finally to Justin Timberlake and Ryan Gosling. And, since the mid-1950s, visiting a Disney amusement park became a sort of rite of passage, attaining synonymity with childhood and adolescence in the minds of many US citizens. It is thus ironic that such an icon of US culture, symbolic of corporate entertainment, stands as a representative of the degree of contrast in fortunes in our country when it comes to immigration status. In a move highly indicative of disparities imposed by the economic dynamics of globalization, in which corporations are increasingly able to cross and surpass—and even transgress—borders at will while many immigrants of various nationalities

MIGRA MOUSE, 1994

The namesake of this book, Migra Mouse is perhaps my most well-known cartoon, at least on the immigration topic. Migra Mouse represents the corporate interests of the Walt Disney Company, which donated money to then–California Governor Pete Wilson's re-election campaign. Wilson was exploiting the illegal immigration issue in the most divisive way, so I felt it was necessary to point out that wholesome Disney was affiliating itself with Wilson and Proposition 187, a xenophobic state ballot initiative. To be fair, Disney also donated to the Democratic opponent of Wilson, Kathleen Brown.

This parody of Mickey Mouse in Border Patrol garb happily pointing immigrants toward Mexico became a widely seen image. Pro-immigrant organizations asked to reproduce the image, and one printed 10,000 large glossy posters in Mexico, which it then distributed to labor groups in North and South America, and in Europe. I was told this poster was proudly picketed in front of Paris' Euro Disney theme park.

And no, the Disney Company has never contacted me to complain, as the image is completely protected under the First Amendment, but thanks for asking.

Migra Mouse, 1994. Cartoon appears courtesy of the artist Lalo Alcaraz and Universal Uclick Syndicate. All rights reserved.

struggle to enter the country by way of its border with Mexico, one of the country's most traditional and celebrated entertainment companies has, since its early days, grown accustomed to a steady influx of cheap labor, embodied by thousands of international students.

As I stated, Disneyland has been part of the US imagination since the mid-1950s. By the time its much larger sister park opened in Florida in the early 1970s, the need for a young, upbeat workforce was very palpable. With a peak area of roughly the size of the city of San Francisco, it was clear the site was going to demand a much larger workforce. Thus, while many international-recruitment initiatives operated over long periods of time, designed to provide an affordable multilingual staff for a full-blown experience of Americana—witness the contradiction between a scrupulously monolingual society hard-pressed to serve in many languages and cultural contexts—Disney consolidated its programs in the early years of the twenty-first century, bringing some order to its wide array of staffing efforts. After all, what is Epcot Center if not the standardization of the world under a thoroughly ethnocentric view—that is, a view of the globe through a thoroughly normative US lens? Quite certainly, when visitors amble through Main Street, USA, a great deal of their enthusiasm comes from consuming a sanitized and truncated view of the world, from the Matterhorn to Polynesian Village. It *is* a small world after all, for the joy of many US citizens who would rather consume this version than risk venturing into actual travel abroad, especially after September 11, 2001.

In her research paper for the *Florida Law Review*, "The Wonderful World of Disney Visas," Kit Johnson, an associate professor of law at the University of Oklahoma, discusses the ways in which the Walt Disney Company has benefited from immigration policy.[6] Chief among these ways is the procurement of a readily available workforce—international students—thanks to a very advantageous implementation of the J and Q visa programs. In the case of the Q visa, Disney single-handedly supported this piece of legislation, keeping its massive need of labor for its Florida operations in mind. In the case of J visas, a program started during the Cold War that hoped to "increase mutual understanding between the people of the United States and the people of other countries by means of educational and cultural exchange," people from around the world apply and pay between $3,000 and $6,000 to a sponsoring organization, dutifully accredited by the State Department, to enjoy this opportunity to mediate. In exchange, they obtain employment in US companies like the Hershey Company (which also owns an amusement park) and Disney. Along the way, these companies save a fortune on wages, state and federal taxes, health care, housing, and pension plans. In the case of Disney, according to Johnson, the company saves more than fifteen million dollars a year thanks to its international labor force.[7] In this sense, it is evident that immigration policy works to Disney's benefit. While the company may not be infringing the law, it serves as an ideal example of the proximity between the interests of the private sector and policies enacted by government, both at the federal and state levels. Thus, it is government's catering to the whims of its financial supporters that could strike many as the true problem. One final note: it is also relevant to consider how Disney has developed as a company with its cruise line; most of the staff aboard their cruise ships usually have a crew visa, which allows the corporation to operate its line in an analogous fashion to that of the workers at its amusement parks.

Jean Beaudrillard, the French theoretician, would certainly have been amused.[8] His view of the United States as an exercise in simulation, as an extension of a Disneyesque paradise or inferno, did not contemplate the most scathing fact of all: that, in a sort of accelerated rehearsal for the invisibility of difference, the thousands of yearly visitors at Disney's amusement parks learn to ignore the multilingual, international staff, which fades into the background and, though usually helpful and ever-present, is seldom noticed or acknowledged. As a matter of fact, one could argue that this invisibility is viewed as something positive by Disney because it contributes to the impression of seamless operation. On a general basis, comprehensive management of amusement parks, which involves such time-intensive efforts, is not supposed to be too evident to visitors. While ushers and tour guides direct and address crowds in friendly fashion, their presence must not be perceived as preponderant within the overall scheme of things. In sum, not only does Disney benefit from international workers in a stealthy fashion, but it also accustoms its visitors to ignore veritable signs of diversity. In a place where everyone has an accent and may display a tag advertising another nationality, difference becomes the unheeded norm. Hence, it could be argued that, amid a sea of helpful foreigners, Disney acquaints its guests with the notion of a comfortable life around undocumented, multilingual individuals. In this context, the hypocrisy of supporting a bill like Proposition 187, which called for a state-run screening system in the hopes of keeping illegal aliens from using health care, public education, and other social services, when the very company advocating the measure benefits from a large pool of imported workers—granted, most of them at the other end of the country, given the disparity in size of Disney's operations—seems even more outlandish. Thus, the figure of Mickey as perhaps the most memorable image during this phase of Alcaraz's production is particularly pertinent, not only for its national quality, but also for its representation of rampant duplicity in migratory measures.

On the other hand, Proposition 187 deserves a special place in the record of a long history of disenfranchisement. Most significantly, it was the first time that a state attempted to legislate immigration, usually an issue handled exclusively by the federal government. In the early 1990s, Californians became concerned about the strain on the state's infrastructure and institutions by a growing number of immigrants, a percentage of which were undocumented. Thus was born Proposition 187, originally concocted by Republican assemblyman Richard "Dick" Mountjoy, a Korean War veteran from the city of Monrovia, located in the foothills of the San Gabriel Mountains. As any skillful politician would have done, Governor Pete Wilson happily embraced the bill as an opportunist advocate, seeking an issue that would fuel the fire, generate animosity, and radicalize the electorate, thus motivating people to go to the polls in large numbers. This is, we all know well, a basic rule of politics: issues must be identified that encourage the electorate to perform (to attend the polls on a given day) in order to achieve the desired result. Then again, things are not that straightforward when it comes to accomplishing this objective. An awful lot of campaigning and image manipulation must first take place.

In "Disassociating Myth and Practice: Pete Wilson's Campaign against Immigration," Miller and Lotterman discuss some of the specific strategies of the anti-immigrant argument in the course of the Proposition 187 vote.[9] Dissociation, the separation of a unified idea into two concepts, in which one is perceived positively (idealized) and the other negatively (demonized), plays a key role in this context. Miller and Lotterman make a point of describing the importance of language during the campaign, because it enabled framing of the issues in a particular light. Despite the theoretical sophistication of today's electorate, as a rule, contemporary politics remains a contest to frame things in easily manageable, occasionally simplistic terms, through efficient communication and dependable connection with the public. Only when a candidate manages to describe an issue in its full complexity and is able to share a more nuanced view with voters is it possible to override this picture. And so, semantics matter a lot in modern politics because explaining a complex issue is no easy task, and because it can turn off or be misunderstood by the public. Miller and Lotterman describe how the "pro-immigration" argument identified immigrants as a noble and just people, framing illegal immigrants with the opposite characteristic: the will to hoard scarce resources, taking advantage of the system and "invading" the country. In this sense, the anti-immigrant lobby established clear distinctions between both groups. According to them, illegal immigrants had a free choice in their actions: they moved into the country and chose to harm legal residents intentionally through their takeover of public-assistance programs. To substantiate the idea of a "takeover," the lobby claimed that undocumented immigrants were invading the country. At the same time, the lobby redefined the term *invasion*. Its rhetoric was sprinkled with images of violence resulting from a "flood of immigrants" (which immediately elicited fear). Also, thanks to Ronald Reagan's assault on the welfare system, the denotation of terms frequently used when alluding to undocumented immigrants, like *truly needy* and *safety net*, had shifted, although the subtext remained unchanged. Thus, voters could feel good about themselves by voting to solve a problem (fixing a system that would take care of the poor) while simultaneously forsaking a group (only those who qualify should be assisted). Finally, through the adoption of a new vocabulary, it became difficult to imagine undocumented immigrants in an individualized fashion, as in the person who takes care of my lawn, cooks food for my children, or takes care of my father. (In this way, Californians could feel at ease with Latino workers while they visited the polls and voted against them.) Rather, through reiterated descriptions of them as aliens, criminals, and health risks, undocumented immigrants were dehumanized. Regardless of the context surrounding the Proposition 187 campaign, this is a generalized practice in mainstream US media and at an institutional level.

In "The Cultural Production of Mexican Identity in the United States: An Examination of the Mexican Threat Narrative," Aguirre, Rodriguez, and Simmers focus on racial-profiling procedures utilized by the US Border Patrol that criminalize Mexican identity to illustrate the application of the Mexican threat narrative. Their research discusses how the cultural production of Mexican identity in the US media fuels a Mexican threat narrative that, in turn, serves to legitimate the racial-profiling practices utilized by the US Border Patrol. And, using media as a reliable primary news source, they concentrate on work by the *Los Angeles Times*, given its coverage of US-Mexico border issues.[10] In contrast with those targeted by the Border Patrol, the thinking went, legal immigrants did not harm anybody when they came into the country seeking a better life. Unlike recent (and illegal) arrivals, early (and legal) immigrants were said to possess useful skills that contributed significantly to the development of US society. Legal immigrants exhibited strong values and moral character; undocumented immigrants did not. Moreover, while unemployed immigrants were portrayed as victims, because of undocumented workers' willingness to work for less, the latter were blamed for all sorts of problems, like failures in the education system and the health-care industry, thus externalizing any sense of accountability among voters. In general, legal immigrants were described in a way that legitimated the mythical view of migration as a US ideal, so people could identify themselves with such an appeal and, at the same time, respond powerfully to the demonization of others.

With this context in mind, Lalo Alcaraz plays from the opposite corner. The object of his work is not only to materialize so-called alien identity for his readers, but also to generate empathy through the use of parody and irony, continuously fostering a critical approach to the immigration issue. His audience needs to be able to imagine what it is like to be somebody else, so that, through theory of mind, they can come to a less rushed conclusion. From Alcaraz's point of view, however, Proposition 187 is a key theoretical cornerstone because, by way of legally condoning discrimination, it allows him to read migration as a basic human right. For Alcaraz, migration is motivated economically; it is as simple as that. People need to work, so they migrate to the places where someone—and there is always someone, especially in the United States—is willing to hire you. In this sense, people are only doing what is necessary for their survival. So, when politicians advocate for the stringent application of repressive measures during demonstrations or raids, Alcaraz's work frames them as extremists, in a manner historically inscribed in US history. By throwing the weight of history at them, by placing their response in the context of a version of events common to a national memory, Alcaraz hopes to achieve a more balanced result in terms of political perception. That is why, when he compares figures like Pete Wilson and Ron Unz to other historical characters, he codes them in such a manner that his critique of them is contextualized within a scenario familiar to US culture, further ratifying his cultural production as a form of US identity. To criticize these kinds of personalities is to practice dissent, therefore enacting freedom of speech—thus, Lalo Alcaraz delineates himself as a US voice. If his response is interpreted as a legitimate form of Americana, his critique of immigration-reform opponents will be more valid. In plain terms, to disparage politicians, Alcaraz employs aesthetic and thematic arguments rooted in US culture, so readers accept his criticism as an exercise of US identity, which speaks for those who cannot speak for themselves, as a legitimate form of national disposition (in contrast to the restrictive definition articulated by Republicans). In this way, his cultural production becomes a tit-for-tat contest with politicians, one form of US identity competing against another. Within this scheme, once migration is connected to economic need, a negative response can be effectively portrayed as heartless, appealing to the electorate's sense of sympathy.

Now, this is all good—except for one problem. It is justifiable and understandable that Alcaraz tries to frame things in terms of US culture, but it does denote a lack of progress in his assessment of cultural norms, at least at this point in his career. Later on, in his work on *La Cucaracha*, Alcaraz will evolve, but at this particular point in time, the cartoonist does not yet issue a pragmatic critique of a prevailing cultural norm, formulating options or offering a resolution. In a way, his early production denotes a less adventuresome analysis of the concept of identity. Alcaraz has not yet devised approaches beyond a complicit engagement of US culture that, in one way or another, fails to push forward a better result for Latinos. He limits himself to criticizing that which he views as wrong and, to contextualize it, he sets it in the context of the normative culture, to validate his arguments as part of the greater order of this culture. Hence, he ends legitimating its hierarchy. Motivated by a concern for communication, the cartoonist embraces the prevailing cultural norm—Disney, Mickey, Americana, dissent as national tradition, and so on—so readers will be able to consume his criticism. As I've mentioned, this is all good, except for the fact that, initially, as a cartoonist with a critical voice, Alcaraz plays too much into the system. Beyond that, when it comes to immigration, the cartoonist limits his work to a censure of the double standards of the system, indicative of rampant economic disparity. In all, it seems an inquiry from the perspective of a witness.

Such an argument is not uncommon among cartoonists. A close look at Joe Sacco's *Journalism* will illustrate the many similarities between undocumented Latinos in the United States and African immigrants on the island of Malta, which, for the most part, replicate conditions found along the entire Mediterranean, from Spain to Greece. (The recent exodus from Syria has only intensified this situation.) Sacco is correct to point out that, when it comes to migration, the reigning contrast is between the haves and the have-nots, and not between Europe and the United States, hence condoning Alcaraz's point of view. A case in point: Italy, once a net exporter in terms of population, has become a hotbed of immigration. Its shores have been teeming with recent arrivals since the 1990s, following the fall of the Iron Curtain. Gianni Amelio's powerful *Lamerica* (1994), which itself toys with the notion of the United States as a land of promise (while thematically displaced to Italy), is indicative of this crisis, even though it failed to anticipate the dimensions of the population coming from Africa and the Middle East (the movie is set in Albania). According to the United Nations, about 32,000 migrants reached Italy and Malta by sea in 2013; in 2015, by April 30, 26,644 had landed in Italy alone, so the numbers are increasing steadily.[11] While vacationing around the southern shore of Sicily, I had the opportunity to talk with some of these African recent arrivals, many of whom sold trinkets at the beaches during the summer and then migrated to northern Italy during the colder months. In their minds, the United States figured as a possible ultimate destination, given European backlash. At the time, Italian media were ablaze with news of a ship rescued by the Coast Guard after numerous days adrift in the Mediterranean and with many of its passengers suffering from malnutrition, dehydration, and heat exhaustion; six were reported dead, in a story dutifully covered by the BBC.[12] A few months later, in October, news came of a boat that capsized near the shores of Lampedusa, a tiny island south of Sicily, with scores of immigrants feared dead or missing.[13] In 2014, 3,279 were reported dead as the result of their journey across the Mediterranean to Europe.[14] In 2015, the figure increased to 3,771.[15] At the time of this writing, with the Syrian exodus, from a grand total of 157,801 immigrants to Greece, 56,227 to Italy, and 1,352 to Spain, 2,868 are believed dead or missing in the course of 2016.[16] Unable to deal with such an influx of immigrants and short of resources, Italy is beginning to advocate for more effective (and perhaps repressive) means, framing the situation as a European, rather than a national, predicament, for it is clearly beyond the scale of its control.

As Sacco points out, events of this nature are part of a steady stream of migrants fueled by conflicts in other latitudes, like the war in Syria and Iraq, instability in Libya, and conflict in Sudan, Eritrea, and Somalia, situations that, in one way or another, are also connected to European and US interests. Nowadays, hardly anything takes place in the world in an independent, isolated manner. Everything tends to be interwoven and interconnected, and what happens in one corner is, most likely, closely linked to what takes place in another. Migration is a global issue and, until the world of haves and have-nots balances out, it will continue to signify oppression and repression at both ends of its trek. As long as circumstances of this nature fuel social exclusion in other latitudes, people will continue to risk their lives in search of better futures. It is no coincidence that the United States is not the only place with a general issue of mass illegal migration. In today's world, in which images and sounds circulate easily around the globe, people don't think much before daring to migrate. Most commonly, they migrate out of sheer economic necessity, frequently out of desperation and fear of starvation. In many cases, this desperation is the result of change sparked by globalization, occasionally personified by consequences from the implementation of trade treaties between the United States and other economies. In fact, during the initial years of NAFTA, when the commercialization of national corn became impractical in Mexico as a result of the importation of heavily subsidized corn from the United States, the number of farmworkers illegally crossing the US-Mexico border spiked out of control. Because of this situation, many Mexican farmers could no longer make a living and, rather than suffer informal employment or poverty in many Mexican cities, they resorted to migration to the United States. At the same time, many people in the United States failed to recognize the connection between local government policies intimately linked to the support of corporate farming and a spike in the incidence of illegal immigration across the border (and hence in the streets of US metro areas). Thus, like Sacco, Alcaraz's work in defense of Latino immigrants is a critical reflection on the lack of appropriate mechanisms to deal with situations of this nature in a realistic, hands-on manner. As I have mentioned, at this point in his career, Alcaraz's main shortcoming is that he refuses to advance a critique beyond the mere identification of inequality and resort to more effective devices in terms of resolution.

Following their politics of demonization, politicians habitually allude to the illegal nature of migration; that is, as an infringement of the laws of the receiving country. Laws may exist against enterprises of this variety, but immigrants seldom come from places where laws work the way they should. In 2014, the arrival of many children from Guatemala, Honduras, and El Salvador stands as further proof of this fact.[17] For this reason, it is feasible not to contemplate legal obstructions to a matter of life and death. When you fail to imagine a legal order, given its lax implementation in your home country, little does it count against personal initiative and misery. Just as laws do not automatically make something inherently wrong, the fact that a law exists does not necessarily make something else right or moral. A law may exist, but it may condone a double standard in the population, whereby people with means may transgress while others follow. Laws are a cultural product of humankind and, as such, they are open to the changing temperament, mores, and values of the population. What at some point was considered to be morally or socially unacceptable may not be thought of that way after a number of years. Witness the fluctuating postures in the United States with respect to the alcohol industry (made illegal during Prohibition), abortion (increasingly obstructed in a number of states, risking insecurity and violation of women's rights), drugs (with medical or recreational marijuana legal, as of this writing, in twenty-four states and the District of Columbia, and growing), and same-sex marriage (which became the law of the land in June 2015, after attaining legality in thirty-six states previously). In other words, just because there is a law mandating that certain children do not attend schools or that sick people are not to be accepted by the health-care system, it does not mean that it is right or morally sensible for a segment of the population to grow without education or for others to fall sick and possibly die. This is the basic motivation of most of the material included in *Migra Mouse*, which although it poses an alternative, usually very critical view of issues pertaining to the Latino/a population, in many cases it applies to dilemmas faced by nationalities elsewhere.

THE CARTOONS: AN INITIAL CRITIQUE OF US SOCIETY

When it comes to images, Alcaraz makes it quite clear—with his opening salvo—that, amid the fluctuating historical and political context, moral correction is unstable, shaky ground. With this in mind, he includes a cartoon depicting Pilgrim ships arriving on the shore of the United States, where, on a rock, there is a billboard stating, "Welcome to America / The Illegal Immigration Country / Don't let this happen to your country / Call 1 (800) NO

PILGRIMS." According to the caption, the image echoes a billboard erected by an anti-immigrant group as people entered California from Nevada. Alcaraz then alludes to two key considerations: on the one hand, he mentions his Amerindian descent via Mexican heritage, which means that, according to a popular theory on migration, his lineage dates as far back as when Asians first arrived in the Americas by way of the Bering land bridge; on the other hand, he reminds the reader that, even the Pilgrims, who were European outcasts arriving at a time when Amerindians clearly outnumbered them, were given more humane treatment, purportedly sharing a meal that, following the co-optation of this event by official history, has turned into a national ritual—that is, Thanksgiving, which almost certainly never happened as in the rosy version promulgated by the government, although it most likely took place. All this happened even though, as the cartoonist suggests, the Pilgrims arrived with an invasive demeanor, not even considering for a second that the land they were about to live on was already inhabited by others. One could argue the natives were not so arrogant or greedy: unlike the Europeans, they did not believe the land belonged to them; rather, they felt that they belonged to the land, thanks to an ever more generous logic than the Western notion of private property. (This is not to say they could not be ruthless; let's not convey the impression of glorification or idealization.) As US history would come to prove, the locals were on the losing end of the stick. The Amerindians may have lacked an understanding of property according to capitalism—Niall Ferguson suggests a pragmatic, institutionally supported implementation of private property as a key component of the rise of the West above the rest[18]—but the arriving Pilgrims were fairly well acquainted with it and knew what their enterprise entailed in terms of a land grab. The gist of Alcaraz's argument is quite clear: in the United States, we are all—from Native Americans to the most recent imports—immigrants, so it is very hard for anyone to claim that they are entitled to the right to deny immigration to others. At the very least, it strikes as phony or insincere. In the context of this particular image, nobody is in the position to judge and state whether it is correct for anybody to migrate into the country. Then again, the hope would be that, in an increasingly globalized world, economic disparities and political realities would evolve in such a manner as to discourage widespread, uncontrolled migration. To make things even more ironic, Alcaraz talks about "a God-given right to migration," reclaiming the kind of language favored by more conservative groups attacking undocumented workers. The mention of a superior being, and the fact that it has granted a right—never mind the thought that the grantor may be the product of the grantee's imagination, a commodious conflation, to say the least—demonstrates how, when it comes to arguments and tricks, anything is fair game. So, by way of example and the exercising of a basic right—the

CHAPTER 1: OUR ILLEGAL FOREFATHERS

Welcome to the Illegal Immigration Country, 1998
The cartoon above is based on a controversial billboard erected by an anti-immigrant group in California who were trying to make their divisive, xenophobic viewpoints known as you entered the stateline from Nevada. The U.S. was founded on immigration. My ancestors who walked over the Bering Straits, or whatever method they used to get from Asia to North America and down to South America, were using their God-given right to migration. Even the illegal immigrant pilgrims who invaded Indian Country and begged at the first welfare line were deserving of humane treatment, or at least a free turkey drumstick.

Welcome to America, the Illegal Immigration Country, 1998. Cartoon appears courtesy of the artist Lalo Alcaraz and Universal Uclick Syndicate. All rights reserved.

freedom of speech consecrated by government—Alcaraz manages to subvert anti-immigrant assertions.

From this perspective, however, it is not that everything is relative—although this is an argument Alcaraz will embrace at other times. Rather, it is the opposite. If we are to embrace extremes and dictate that it was right for some to come into the country and thrive, and it is not appropriate for others to follow, then, it is clearly a matter of a double standard. Therefore, it is, above all, a matter of being consistent. Within this stringent application of the law, the same rule should apply to all because, for the most part, the conditions of arrival for most of the people have been similar: an economic need—disguised as political, religious, or even cultural sanctuary—that has served as their motivation. After all, it is highly likely that the people associated with the group supporting the billboard are descendants of those who benefited from a more generous approach to immigration by the US government, when the quota system prevailed, regulations were less restrictive, and European descent was prioritized. Their ancestors may come from a wide variety of nationalities and ethnicities, but, given the historic record, it is more than likely that these activists' ancestors came from northwestern Europe; in this case, economic need figured prominently among the rationales for immigration, just as in the case of undocumented Latinos crossing from Mexico into California. The rest, as people tend to say, is history.

This initial cartoon by Alcaraz denotes what I have stated previously: in this first stage of his production, the cartoonist's main strategy is to put forward a critique by setting a new reality—usually, the one pertinent to Latino/a immigrants—in the context of the normative narrative (the Pilgrims, the *Mayflower*, and so on) and validate his production as Americana. Now, we are able to see why. As a Latino cartoonist, Alcaraz's concern is to be consumed and accepted as an Anglophone cultural actor. The main problem with this strategy is that, to accomplish this translation of cultural understanding, he is in some way validating the cultural codes of the established normative narrative, one that, increasingly, provides the cues for the exclusion of Latinos as an alien body. Simply put, at the start of his career, while Alcaraz shows the initiative and spirit to come forward and to denounce prejudice, he has yet to conceive of more committed and practical ways of criticism in which, rather than just exposing what is wrong, he goes further, envisioning new arrangements for the cultural order. And beyond this, he has yet to figure out a way of posing a critique without playing too much into the system, a key concern if you happen to criticize society from an allegedly peripheral viewpoint. In a way, this approach embodies a bit of a contradiction because it shows Alcaraz negotiating how to attack the system with viewpoints from the outside by means of a position in the inside.

In a succeeding cartoon, to highlight his position with respect to Disney and the historical record on immigration, Alcaraz illustrates an encounter between Pocahontas and John Smith, embracing the aesthetics of the entertainment company. Although Alcaraz does not tend to change much his style of drawing, occasionally he will emulate a famous cartoonist (e.g., Schulz, Ketcham, Guisewhite) or a style of illustration (Disney). In this way, quite literally, Alcaraz embraces the status quo—thus legitimating it—even if ironically. In the few instances when he does so, Alcaraz is a master at imitating illustration techniques. Drawing in a style close to Disney's was undoubtedly a part of the cartoonist's objective, as he hoped to problematize how the entertainment industry contributes to a revisionist view of history in most of its projects. Imitating the strokes of Disney's art with perfection, Alcaraz shows Smith giving smallpox-infested blankets as a gift, which will decimate Pocahontas's people in due course. Nonetheless, the cartoonist's ploy escaped an infuriated reader, displaying a lack of depth in interpretation. The reader's letter, which Alcaraz includes on the opposite page, criticizes the cartoonist's "Savage [sic] blood" and chastises him for not portraying the "REAL" Pocahontas, "ugly" and with her hair cut off "to where she was bald." Like any other cultural construct, beauty is subjective and most certainly in the eye of beholder, yet feedback of this nature surely comes across as mean-spirited. The sentence that follows in the letter clarifies this stance even further. In it, the reader reminds the cartoonist how the Native American woman, ever the embodiment of perdition for European settlers, "danced naked in front of the white pioneers." At this point, it is apparent that irony deficiency is even more widespread than initially surmised. With a stroke of the pen, the Pilgrims have evolved from outcasts into "pioneers," granting their effort a positive connotation, and Pocahontas has discarded her ugliness to exude sensuality and allure before a group of venturesome Europeans. By including the letter, Alcaraz shows his capability to steer the meaning of images within the context of the normative cultural order. A text initially designed as a bitter critique turns out to be an ally. At the same time, Alcaraz reiterates how history is a narrative of the victorious, how particular versions are supported according to personal interests—including, most decidedly, the letter writer—thus theoretically striking at the foundations of arguments against undocumented Latinos hypothetically established on historical precedent. In this way, throughout Alcaraz's production, the artificial nature of history's fabricated discourse comes to the forefront, never mind the fact that the cartoonist employs the very discourse he censures to substantiate the basis of his argument.

Needless to say, Alcaraz is remarkably adept at reclaiming what others have thrown at him as attacks and making enhanced readings of images with other purposes. This twist seems to have been the platform for the initial

Smallpox Infested Blankets? 1995
I received the following hate letter about this Pocahontas cartoon. The author didn't quite get that I drew the idealized Disney version of Pocahontas as a goof (right).

Smallpox Infested Blankets?, 1995. Cartoon appears courtesy of the artist Lalo Alcaraz and Universal Uclick Syndicate. All rights reserved.

evolution of his humor, apart from its oblique validation of a cultural norm. At times, he even simply appropriates what is readily available in the course of daily life in Southern California. Most relevantly, in 1994 he appropriated the "immigrant crossing" freeway signs used by the California Highway Department (Caltrans) along many freeways in the Southern California area and embraced them to rebuke politicians. Paradoxically, it was graphic artist John Hood, a veteran of Navajo ancestry who was raised without electricity or running water in a reservation in New Mexico, who designed the image for Caltrans—that is, a descendant of Amerindians came to the protection of people trying to migrate into the land of his forebears. The sign is a common sight along many highways of the region—for example, the I-5 corridor—and was adopted as an attempt to address the unsafe presence of pedestrians on the roads.[19] After crossing the border, many *pollero* and coyote vehicles would drop off their human cargo along the way, hoping to avoid nearby Border Patrol checkpoints. As a result, drivers would suddenly encounter people running across multiple lanes. To deal with this situation, Caltrans commissioned an image that would convey, at a swift glance, the possibility of pedestrians on the highway. The image has become so iconic that it has been reclaimed by many Latinos in California, used in murals and on T-shirts, and even adapted for commercial purposes, such as an image that shows a family holding surfboards that suggests a more entertaining alternative with a local pastime in mind.

The original Caltrans image for "immigrant crossing" shows the silhouettes of three humans—a man, a woman, and a female child—running as one. Although the man does not hold the woman's hand (in Alcaraz's version, he does), his image is connected to hers by way of their legs, which blend together. In this sense, purportedly, the man and the woman run as equals. It is the woman who is explicitly holding the hand of the child, whose main suggestion of gender is the fact that her hair is tied into pigtails. A politically correct reading of this feature could argue that it draws on a more conventional view of gender roles, as the man and woman do not seem to share equally their concern for the child. Then again, from a design perspective, an image with the child between the couple might not have worked so well. Also, from a certain point of view, one could even contend that the undocumented immigrants in the image honor Latinos' alleged deference for family structures, as they are portrayed as a close-knit family unit (running as one). This aspect is not to be dismissed lightly; in terms of cost efficiency, the elaboration of an image based on a single outline (common borders) tends to be less costly. And cost is, after all, a resounding priority for a bureaucracy responsible for the operation and maintenance of some of the most heavily traveled highways in the country.

A second reason that the three family members are portrayed as one contour is not as nuanced. Aside from cost efficiency, it is the result of another practical consideration: the avoidance of accidents on the road. The essential aim of the image is to alert drivers about the presence of individuals at unexpected points along the highway network. In addition, given the speed at which drivers typically are approaching, the sign had to convey a sense of motion to inspire alertness in the public. With this consideration in mind, a little girl with flowing pigtails worked a lot better than a boy, claimed Hood.[20] In sum, the main object of the Caltrans design is for drivers to be cognizant of the fact that, where there is a father, there sometimes follows a mother and, eventually, a child. That is to say, undocumented immigrants racing across the highways of California seldom travel alone, never mind the underlining of a patriarchal mind-set (after all, this is a rather dated way of imagining a family, which now comes in all sorts of arrangements). Thus, if you are driving and you see an immigrant racing across the asphalt, it is appropriate for you to diminish your speed as another immigrant is very likely to follow. So, with all these points in mind, it is quite evident that the sign's motivation is not simply to protect the transgressors' lives. Ostensibly, if someone is struck, there has been an accident and that should be the end of things (assuming the driver's goodwill, who should stop to attest her or his responsibility). The fact that the admonition stresses sequentiality makes clear that the intent of the sign is, most particularly, to protect the motorized vehicle, which happens to be using the road. As the intended *subject* for this image—the image is drawn from the driver's point of view—it is the vehicle's driver who will face the sequential challenge to her or his senses. It is her or his decision to brake and save a life. In turn, as *objects*, it is the immigrants who are portrayed as out of place, hurried, and reckless. These are, most definitely, people who *should not be at this place* (but, unfortunately, happen to be). This sign, like much of the infrastructure in Southern California—for which Caltrans happens to be responsible—as well as that of much of the rest of the country, has not been designed with the best interests of pedestrians in mind. With this mentality in consideration, cities like the District of Columbia, New York, San Francisco, or Chicago stand as proverbial exceptions. For that matter, rather than build a set of pedestrian bridges, Caltrans soon fenced the median at key points of transgression, effectively putting an end to the issue. Thus, it becomes glaringly clear that, for practical purposes, Caltrans does not seem to be singularly concerned about the health of undocumented Latinos who, by definition, are infringing the law—in the end, they are cutting across a road where there is no marked pedestrian crossing—but is perhaps more anxious about the well-being of the users of its lovingly maintained network of roads (though Californians critical of the conditions of their roads would state otherwise). After all, it is assumed that these drivers are the taxpayers who have funded construction of this infrastructure. While this might be a justifiable approach—like any institution, the first priority of Caltrans is to look after its own, the customers who enable its survival—a closer analysis of the implementation of this safety measure sheds light on the distinctive value being assigned to life. In this sense, the billboard takes an unintended stance in the struggle for recognition of undocumented workers. Following a more inspired approach,

Signs of the Times, 1994
This cartoon and several others throughout this book are based on the famous "Immigrant Crossing" freeway signs that grace the Southern California area. They are seen by many as an inhuman rendering of immigrants, sort of like a Deer Crossing approach to representing undocumented immigrants. Caltrans, the California Highway Department, probably had safety in mind when they first posted these near high immigrant traffic areas where "illegals" braved high-speed freeway traffic in search of a better life. Regardless, they have become an icon, and very useful to artists and cartoonists looking for familiar symbols. This cartoon, "Signs of the Times," captures the anti-immigrant hysteria that poisoned California in the early '90s and spread throughout the U.S.

Signs of the Times, 1994. Cartoon appears courtesy of the artist Lalo Alcaraz and Universal Uclick Syndicate. All rights reserved.

one could go even further, questioning whether distinctions of this nature are compatible with the avowed spirit of our nation, so quickly claimed by conservative groups.

Lalo Alcaraz tries to turn this sign on its head. On one page, he copies it faithfully; on the other, he includes an analogous sign portraying a couple (holding hands, no kids) chasing the immigrants. Above the couple, rather than the word *Caution*, the cartoonist places the word *Politicians*. The man on Alcaraz's version of the image holds a bat in his hand; unlike the running immigrant, he sports what seems to be a jacket (its edge hangs above his right leg), and his profile, with a long, pointy nose, is suggestive of that most renowned of California Republicans: Richard M. Nixon. In short, the man could pass for an angry, white-collar crook. Unlike the mother in Hood's design, who wears flat shoes, the woman in Alcaraz's parody runs in high-heeled pumps, an impractical measure and an affirmative indication of her social status. Both display open mouths, angled irately, alluding to the vocal quality of their outrage. In addition, the absence of a child may be construed in one of two ways: either they are empty nesters, who tend to be older and more conservative in their political preferences (particularly among baby boomers), or they belong to the double-income, no-kids (DINK) segment of the population, which also tends to be identified as selfish and/or egotistically driven, typical of the beneficiaries of the economic boom in California in the 1980s and 1990s. In one way or another, without declaring it explicitly, Alcaraz is trying to make clear that this pair most likely sides with Republicans, a party allegedly mindful of a dream of self-sufficiency and financial independence. Rugged, individualistic self-sufficiency is easy to claim if you do not account for the government's implementation of a working economy, which provides everything, from cell-phone communication to running water to a decent job and education to viable investment opportunities. Also, by proposing a dialogue between these images, Alcaraz talks about the transformation of state politics in the context of Republican administrations. In this light, the illustration can be read literally: in California, working-class families of Latino/a descent are being chased out of the state by rich, greedy folks with little else on their mind but their own self-interest. Thus, just as the drivers are to be cognizant of the risk on the road, Alcaraz's audience is to be markedly aware of selfish people of this nature and irritated by the fact that others are willing to partake in their prosperity. The cartoon is aptly titled "Signs of the Times," playing with the meaning of the phrase, in the sense of billboards and zeitgeist. In 1998, Alcaraz revisited the Caltrans image and gave it a more sinister twist. In front of a billboard, with the sun at its back, lay the skeletons of three immigrants—a man, a woman, and their daughter—exactly in the same pose as in the billboard, only with an empty water container next to the woman's cranium. In this new permutation, the billboard acquires a prescient air, foretelling the death of the entire family. The desert, which looms large across the US-Mexico border, particularly around portions of California and Arizona, is an inhospitable place. In the end, however, regardless of his adept use of the Caltrans image, Alcaraz also substantiates the notion that people running across the state's superhighways happen to embody a risk for the average citizen. That is the implicit hazard in taking someone else's narrative and appropriating it for reasons of mockery. Criticism may work, but only as

Signs of the Times, 1994. Cartoon appears courtesy of the artist Lalo Alcaraz and Universal Uclick Syndicate. All rights reserved.

long as readers are able to relate to the initial image as a cultural reference. Thus, for humor to work, a certain degree of validation must be present.

At certain points, Alcaraz might come across as too extreme in his criticism, giving the impression of embracing personalities for the sake of controversy. His critical disposition is always willing to undertake enhanced readings of figures and situations and, to this effect, he relies on a series of customary mechanisms. Part of his strategy resides in the proposal of parallels between characters. In another image titled "Separated at Birth?," he displays Pete Wilson next to a hypothetical doppelgänger, the German dictator Adolf Hitler. By embracing Hitler as model for his critique, Alcaraz is resorting to a cultural milieu: the national entertainment and cultural industry's habitual appropriation of Hitler as the definitive embodiment of evil (from *Hellboy* to *Captain America*). Now, it is one thing to represent Hitler as object of derision, and another very different one to use him as a point of reference for a critique. It is not Hitler who is being criticized, but rather the other character who is portrayed as his analogue. Wilson is framed as an evildoer, but only in the most US-centric way possible, so that readers are able to recognize this brand of criticism as a practice of US origin, culturally coded as Americana. But, is there any risk here that, while critical engagement is being celebrated as tradition, the enactment of extremism is also being substantiated? In truth, Alcaraz draws Hitler and Wilson using the same outline, except for the hair, mustache, and attire. Hitler sports typical Nazi regalia; Wilson wears a suit. The stance, facial expression, and tie are the same. While Hitler fumes at Jews, Wilson blames Mexicans. Both minority groups are labeled as being evil. The analogy between how the German chancellor used anti-Semitism as a measure of political gain and the way in which Wilson blamed Latinos—and Mexicans in particular—for all the troubles in his state points out a basic rule of thumb: the advantageous exploitation of otherness. When in trouble, always blame a scapegoat. Through this representation, Alcaraz is not only appealing to Latinos, who may equate Wilson's misuse of an issue with racism and fascism, but also to the influential Jewish population in California, so closely linked to the entertainment industry. This is a very age-determined piece of criticism, especially as the last remaining Holocaust survivors begin to fade away. The cartoon may be Manichaean, replicating the tactics of division popularized by the Republican governor, but this does not detract from its effectiveness. In humor, the range of admissible arguments tends to be ample. In a sense, it is as though Alcaraz was answering Wilson with his very same set of tools. The fact that both parties—Nazis and Republicans—represent political entities with a propensity toward a world in black and white—a viewpoint so adamantly enforced by George W. Bush—aligning themselves at the right end of the political spectrum, a segment where nationalist militancy, hawkish tendencies, private consolidation, economic self-reliance, parsimony in government, and disregard for difference coincide, makes for a droll comparison. Under the guise of economic rationales, the object of this strategy seems to be the preservation of the privilege of the 1 percent at almost any cost, rather than to share and coexist in prosperity.

Hitler is not the only character used by Alcaraz to compare with Pete Wilson. Alcaraz is an equal-opportunity critic, yet he resorts to figures that promote extreme views, giving his production an equal air, a facet that may not always result in effective denunciation. It may not be a good thing if your cultural production is perceived to be as radical as that which you intend to disparage. From a reader's perspective, it may render your criticism useless. Once he has singled out certain features of his target, Alcaraz favors multiple modes of comparison, no matter how controversial. And to accomplish this, he sporadically contravenes racial boundaries. In a way, Alcaraz may give the impression of resorting to the very tactics he criticizes. In another cartoon, he

Separated At Birth, 1994

Separated at Birth?, 1994. Cartoon appears courtesy of the artist Lalo Alcaraz and Universal Uclick Syndicate. All rights reserved.

depicts the governor as a member of a group similar to the notorious Nation of Islam (NOI). Alcaraz illustrates Wilson with a suit, bow tie, and hat similar to those worn by the Fruit of Islam, the male-only paramilitary wing of NOI. In fact, the hat displays the initials *FOI*, which in this case, the cartoonist clarifies, stand for "Free of Immigrants." In the image, Wilson is labeled "most honorable," à la Louis Farrakhan, and the illustration calls for the celebration of a "historic Million Mexican March," very much in the spirit of the march called by the leader of the Nation of Islam that was held on October 16, 1995, at the National Mall in Washington, DC. Alcaraz's imitation is obviously tongue in

Million Mexican March, 1995

Million Mexican March, 1995. Cartoon appears courtesy of the artist Lalo Alcaraz and Universal Uclick Syndicate. All rights reserved.

cheek, as the cartoon calls for the attendance of "only men, women, children, and elderly relatives." In other words, the hope is that "only" everyone will attend, that not a single Mexican be left out, since the directions for the event are quite clear: "Head South!!" The fake event, it turns out, is a spoof of the Million Man March simply because it wants all Mexicans heading south together—out of the United States! If Lalo Alcaraz is a cartoonist well known for his critical vein, it is equally discernible that Farrakhan strikes as a no less polemic figure, given his statements of anti-Semitic and sexist nature. In fact, in an attempt to suggest a lack of a distance, in terms of intolerance, between Farrakhan and the German leader, journalists and figures associated with the Jewish community have sometimes called him a "Black Hitler."[21] A comparison to the head of the Nation of Islam situates Wilson in the context of a master manipulator, suggesting the use of ideology for personal gain—in the case of Farrakhan, his appropriation of religion, be it Islam or Dianetics (Scientology); in the case of Wilson, an improvised form of nationalism and/or populism based on a lax understanding of ethnicity. From this perspective, both are, by and large, figures well acquainted with the corrosive potential of the politics of division, bent on the demonization of difference. As in the case of Hitler, Alcaraz's embracement of Farrakhan as model for criticism also identifies the cartoon as a thoroughly culturally determined practice of US identity, to be understood and digested mainly by readers accustomed to Americana. As a result, Alcaraz inscribes himself more and more into the US cultural mainstream as a cultural actor associated with extreme views, be it as subject or object.

Alcaraz's approach to humor can also be light and whimsical. Thanks to the amplitude of US culture, he need not tread far in this direction. Mickey is not the only US icon lampooned by Alcaraz. In another cartoon titled "Dennis the Mexican Menace," the cartoonist appropriates Hank Ketcham's character, so illustrative of the bland, clean-cut, suburban nation of the 1950s. The basic tension of the story in this comic strip, set in the city of Wichita, Kansas, is the rivalry between Dennis, a precocious, freckle-faced kid, and Mr. Wilson, his cranky, cantankerous middle-aged neighbor, whom the boy seems to love (despite the fact that the child constantly irritates his elder). In Alcaraz's Dennis, he preserves the use of his overalls, ditches the striped T-shirt for a plain-colored one, and flaunts dark hair, revealing himself as a Mexicanized version of the white-bread boy from middle-of-the-road Kansas. Dear reader, there is a feeling we are not in Kansas anymore (talk about a cultural matrix, if there was ever one!). Quite evidently, the cartoonist is referring to the situation in his home state of California. Following this approach, Alcaraz Mexicanizes Dennis in a single vignette.

Within the arc of the original comic strip, Dennis's youthful misdeeds are the customary source of amusement and constitute the heart of its plot. Faithful to Ketcham, Alcaraz renders a Dennis who has mistakenly gotten his neighbor wet while watering the lawn. The caption reads, "Mr. Wilson hired me to water his lawn and then he called me a *mojado*." The term *mojado* means *wet*, but, in the context of Mexican American Spanish, it connotes *wetback*, the pejorative expression for immigrants who have arrived to the United States by wading across the Rio Grande while carrying their clothing in sealed plastic bags (thus their wet backs once they have dressed at the other side of the river). Mr. Wilson, the mustachioed grump with a heart of gold (in

Dennis the Mexican Menace, 1995

Dennis the Mexican Menace, 1995. Cartoon appears courtesy of the artist Lalo Alcaraz and Universal Uclick Syndicate. All rights reserved.

the original story, he is secretly fond of Dennis), has transformed, most obviously, into Mr. Wilson, that is to say, *Mr. Pete Wilson*, the California governor. So, when Dennis claims to have been hired to water the lawn, his assertion acquires a different quality, alluding to a habitual perception of Latinos as gardeners or landscapers (like Alcaraz's father). At another level, Dennis's love for the man, traditionally predicated on the child's need for affection, acquires a different connotation: as a Latino, as a new enactment of US identity, the Dennis of Alcaraz's imagination demands acceptance and validation in a dignified manner, rather than the discriminatory and prejudiced way in which he is viewed and treated by his temporary employer. Furthermore, the game with water, while it works at a superficial level—the child does not understand why he is called *wet* when it is his neighbor who has been soaked—can also be interpreted in another way: when it comes to migration, whose presence is more valid? The one of a descendant of Anglos who arrived in California (as the image is no longer supposed to be set in Kansas) as the result of the 1849 gold rush or the post-WWII suburban boom, or the one of progenies of Amerindians and Spanish conquerors, both of whom inhabited the area long before the arrival of the Anglophone? All the same, by embracing the term *menace*, Alcaraz also plays with recent US history, in which the word immediately recalls the witch hunts of McCarthyism and the context of the Cold War, when, amid endless theories of international conspiracies, anyone remotely linked to left-wing movements was instantly designated as suspicious. Thus, by appealing to a historical narrative, Alcaraz even manages to frame his version of Dennis in a context of extreme politics. By echoing paranoia and finger pointing, Alcaraz delineates Wilson and his opportunistic politics within the same tradition. Then again, it all falls within the framework of the cartoonist's production at this point in his career, when extremism served him well in his cartoons, despite the potentially counterproductive result.

The cartoonist's repertoire of targets and icons oscillates between individuals and institutions. As I have stated previously, the Republican Party plays a key role in the cartoonist's production. In the late 1990s, amid the shortsighted economic boom of the Clinton years and the revival of conservatism sparked by Reagan and Thatcher, the presence of undocumented Latinos waiting for work at particular corners of working-class districts, where they would be promptly picked up and hired by contractors, became a common sight in many metro areas of the nation. Soon enough, the higher visibility of these workers sparked a nascent backlash, which would grasp hold of xenophobe factions of the right-wing political establishment. In August 1996, the California Republican Party held its national convention in the city of San Diego, the cartoonist's hometown. Bob Dole, the former senator from Kansas who would eventually win the nomination and lose to Bill Clinton, competed against conservative political commentator Pat Buchanan, publishing executive Steve Forbes, political activist Alan Keyes, and legal scholar Robert Bork, a colorful array of pundits, and then some. Alcaraz could not miss the opportunity to get back at these politicians. Yet, rather than get personal and dilute his critical verve among personalities, his approach instead was to focus on a more homogeneous objective: the delegates, who invaded the city of San Diego and nested in its many hotels, unaware of their embodiment of difference. Thanks to the presence of the military, the defense industry, and a

San Diego Republican Convention, 1995
The GOP delegates enjoy another Southern California morning, thanks to immigrants.

San Diego Republican Convention, 1995. Cartoon appears courtesy of the artist Lalo Alcaraz and Universal Uclick Syndicate. All rights reserved.

community of retirees, San Diego has long had a solid reputation as a conservative enclave. However, to compare a Californian conservative with a run-of-the-mill, middle-of-the-country conservative is like comparing apples and oranges. That is why Alcaraz must have felt the contrast between the Waspy delegates, so eager to enjoy the Southern California weather, and the staff from the hotels, typically composed of working-class stiffs—and thus more representative of regular folks close to the border—would elucidate a fitting view of the political party's double standard. On the one hand, he illustrates a mustachioed waiter named José offering cocktails to a pair of delegates; another mustachioed worker, a landscaper, pruning a tree by the pool; and a third, a dark-haired chambermaid, pushing a housekeeping cart on her way to the rooms. All three occupations are commonly held by minorities, which, in the case of San Diego, are usually Latinos of Mexican descent. On the other hand, the female delegate inside the pool, so representative of the detached lifestyle of suburban housewives, is asking her husband, who lies sunbathing and relaxing on a pool chair, "Honey, what time is our anti-immigration delegate meeting at?" Thus, the image is highly symptomatic of the double standard implicit in people willing to chastise others for attempting to find a better life in this country, yet benefiting complacently from the comfort provided by their services. Who do these people think they are, the reader could surmise, to expect pampering from an underclass whose rights they so vigorously deny? How can they impart such treatment to others without any admission of the contradiction latent in their behavior? At first glance, their attitude smacks of entitlement because of the contrast between the lazy, overweight delegates, who could easily personify people from a less diverse and culturally isolated mainstream USA (think of the *TIME Labs* map quoted previously), and the busy hotel staff, agents incarnate of the "browning" of the country, which showcases in one quick stroke the chasm between classes in the United States. In this way, Alcaraz is speaking about two nations that, for the most part, do not talk to or interact with each other. Unfortunately, while the criticism may be valid, it also manages to situate things in a simplistic binary order, which tend to present matters in terms of black and white, hence ratifying a polarized outlook. In other words, though in a different manner, this particular cartoon emulates the extreme dynamics of the previous ones, only through a distinct tactic. The subjects of this illustration might exchange pleasantries at the time of commercial or service transactions, but true dialogue and acquaintance remains a distant possibility. In this way, San Diego, a city by the US-Mexico border and Lalo Alcaraz's birthplace, enacts the margin within US society.

ALCARAZ ON LANGUAGE: THE ENGLISH-ONLY MOVEMENT

Within the variety of topics covered by the cartoonist, bills and policies of dubious logic also play a significant part. The English-only movement, sparked by the latent insecurity of monolingual Anglo voters, occasionally uncomfortable with the fact that others—Latinos, Asians, Africans, and so on—speak more than one language, also plays an important role in his production. In the course of the twenty-first century, as the population of the United States varies and the number of Euro-Americans decreases comparatively, the country will become an increasingly multilingual enclave. Such a shift does not occur sans friction. In 2000, echoing the events in California, Arizona voters passed Proposition 203 by a margin of 63 percent, limiting the type of instruction available for English-language learners. For practical purposes, the vote reflects a decreasing support for multiculturalism and the widening consecration of total cultural assimilation. It remains a remarkable fact that, for such a diverse and vast country, so allegedly celebratory of difference, some segments of the United States remain obstinately, fiercely attached to a monolingual agenda, completely blocked to the possibility of other linguistic traditions—a pointless, unexplainable attitude in an increasingly globalized world—to the extent that, given likely psychological impediments, some of its inhabitants will perform poorly even when awarded the opportunity to learn another language. The denial of a second or third language in a global world is not only culturally shortsighted, strategically speaking; as the demise of an advantageous commercial tool, it also spells out a tragedy.

When I shop for groceries in Georgia and speak to my son in Spanish and he answers in English—a logical consequence of the predominance of Anglo tradition at his school (we live in a community with few middle-class Latinos, despite its claim to diversity) and in his family (I am the only Spanish speaker), even though his district is one of the few in the state to offer Spanish classes for all grades, from pre-K to high school—people stare at us, baffled, as though we were accomplishing a singular feat of strength. It is not necessary to protect the English language, I would contend. The legacy of Shakespeare and the British Empire can take good care of itself, as society, school, friends, and general society will nourish it—not to mention adolescent propensity to conform. When previous generations worried about assimilation, they underestimated the overwhelming appeal of the English language in everyday life. English represents a fiercely normative linguistic view of US society. It is the other languages that should be protected, I would argue, because, according to statistics, they will perish within three generations, failing to do wonders for the US economy. In the coming years, the rapid development of translation technology will make this trend toward linguistic homogeneity even more acute. (Skype, for instance, is already toying with translation technology in its software.) A key tool for the enrichment not only of our culture but also of our entire economy stands in the survival of these other languages, given that we need to have the tools to engage trading partners and allies in a more competitive fashion. At least superficially, Alcaraz's artistic production appears to be cognizant of this fact.

In this regard, the United States replicates closely the behavior of other cultures that, when they feel threatened culturally—such as France or Spain, which, after forcing their culture upon the Americas, still oppresses regional heritages within their states—resort to intellectual disqualification and vilification of difference. This behavior, I maintain, represents a remnant of the trauma of the melting-pot experience, which pursued so aggressively the elimination of traces of cultures from many home countries. In this respect, however, Latinos are said to behave differently. Had the Irish, Italians, Dutch, and German enjoyed the Internet back then, Eurocentric cultural diversity would be even more widespread and established around the country. And this kind of mind-set is not the privilege of the Anglophone. In many ways, it is a historical constant. Conceivably, it is also a behavior that mimics the dynamics of the forceful conversion of Jews to Catholicism during the Inquisition, when fresh *conversos* instantly became rabidly protective of cultural homogeneity, hoping to dispel any suspicion of difference until they eventually forgot why they professed such a militant brand of religious creed. As we say in Spanish, their behavior was *más papista que el Papa* (more partial to the Pope than the Pope himself).

All things considered, US identity is the result of an intimate contradiction: in a country with people of all classes, races, creeds, and sexual orientations, so bent on the appeal of difference, we are continuously reminded that there is nothing as national as coming together as one: *E pluribus unum* (Out of many, one), as proclaimed on the seal of our country. As a consequence, unlike other nations, which preach homogeneity, the United States can claim to preach heterogeneity—that is, as long as, ultimately, everything falls under one category. This smacks of lip service to difference. In plain terms, we must all be different. There is no alternative. We live in the prison-house of difference. If you do not embody difference—and here is where things tend to get tricky, given the idea of difference being a cultural, and thus fabricated, man-made construct that is conceived, endorsed, and supported by a cultural and political establishment—you are likely to be not playing your part as a good citizen. Nonetheless, there are various ways of being acceptably different and, in the United States, linguistic difference is not one of them. You can be different racially, socially, and even sexually, but do not dare contest Anglophone linguistic hegemony, the mainstream's refrain seems to say. (The elitist establishment tends to be more pragmatic, nurturing fluency in other languages as a sign of privilege.) Otherwise, you will not be like everybody else (who are acceptably different) and will stick out like a sore thumb. We must all be the same in that we are all acceptably different in the very same ways, excluding things like cumbersome meddlings by the tongue of Cervantes and García Márquez, as Alcaraz's cartoons on the English-only movement tend to attest.

Within this context, difference reigns supreme as long as it is practiced in the way construed, dictated, and celebrated by the government. After all, our culture is a veritable machine of identity, swiftly co-opting any discourse that comes even remotely close to questioning the government's particular implementation of the idea of nation, from the riffs of "The Star-Spangled Banner" by Jimi Hendrix to barred and starry outerwear during the 1970s. In view of these considerations, the work of Lalo Alcaraz attempts to act as a safety valve for US identity, effectively establishing a historic record in which many notions and concepts begin to register as examples of Americana. This is the price to be paid by coding your cultural production as *Americana*. By way of narrating the Latino experience in his cartoons and comic strips, Alcaraz is enhancing the overall spectrum of consensual behavior, including his extensive use of Spanglish. From this perspective, it is perfectly consonant that, unlike many other nations, the United States lacks a specific mention of an official language in any of its political charters. Such an absence is not the product of an oversight, I suggest. Rather, it is a sign of self-assuredness—cultural hubris, if you will. It is a measure of the degree of certainty about the correct way in which a particular idea of nation will be implemented by its corresponding material embodiment, the US government, so long as a privileged elite, at the wheel of a national project, follows precisely the dictates of charters. After all, what is not the state but the materialization of the correct implementation of an idea of nation? Think of Voldemort slowly attaining materiality during the Harry Potter saga. Something that initially stood as a vague notion in the minds of Jefferson, Franklin, and so on, once accurately communicated on paper, took on a life of its own, until it morphed into a superpower, chock full of aircraft carriers and nuclear weapons. English is such an uncontestable part of the way in which national identity has been implemented in the United States that, most likely, to those who first conceived the idea of a state in this country, the need to spell out linguistic hegemony did not seem necessary. Other languages would be welcomed (and digested) because, through eventual co-optation by the machine that is national culture, they would enrich tradition and never come close to threatening the vast supremacy of the English language, theoretically intrinsic to the understanding of democracy and capitalism manifest in our charters, according to some very ethnocentric Anglophone theoreticians (à la Samuel Huntington). Following this train of thought, only individuals with latent insecurities need to repeatedly ratify their cultural preeminence; for example, searching for official ways to consecrate English as the language of the state. It is no accident then that, unlike Romance languages, which espouse entities that look obsessively (and belatedly) after their corresponding tongues, the closest thing of this nature in English tradition is the *Oxford English Dictionary*, hardly an equivalent for the Académie Française or the Real Academia Española (or any of its Hispanophile versions in the Americas). Taking everything into account, English has a far superior ethnocentric tradition, empowering its speakers to conquer the globe in just five centuries. Most cogently, the corollary to this affirmation is that people who vie for the concrete mention of English as the official language in government documents are rendering a disservice to the implementation of this supremely confident idea of nation authored by the founding fathers.

Millionaire software developer Ron Unz, who pushed for Proposition 227 in 1998, may qualify as one of those. Despite opposition from language-education researchers, Proposition 227 aimed to transform California's bilingual education system into an opt-in, structured–English language educational system. Although it contemplated granting exemptions for people willing to remain in English-immersion classes, these were limited. Also, it included punitive measures for instructors unwilling to perform in an English-only environment. In the cartoon that satirizes Unz, which mimics James Montgomery Flagg's famous Uncle Sam recruitment poster—once again, the US-centric cultural matrix—Alcaraz portrays Unz as a dunce, playing against type because the millionaire recurrently boasted of a reputation for his high IQ during his unsuccessful bid for the Republican nomination for governor of California in 1994. Instead of 214—Unz's alleged IQ—the button on his jacket displays the number 227. Also, the phrase "I Want You," so evocative of the armed forces' recruitment poster, appears above "to speak one language," in a manner more exclusive to the language controversy in California. In this way, Alcaraz compares the issue, the product of anti-immigrant hysteria in the late 1990s, with corresponding knee-jerk reactions in the culture, to the evolution debate in some parts of the South, such as when renowned orator William Jennings Bryan sided with state laws banning public schools from teaching evolution in the famous 1925 Scopes trial.

When it comes to the English-only movement, there is always space for a few turncoats. Bolivian Jaime Escalante, the famed math teacher memorialized by Edward James Olmos in the film *Stand and Deliver* (1988), is, sadly, another one of those standing on the wrong side of history, clinging to an English-only campaign that would rob many children of the opportunity to be bilingual and bicultural, a treasured value in a progressively diversified world. During the 1990s, Escalante spoke in support of English-only campaigns and, in 1997, joined the English for Children initiative, which campaigned against bilingual education. Alcaraz spoofs Escalante with the language of math, with statements like "speaking Spanish only causes division" and "bilingual Latinos tend to over multiply" coming from his mouth. Finally, he draws the Bolivian teacher with a writing pad, on which he has scribbled a nonsensical "$2 = -0$." Escalante, it turns out, is trying to find a mathematical equation that encapsulates his main claim in the cartoon: "I'm positive: two languages equal a negative," which in the end he must admit "doesn't add up." Escalante's participation in the English-only movement represented a low point in his career and happened when he had left Garfield High School, the place where he became famous for his masterful instruction. It is likely that positions of this nature did not make him popular among many Latinos. Alcaraz situates him with other minority figures known for speaking against the best interests of their own groups.

In yet another editorial cartoon, framed as a comic strip, Alcaraz lambasts controversial figures Richard Rodriguez and Linda Chavez. Rodriguez, a best-selling author on the subject of the Mexican immigration experience and assimilation into US culture, is well known for his opposition to bilingual education and affirmative action. As for Chavez, a FOX News analyst who served as White House director of public liaison during the Reagan years, her conservative politics and active participation in the Republican Party have alienated many Latinos. Alcaraz represents Rodriguez as a talking Olmec head, preaching his hatred for "La Raza" in a plug for an imaginary book titled *Brown Like Me*. The Olmecs, the first major civilization in Mexico, lived in the tropical lowlands of present-day Veracruz and Tabasco; they are well known for their stone carvings of huge heads, some of which can weigh well over fifty metric tons. The image used by Alcaraz, in particular, appears to be similar to the heads from the archaeological site of San Lorenzo Tenochtitlán in southeastern Veracruz. In this way, employing literal big-headedness, Alcaraz criticizes Rodriguez's arrogance and intellectual presumption, exemplified by the fact that most of his books seem to share a common, favorite topic: himself. The cartoonist also encapsulates in Rodriguez his dislike for Latinos who embrace postures that devalue the importance of linguistic heritage and Latinos' lack of access to opportunities in education and employment, given the conservative author's emphasis on monolingualism and callousness toward immigrants. Alcaraz shows the book's manuscript, which resulted from Chavez's commission of a text that disparages Mexicans—for the laughable sum of five dollars a day, meant to mimic immigrant wages—in which Rodriguez claims to address the question of what it is like to be a Latino, since the Californian author has made such a huge point of his Anglicization. To accomplish this, Alcaraz describes Rodriguez embracing brown makeup, a sombrero, Kmart pants, huaraches, and a can of malt liquor; in other words, embracing a cliché-ridden set of elements emerging from a prejudiced view of Latinos. After he strolls through the city in this getup, the Toltec head expresses its discomfort with the experiment. It then reaches out to its literary agent to pitch the manuscript, which the agent assures him will sell well among Anglos, who are avid for the consumption of normative difference. Finally, the head requests that the book not be marketed as a Latino volume, since Rodriguez claims to hate when minorities capitalize on their ethnicity—but instead requests that the book be pitched as a Chicano studies text!

Thus, through a mocking appraisal of tokenism, what Alcaraz is actually criticizing is the conditions for the production of a discourse that appeals to the claims of conservative pundits (à la Pat Buchanan), who have gone as far as decrying the negative impact of Latino/a culture and the Spanish language on the Anglo mainstream. In 2002, he produced a similar comic strip against Buchanan, portraying the Republican at his best, like a talking head, pitching his book *The Death of the West*, which warns about the collapse of Western civilization due to declining birth rates and sweeping immigration from places like Africa, Asia, and Latin America (also à la Huntington). Buchanan is depicted blasting Latinos and MEChA, the student organization Alcaraz used to belong to, while he orders food at Taco Bell. To counteract Latino propensity to breed like rabbits, Buchanan will strip naked and visit the ghetto, hoping to stunt the community's sexual desires with his homely appearance.

Yet Buchanan is not the only talking head ranting against MEChA. In 2003, just as the recall election for California's governor was taking place, Alcaraz depicted FOX News personality Bill O'Reilly (although Alcaraz calls him "O'Really") discussing MEChA as a way to demonize the Democratic candidate, Lieutenant Governor Cruz Bustamante. O'Reilly had condemned Bustamante's participation in MEChA during his college years at Fresno. According to Alcaraz's version of O'Reilly, MEChA's objective is the takeover of California and its eventual return to its rightful owners, people of Mexican descent. To be exact, during the political campaign, O'Reilly actually described MEChA as a racist organization whose primary purpose is to return the states of California, Arizona, New Mexico, and Texas to Mexico, so Alcaraz's version pales next to the truth.[22] Nevertheless, to accomplish such a perfidious objective, according to the cartoon, MEChA dares advocate the radical notion that young Latinos get a college education! Like Chavez, Rodriguez, and Buchanan before him, O'Reilly seems dramatically out of touch with US society when it comes to the availability of better opportunities for Latino/a immigrants. In such cases, meritocracy—be it by way of bilingualism or English-only—is out of the question.

In those days, California was not the only state behind efforts of this nature, which demonized the use of other languages. Alcaraz alludes to a right-wing shift in Colorado politics by drawing a highway billboard welcoming drivers to a place called "RED," as in a red state, signaling the growing power of the Republican Party. The color red has been associated with Republicans since journalist Tim Russert used it to track the votes, outlining the nation's political divide, during the 2000 presidential elections, notwithstanding the fact that red has usually borne a left-wing connotation, an ideology diametrically opposed to the Republican agenda.²³ (This inappropriate choice of colors to signal right- and left-wing proclivities speaks volumes to the degree of political illiteracy in the country and US ethnocentrism, clearly unconcerned about these colors' political connotation elsewhere.) In the late 1990s and early 2000s, Colorado leaned heavily Republican, ominously foreboding initiatives similar to the ones voted in California. In Alcaraz's cartoon, the billboard identifies the place as the "home of the next anti-bilingual education initiative." In fact, on November 5, 2002, Colorado voters rejected Amendment 31, the local version of Unz's anti-bilingual, English-immersion initiative, by a margin of 56 percent to 44 percent. As it happens, between 2000 and 2002, Unz made repeated trips to Colorado, heading the effort behind the proposal. In "Breaking the Code: Colorado's Defeat of the Anti-Bilingual Education Initiative," Kathy Escamilla et al. chronicle the efforts of Coloradans to defeat this measure.²⁴ The article includes a list of ten factors that contributed the most to the defeat of the measure, key among which are the building of broad-based, bipartisan coalitions; great focus and attention on the message; the relevance of fund-raising; and good timing. The event is all the more remarkable if we consider that, on the very same night on which Coloradans rejected the measure, a sister initiative, Question 2, passed by a wide margin (68 percent) in Massachusetts, a state with traditionally progressive leanings. It is plain to see that, when it comes to linguistic conformity, even conventionally open-minded communities exhibit a regressive streak. Thus, Alcaraz was correct in his need to warn Coloradans about the risks associated with Unz's politics. However, by playing with the name of state, Alcaraz not only alludes to Republicans. He also reclaims the location and situates it in the same light as California: as a place where Spanish heritage preceded English culture. The double entendre with the state's name only makes sense because the meaning of *colorado*, in Spanish, is red-colored. So, by bringing attention to its English equivalent, it may be argued that Alcaraz is emphasizing the Anglicization of historical onomastics and underscoring the state's heritage. From this perspective, the term points out how the name came from Spaniards who explored the region, naming the place after the reddish color of the river that runs through it. In fact, coming from the Mexican Cession of 1848, which resulted from the Treaty of Guadalupe Hidalgo, well over half of Colorado used to belong to Mexico. Like Nevada and Montana, Colorado belongs to the group of western states with names of Spanish origin. Colorado's naming might not be as deeply rooted in Spain's learned tradition as California's, but it is still representative of the weight of historical record. Hence, Alcaraz is willing to summarize the many similarities in context between both states in a single image. In this sense, there is a shift in his arguments with respect to the English-only movement: consciously or not, Alcaraz is beginning to support his criticism with a cultural context that strays from the version of history supported by the monolingual, Anglophone establishment. Quite clearly, the cartoonist is seeking a way beyond the strict validation of criticism through the normative order of Americana.

ON VIOLENCE BY THE BORDER: VIGILANTISM, EXPLOITATION, AND HARASSMENT

In 2000, Alcaraz published another billboard cartoon. Denoting a return to his earlier approach, it represented a new take on Hood's Caltrans image: this time, the immigrant family appeared to be running away from a cowboy-hat-wearing assailant, who aims his rifle at them. The billboard's message read "Bienvenidos a Arizona" (Welcome to Arizona), a frank allusion to the rise of vigilantism in the state. In May 2000, the Mexican government hired a US law firm to help gather evidence and bring charges against Arizona ranchers, alleging they illegally detained immigrants through vigilante actions. At a news conference, the Mexican foreign minister Rosario Green said thirty-two incidents of vigilantism had been committed against Mexican immigrants in the United States since January 1994; of those incidents, twenty-seven were in Arizona. According to the *Los Angeles Times*, Mexico decided to take action against the ranchers after a Texas man was charged with killing a Mexican immigrant on his ranch and after a television station showed Arizona ranchers allegedly holding immigrants at gunpoint.[25] The Texan rancher in question is seventy-three-year-old Samuel Blackwood, a retiree from Arkansas, described in a story by Tim McGirk and Ronald Buchanan for *TIME* magazine that chronicled the growing tensions around the US-Mexico border at the time.[26] On May 14, 2000, Blackwood shot twenty-two-year-old Eusebio de Haro Espinosa in the groin and left him to bleed to death after he stood fifty feet from his ranch's door begging for water. According to witness Javier Sánchez—who, together with De Haro, had hiked nearly two days to Blackwood's trailer in Brackettville, Texas, forty-five miles north of the border—after they asked for water, which a woman refused to give them, they took off down the road, and the couple (Blackwood and his wife, Brenda) followed them in a truck.[27] When they spotted them again, the couple stepped down and ordered them to stay put. As soon as he saw the gun, Sánchez fled. From a distance, he saw how De Haro begged for help after being shot in the back of the leg while he ran (the autopsy confirmed he was shot from behind), and, to the couple's indifference, bled to death. Later, a 2005 documentary by brothers David and John Eckenrode and John Sheedy, *El inmigrante*, would recount his demise. Actually, De Haro was the third Mexican shot by south Texas residents since November 1999. At the time of De Haro's killing, a sixteen-year-old boy had also died. Given this string of events, it became increasingly obvious that some people were more than willing to take the law in their hands and hunt down immigrants. However, taking into consideration the statistics that the Mexican government was collecting, Arizona—not Texas—was a primary concern. Proportionally speaking, although people of Mexican origin are equally represented in both states, the number of fatalities in Arizona tilted the balance heavily in its favor as the target of an initial legal action. This much is evident in Alcaraz's cartoon, which combines imagery from California's highway system with Arizonan vigilantism. The cartoonist was well aware of the fact that, although the sign serves as a general measure in highways near the border, it was in Arizona rather than California that undocumented immigrants were being targeted like prey. Thus, by taking this information into consideration, Alcaraz is showing that, while he pays heed to details relevant to Latinos, he remains adept at the appropriation of imagery supporting the normative order.

In 2002, Alcaraz raised the stakes, producing a cartoon about Arizona border snipers, establishing a contrast between the uproar generated by the Beltway sniper attacks around the Washington, DC, area, in which John Allen Muhammad and Lee Boyd Malvo killed ten people from a Chevrolet Caprice sedan, and the lack of interest for the actions of snipers along the US-Mexico border in Arizona. In the cartoon, a pair of white men express their outrage regarding the Beltway shootings while, on the side, their shadows stand out behind a cactus, just as they are ready to aim at immigrants walking across the desert. The juxtaposition of characters in two contrasting settings informing the debate on policing the border is meant to convey the binary, oppositional fashion with which much journalistic coverage has framed the issues. In this cartoon, nonetheless, the drawbacks of a nationalist mind-set become evident. The value of life is colored by national affiliation, introducing harsh distinctions between fellow nationals and outsiders. This, I suggest, is a reductive mind-set that nourishes hatred and intolerance because it allows individuals to disparage difference. While the deaths in the District of Columbia received significant coverage, those by the border barely registered. In other words, death only matters when it befalls a US citizen. The sad twist of the story is that later, perhaps incensed by the inaction against sharpshooters targeting its fellow nationals and exhibiting equal capability in the vilification of others, Mexican drug cartels and coyotes started using snipers to target Border Patrol agents. Sniper incidents against border agents date as far back as the 1990s, but now that vigilantism was on the rise in places like Arizona, they acquired a different quality as a form of retaliation for the mistreatment of fellow nationals.[28] On the other hand, the shootings of Mexicans have continued, and they are not exclusively because of the zeal of vigilantes. On June 11, 2013,

Border Snipers, 2002

Border Snipers, 2002. Cartoon appears courtesy of the artist Lalo Alcaraz and Universal Uclick Syndicate. All rights reserved.

the *New York Times* reported, "Shootings by the United States Patrol agents have caused the deaths of at least 15 people and increased border tensions with Mexico."[29] It is a result of such developments that author Todd Miller, in words echoed by many others, has argued in an op-ed article that "the US-Mexico border has become a war zone and the Border Patrol has become an expensive military apparatus deployed to police and capture immigrants."[30]

At another point in his book, as I mentioned previously, Alcaraz adheres to US cultural history, seeking a normative frame of reference for his criticism. In an image from 2001, he portrays a Latino worker with a "5-year" ball and chain around his neck. In the cartoon, the character is a participant on a remake of an imaginary 1950s classic TV show called *The Bracero Program*, the name of the policy created by Congress in association with the agribusiness sector. The episode is titled "Indentured Servitude," immediately establishing parallels with early US settlers, who would labor for a number of years to cover the cost of their passage to the British colonies. From Alcaraz's viewpoint, the revival of the bracero program—*bracero* being the Spanish word for someone who uses his arms (*brazos*; i.e., a manual laborer)—proposed at the beginning of the twenty-first century was tantamount to indentured servitude, as it demanded that workers labor for five years before gaining amnesty. The original program operated from 1942 to 1964, covering the entire decade of the 1950s. In the end, echoing a similar note to today's criticisms, it was terminated under the claim that it contributed to the exploitation of Mexican workers and deprived US citizens from salaried jobs. In this sense, Alcaraz is toying with the reference provided by normative history in terms of an official national account, while at the same time his allusion to the aesthetics of a TV show from the 1950s hints at familiarity with mainstream cultural codes. Quite obviously, Alcaraz's critical approach has not evolved drastically; his main concern still pertains to the viability of a peripheral critique from the very insides of a culture.

In 2001, prior to the September 11 attacks, the George W. Bush administration and its Mexican counterpart, headed by rancher Vicente Fox, were actively discussing the implementation of a new guest-worker policy, including the possibility of an amnesty, a term that, with time, consolidated its loaded meaning. According to public defender Camille Bosworth, Bush's plan prior to 9/11 included the possibility of amnesty provisions granting legal residency status to undocumented foreigners who held jobs and paid taxes.[31] However, unlike the Immigration Reform and Control Act (IRCA) of 1986, by 2004, Bush's suggestion of an amnesty had elapsed. After 9/11, Bush's position evolved, eventually supporting a guest-worker program favoring a period of three years and an increase in the immigration quotas, to handle potential immigrants surfacing from the three-year scheme. In contrast with the rest of his party, Bush tried to appeal to Latinos. Conscious of their potential for votes, he worked aggressively to increase the GOP's share of their historically Democratic vote. On the other hand, the business community, generally friendly to Republican fiscal policy, also supported a guest-worker plan. It was no coincidence that, when the time came to announce Bush's guest-worker program proposal, it was Senator Saxby Chambliss, from Georgia, who announced it because Georgia's farmers have traditionally cried for help from the federal government when it comes to farmhands. In this sense, Alcaraz was upping the ante. By framing the possibility of an amnesty within the general context of US history, he was comparing treatment of Mexican guest workers to impoverished indentured servants during the colonial period. In this manner, Alcaraz counteracted the way guest workers had been portrayed by the media, similar to the way immigrants had been represented during the Proposition 187 debacle. By comparing them to indentured servants—immigrants who had toiled arduously to gain social stature—the guest workers immediately benefited and their efforts earned moral stature. In this manner, as potential immigrants compared to victims of the past, they were inscribed within the overall context of US history. Once again, this is an example of Alcaraz's initial approach: rewriting outsiders from the inside. Back then, though a distant possibility, amnesty seemed feasible and the immigration-reform debate was not as poisoned as it stands today. In another cartoon of the same period, Alcaraz even represents Bush and Fox as bedfellows, both dreaming of amnesty to gain more votes. Sadly, as the backlash from 9/11 came to prove, the political honeymoon between these administrations was short-lived. Later, with the advent of the Obama presidency, a new, more recalcitrant leadership arrived to Congress and things ground to a halt.

Alcaraz's relationship with US history is rather accommodating in the handling of events, also alluding to closer incidents. In another cartoon, the caricaturist features his recurring mustachioed character (his take on Mexican stereotyping) suffering a beating from sheriff's deputies. The image is designed to evoke the thrashing suffered by Rodney King, which sparked the 1992 LA riots, in which fifty-eight people died and more than two thousand were injured. Readers may recall it was Los Angeles Police Department personnel that hurt King. However, the switch to sheriff's deputies is no mistake. While the LAPD has had its share of problems, they pale next to the ones faced by the Los Angeles County Sheriff's Department, which figures among the most troubled law-enforcement agencies in the nation. Recent coverage by the press and the fact that a special position has been created to oversee its excesses can attest to this statement.[32] Outgoing sheriff Lee Baca's tenure (1998–2014) has been plagued by scandals, including alleged favoritism for celebrities and inmate abuse at the Los Angeles County jails. In 2016, he pleaded guilty to federal charges of lying during an investigation into civil rights violations at the county jail. Nevertheless, Alcaraz wants to extend his criticism to another event, one having to do with immigrants and generally representative of the nature of excesses in this context: on April 1, 1996, two Riverside County sheriff's deputies, Tracy Watson and Kurt Franklin, were suspended with pay after beating two suspected illegal immigrants, Alicia Sotero Vásquez and Enrique Funes Flores. To their chagrin, a nearby helicopter news crew filmed the incident, which took place at the end of an eighty-mile chase along a California highway, from Temecula to South El Monte. Watson was subsequently fired. Franklin returned to duty as an observer aboard a helicopter. A California Highway Patrol officer who was at the scene was fired for lying to investigators. Vásquez and Flores filed lawsuits alleging civil rights violations and settled for $740,000.[33] In comparison to King's $3.8 million settlement, this sum might appear paltry, but what matters to Alcaraz is voicing his concerns for the mistreatment of immigrants. So, rather than depict the LAPD, the public entity involved in the Rodney King incident, Alcaraz focuses on the Sheriff's Department.

The humorous twist comes from what the man exclaims while he is being hit by the officers: "Only 3 hours in America and already I'm getting treated like a King!" In the first place, the fact that Alcaraz calls it *America* rather than *California* or the *United States of America* speaks to his subjectivity as a national humorist. His focus is not local. It is not even regional; if it was, the character would speak of California or Southern California (SoCal). The fact that he appeals to readers with the term *America* speaks to a more mainstream audience. Beyond this consideration, Latin/o Americans or recent arrivals would tend to be critical of the United States' appropriation of the name for the country, since in Spanish the word is used to designate the entire continent rather than a single nation. On the other hand, when Alcaraz uses the name *King*, there are various conceivable readings. The first, immediately obvious one would be an allusion to Rodney King, who, at this point, had already sued the City of Los Angeles in a federal civil rights case and received millions of dollars as settlement. Given the context, a second one could be to Nobel Prize–winner Martin Luther King Jr., who, as an African American, stands as the most eminent figure of the civil rights movement and is highly representative of the moral stature of minority leaders. Although a champion of nonviolence, King was well known for not shying away from potential abuse by policemen. A third reading would contemplate boxing promoter Don King, famous for his "only in America" catchphrase, which highlights the turns of fortune in US reality. And a fourth, even more ironic one would be to the fact that this is what has to happen to an individual in the United States to receive a juicy lawsuit payment, concluding a march from rags to riches. In both cases, Rodney King's and Vásquez and Flores's, the end result of abuse was a jackpot, speaking volumes to the dysfunctional nature of justice in the country. In a place where one of the best things that can happen to an immigrant is to be abused and then collect precious retribution, things surely are in a sad state of affairs. In other words, this is what needs to happen for someone "to be treated like a king," following a common idiom in American speech. A society that achieves justice through the oppositional dynamics of an overpaid legal system rather than by way of thoughtful progress and due diligence is doomed in the long term, one could argue. So, the term *King*, with its multiplicity of meanings in the US context (rather than in a Eurocentric one), is quite advantageous for Alcaraz's approach, bent at transgressing conventional boundaries with a deceptive touch.

Another example of Alcaraz's re-reappropriation of Americana is a cartoon that he published in 2001: "The Insult That Made a Man Out of Mac," basically, a rewriting of the famous Charles Atlas 1940s cartoon, which appeared as advertising in many comic books of the postwar period. The scenario of the original narrative was that of a couple enjoying a day at the beach. Suddenly, a bully threatens the skinny young man in front of his girlfriend. When he returns home, demonstrating his frustration, the lad kicks a chair and orders the Charles Atlas bodybuilding book. Once he has built up his physique, he returns and beats up the bully, gaining praise from his female companion and locals. As a matter of fact, Alcaraz follows a contemporary practice, in which scriptwriters acquire the rights to old comics, like Joe Simon's *Young Romance*, and rewrite the dialogue, making for amusing entertainment, as in Marvel's *Marvel Romance Redux*. In other words, it is not only in the act of alluding to Charles Atlas that Alcaraz is echoing a US cultural practice; it is also in the act of rewriting the dialogue that he honors the ways of the US entertainment industry, copying the manner in which it takes old narratives and refashions them. In Alcaraz's new version, the skinny guy at the beach is upset about illegal aliens kicking sand in his face and bringing down property values. The muscled-up man, who is now Mexican, claims (in Spanish) that he is in the United States to be able to work and not starve, which the skinny guy takes as a blow to his physical condition. In turn, his girlfriend just comments on how "those people" are ruining her time at the beach. When the guy gets home and kicks the chair, rather than ordering the Charles Atlas book, he applies to the Border Patrol, where, through basic training, he builds up a formidable musculature. He then beats the Mexican while his female companion tells the immigrant to return to the desert. In the end, instead of Charles Atlas's info, there is a Border Patrol logo and praise for Operation Gatekeeper and the new Border Patrol agent that people claim has killed 1,000 Mexicans! The humorous, hyperbolic touch appears in line with the intense viewpoints expressed by the cartoonist in some of this early production.

According to Alcaraz, the cartoon was meant as a critique of Operation Gatekeeper, a measure implemented in the fall of 1994 by the Clinton administration, under which the budget for the Border Patrol was drastically increased so that it could focus its efforts on the westernmost stretch of the border, near San Diego. In a way, Operation Gatekeeper was the opening salvo in the war on the US-Mexico border, which, as we have seen earlier, escalated as the result of the outright militarization of the Border Patrol. To an extent, it is possible to establish a parallel with the consequences of the militarization of many police departments across the nation, which engendered a mind-set conducive to events like the death of Michael Brown in Ferguson, Missouri, in 2014. Alcaraz drew the cartoon in response to a 2001 *New York Times* article in which Diane Rose, then mayor of Imperial Beach (a city fourteen miles south of downtown San Diego and five miles northwest of downtown Tijuana, Mexico), asserted, "When I hear comments that Operation Gatekeeper doesn't work, well, it's worked for us. Suddenly, people feel comfortable walking along the beach with their children in the evening. Your evenings are not disrupted anymore. People want to live here."[34] Quite evidently, the language from the article falls well into the journalistic practice described by Aguirre,

Rodriguez, and Simmers in their analysis of the Mexican threat in US media.³⁵ According to the *New York Times* article, thanks to Operation Gatekeeper, the wildlife refuge at the Tijuana estuary is enjoying newly found peace, and tourists are returning to nearby Imperial Beach, where more people are moving in than out. In addition, the Border Patrol's tighter enforcement is benefiting the occupancy rates at hotels, there is increased attendance at beach events, and the property values have seen a 28 percent increase in the course of a year.³⁶ Thus, a matter of life and death—the possibility that immigrants may find themselves stranded in the desert and perish from heat exhaustion—has turned into a quality-of-life issue for a beach community. Exasperated by the turn of events, which he found as shallow as the classic cartoon's treatment of identity, taking into account the precedence it gave to real estate over the value of life, Alcaraz snagged the Atlas comic strip and rewrote the dialogue. It was not the first time that the cartoonist chastised Southern California culture for not getting its act together. In 1998, Alcaraz published a more succinct version, in which a pair of entomologists marvels at the sight of an endangered border butterfly atop an endangered border cactus, surrounded by the skulls and bones of many deceased immigrants. To Alcaraz, this discretionary tendency toward the compartmentalization of the value of life appears baffling. How can people care about the value of real estate or wildlife when, right across from where they live, people are dropping dead in the desert? The implications of a localist mind-set, which sometimes tends to favor trivial issues at the expense of other, more significant ones, become awfully clear.

Time after time, Alcaraz has inscribed his criticism in the context of US culture. On occasion, he embraces tropes that are mainly familiar to older reading publics, which, statistically speaking, tend to view Mexican immigration across the desert less favorably, failing to contemplate the generosity of the immigration system to their ancestors. By setting the dispute on Mexican immigrants crossing the border near Imperial Beach in the language of a character and advertising familiar to those who consumed comics from the 1940s to the 1960s—various versions of the Charles Atlas ad ran for quite a while—Alcaraz is challenging the sense of difference portrayed in advertising narratives from earlier decades, when the US population imagined itself a lot more homogeneous than it really was. (Even if it was more homogeneous, pockets of difference were concealed carefully, without acknowledgment of their presence.) In other words, by representing the Mexican immigrant as a muscled-up individual straddling the beach—which is not hard to imagine, considering their manual-labor, working-class context—not only is Alcaraz granting the immigrant further visibility, but he is also making a statement about the degree of invisibility of difference in US society during the years of the postwar period, when, amid the economic boom and the rise of the middle class, particularly in communities in suburban California—as in the case of Imperial Beach—the emphasis was on the heavy homogenization of the masses. It is important to note that, located only a few miles from Tijuana, Imperial Beach's largest demographic group is Latinos, comprising almost half of its population. However—and this is an aspect that is sadly missing in Alcaraz's critique but is quite evident in the *New York Times* article—some Latinos raised in the area viewed Operation Gatekeeper as something welcome, forgetting that not too long ago, their ancestors could have experienced a similar situation. This is the classic case of Latinos who, once they have made it, tend to forget about past circumstances and do not empathize with newcomers. As we can see, when it comes to a recollection of the generosity of the immigration system, insensitivity and self-interest know no bounds; they cut across ethnicities and are far from being exclusive to a single societal group.

Perhaps for this reason, Alcaraz's criticism is not exclusively dedicated to other groups. Self-criticism is more often than not a healthy practice. He finds the term *wetback* rather offensive, principally when other Latinos embrace its use, a not altogether uncommon event within the community (similar to the use of the *N*-word). In a cartoon from 1994, he portrays Latinos outfitted like homeboys next to someone dressed like a cowboy (although the belt buckle says "MEX"); the youth are calling the man a wetback. Next, he portrays Uncle Sam, the definitive incarnation of a US Anglo identity, calling the homeboys wetbacks. After all, the concept of Uncle Sam dates to the early nineteenth century, a time when the country envisioned its population in a very homogeneous fashion, completely dominated by a male Anglo imaginary and almost exempt from difference. Flagg's well-circulated image, which dates from much later—1917—gives an idea of how long the country has lasted under a rather harmonized construct of its identity. Then again, by placing the pejorative expression on the lips of Uncle Sam, Alcaraz points out how further validation of the term benefits no one. Indeed, it is not unlike the *N*-word, which is utilized by some African Americans to the discomfort of others. Alcaraz seems more practical. No matter how much an expression is reclaimed by a segment of a community, the very fact that it needs to be set in a certain context for it to appear justifiable deems its use problematic. Words may convey a sense of history, but history does not imply that the use of a symbol—a word, a flag, an icon, for example—needs to be perpetuated to commemorate the past. There are many more constructive ways of celebrating the past without the necessity of giving offense, I propose. After all, language itself changes. Words die out. Neologisms surface. Meanings change. Syntax evolves. Hence, to justify the preservation of an offensive cultural practice exclusively on the basis—the lame excuse—of honoring the past or even reframing it within an ampler context of prejudice is, aside from simplistic, a matter of avoidance of responsibility. In this regard, it is feasible to identify commonalities with the cartoonist.

ALCARAZ AND OTHER ISSUES: LEAF BLOWERS, NOISE, AND 9/11

Prejudice takes many forms. It does not need to be as obvious as the white robe of the Ku Klux Klan or the Nazi swastika. However, when trying to counter prejudice, it is key not to give in too much to the politics of division, lest the end result of criticism turn into a validation of equally harsh views. Witness the Sierra Club's opposition to immigrants, which, until the 1990s, was supported on the basis of alleged concern for nature, theorizing that immigration drained resources and harmed the environment.[37] This sort of stance brought the environmental organization face to face with Latino community leaders for quite a while. Along the same lines, the ban on leaf blowers in Los Angeles, justified on the basis of noise and air pollution, was strongly associated with Mexican workers. The ban reads:

Effective on February 13, 1998.

(c) Notwithstanding the provisions of Subsection (a) above, no gas powered blower shall be used within 500 feet of a residence at anytime. Both the user of such a blower as well as the individual who contracted for the services of the user, if any, shall be subject to the requirements of and penalty provisions for this ordinance. Violation of the provisions of this subsection shall be punishable as an infraction in an amount not to exceed One Hundred Dollars ($100.00), notwithstanding the graduated fines set forth in L.A.M.C. Section 11.00(m).[38]

The problem with the ban was precisely that it was articulated in such a way that it mainly targeted Latinos, who, by and large, were the ones laboring with the devices. Thus, a measure that alleges concern for the levels of noise and the quality of air ends up targeting a specific demographic in a rather incommensurate fashion. In the corresponding cartoon, Alcaraz illustrates a white woman in a gas-guzzling, fumes-emitting SUV yelling at a Latino with ear-protection gear working with a leaf blower (the label on his shirt seems to read "JOSE"; the characters are very small). To convey the volume of her words, the size of the letters of her rather wordy diatribe in the bubble are quite large. In a gesture typical of a clash of classes in the city of Los Angeles, ever expressed by its relationship with the entertainment industry, the woman identifies herself as a scriptwriter. Consequently, the contrast could not be more apparent: on the one hand, a white, upper-middle-class woman who works from her house writing (most likely) for Hollywood; on the other hand, a blue-collar Latino working as landscaper who spends most of his days laboring in the sun. Yet the voice of the woman fills half of the panel, whereas the landscaper's two sentences are locked inside a small bubble. He states, in search of validation, "See? I'm not the noisiest." In this way, Alcaraz alludes to the outlandish scale of the brouhaha regarding leaf blowers as well as to the disparate proportions of advocacy in everyday political debate, frequently determined by the magnitude of economic means. The arguable concern for the quality of the air in the City of Angels, once known as the most polluted metro area in the country (it has now been outdone by other Californian communities), is immediately debunked by the vehicle—so representative of the upper middle class of the 1990s—which, when it comes to pollutants, can readily equate and surpass the damage produced by the leaf blower. Now, it is valid to employ stereotypes to summarize arguments. After all, stereotypes exist for a reason. However, if the stereotype is not properly contextualized, portrayal of identity can appear to be as reductive as many others.

If anything, when it comes to criticism, Alcaraz appears to believe in equal opportunity. Nobody escapes his barbs. In 1996, mocking the idea of a Hispanic heritage month—a period of thirty days starting, roughly, with the celebration of the independence of a number of Spanish-speaking countries (Mexico, Guatemala, El Salvador, Honduras, Nicaragua, and Costa Rica) and ending with the anniversary of the arrival to the Americas of Christopher Columbus—he illustrates a series of clueless characters in a calendar-like arrangement. On September 15, a man asks what are Central Americans, given their rampant invisibility among the general public. With geography skills symbolizing a sore point of the national education system, Alcaraz enshrines the clichéd notion that US inhabitants are dramatically unaware of their international surroundings. In recent academic curricula, the Americas appear divided into North and South, eclipsing Central America altogether. On the sixteenth, alluding to the national holiday south of the border, an old hag questions Mexican dependence on social services. On the seventeenth, *menudo*, a Mexican delicacy made from the entrails of a cow, is said to come from one with bovine spongiform encephalopathy (mad cow disease). On the eighteenth, a country-music fan alleges mariachi music takes away from Garth Brooks's work, mocking the US genre's disdain of other ethnicities. On the nineteenth, referring to public television's snobbery and linguistic hubris, a news anchor reiterates that PBS viewers do not speak Spanish. On the twentieth, a mathematician complains about the high birth rate among Latinos. And so on. For every day of the month, Alcaraz documents a complaint against Latinos, against their laziness, their propensity for graffiti, or even the fact that they may be running from the border. So, a month that is supposed to celebrate Latino roots on a daily basis ends up becoming a time to vent against immigrants, in effect sowing division rather than integration. That is what measures of this kind may accomplish, hints Alcaraz, as the way in which they highlight the profile of a specific group only tends to provide ammunition for criticism. Then again, despite sharing the cartoonist's opinion on the futility of measures of this nature, which serve mostly as lip service, very little is suggested regarding more appropriate ways of integrating alternative identities to conventional mainstream culture.

Two years later, in another multi-paneled chart, perhaps evoking *El Gran Panteón Amoroso*, the piece by renowned Mexican engraver, printmaker, and cartoonist José Guadalupe Posada that parodies the stages of courtship, Alcaraz illustrates a table/calendar with an explanation for weather patterns, sparked by the growing awareness of the meteorological phenomena El Niño and La Niña. In it, the satirist traces childhood, adolescence, adulthood, old age, and death, laughing at what the expressions mean for each age. However, as with everything by Alcaraz, there is a twist to what each expression represents. For example, *la muchacha*, which means "the young woman," passes in colloquial Spanish for "the maid," so she is described as "washes away dirt, grime at your *casa*," in open reference to the number of undocumented immigrants serving as home cleaners in suburban households. *El señor*, or "the gentleman," a middle-aged individual, "blows leaves, cleans yards, you cry," references the large number of middle-aged Latinos laboring as landscapers. Finally, death, or *la muerte*, is "the storm to end all storms." The effect of Spanish, evident in expressions like *La Niña* or *El Niño*, gives way to the admission of everyday contact with immigrant identity, in a fashion consistently more routine than many folks uncomfortable with immigration issues would like to admit. And so, while *El Panteón Amoroso* talks about love, Alcaraz's chart addresses a love/hate relationship with life in the United States, one best left unaccounted by some of its protagonists and audience. The love/hate nature of this relationship, I suggest, could come from the constant fluctuation of identification between the periphery, generating a feeling of disenfranchisement, and the Anglophone mainstream, resulting from the cartoonist's *pocho* condition.

Although acutely critical, Alcaraz certainly does not try to be perceived as a negative person. At times, though, the verve behind his attacks can foster this impression. He occasionally strikes a positive note in his work, as when he re-created the poster for Paul Rodriguez's *A Million to Juan*, a 1994 romantic comedy in which the Mexican-born stand-up comedian plays a character who receives a check for a million dollars, only with a catch: the condition is that he must return it all in a month; in other words, the protagonist must figure out a way to produce as much money as possible with the million dollars so he can keep a good deal of it. The film is loosely based on the 1954 classic starring Gregory Peck, *Man with a Million*, which is in turn based on Mark Twain's short story "The Million Pound Bank Note." In Alcaraz's version, the title transforms into *A Million of Juans*, describing the potential of Latinos as a social contingent, able to deal effectively with the number of pro-Wilson's Proposition 187 businesses, like ARCO and VONS gas stations, Disneyland, Hewlett-Packard, the Gallo Winery, and so on. (All are listed on the sack of dollars Rodriguez holds in Alcaraz's version of the film poster.) In a nutshell, the cartoonist is advocating a boycott of these products as a measure of Latinos' potential impact through political mobilization. If Latinos stop being consumers of these companies, he contends, these California staples will have a better measure of Latino presence and rethink their position with respect to immigrant issues. On Rodriguez's head, rather than an LA Dodgers baseball cap (as on the original poster), he bears a cap with the word "RAZA" inscribed on it, trying to summarize how, upon acting as a whole, Latinos would be able to gain increasing political traction on many issues. This is not an altogether uncommon argument. On both sides of the border, Mexicans have wondered what would happen to the US economy without its steady supply of cheap labor, as in Sergio Arau's 2004 film *A Day without a Mexican*, which speculated about the implications of a shortage of a low-cost workforce and its statistical impact on the California economy. Along the same lines, it has become understood that in order for a group to attain political leverage in the United States, it must first make explicit its economic and commercial might. And, whereas the slogan on the original poster asserted, "Money can't buy everything. Yeah, right," in Alcaraz's spoof, it simply claims, "The odds are in our favor," alluding unequivocally (and positively) to the potential for gains from an exercise in societal and economic visibility. In this respect, this particular cartoon is a novelty within Alcaraz's work because it frames circumstances in a more positive light, looking at the future as a time of hope rather than focusing on the imperfections of the present.

And, as I have pointed out earlier, Alcaraz does not limit his work to the defense of the Latino/a community. More production of this nature would definitely contribute to a less binary (us/them) perception of his work, perhaps resulting in a broader audience. Bigotry and cultural insensitivity are the same for all. That is why Alcaraz has centered on documenting the contradictions or double standards emanating from the backlash in a post-9/11 reality, such as when a group of Middle Eastern medical students on a road trip through Georgia were mistaken for terrorists. On September 12, 2002, during a trip to Florida, Ayman Geith (a naturalized citizen of Palestinian descent); Kambiz Butt (a naturalized citizen born in Iran), from Chicago; and

Omer Choudhary (a US native of Pakistani ancestry), from outside Kansas City, stopped at a Shoney's on Red Bud Road near Calhoun, Georgia, where former nursing assistant Eunice Stone, who was enjoying a plate of fruit with her eighteen-year-old son Josh, overheard their conversation and notified authorities.[39] Geith wore a Muslim skullcap, which Stone described as a "thing on the head." According to Stone, she'd "lived in big cities," so "ethnic minorities were not new to her." Alerted by local law-enforcement agencies, the Georgia Bureau of Investigation immediately notified branches of Florida law enforcement, recognizing that, as a rule, Interstate 75, the highway in question, is used for journeys concluding in the Sunshine State.[40] Stone reported that the men were giggling and joking about 9/11; later on, it became public that the local waitress serving them had started the joking about 9/11. Eventually, the three men were taken into custody near the western end of Alligator Alley, the solitary stretch of I-75 that passes through the northern portion of the Everglades, where more than one hundred law-enforcement personnel congregated. While TV crews in helicopters hovered above, a robot pulled objects from the trunks of their two cars. Three days after the Shoney's incident, which was ridiculed by comedians and praised by government officials, Stone was rushed to the hospital with chest pains. The dialogue in Alcaraz's version highlights the occasional lack of exposure to cultural difference in the countryside—though at times the countryside can be more diverse than a city, given rural industrial investment. The dialogue also builds on the notion of racial profiling and the childhood game of telephone, in that phrases are distorted or misinterpreted to conform to preconceived expectations of threat: "med school" turns into "flight school"; "get down to Miami" becomes "bring down Miami" (Choudhary was actually speaking of purchasing a vehicle in Kansas and "bringing it down to Miami"); and "Alabama" is heard as "Allah." Most important, by highlighting the act of misinterpretation, Alcaraz mimics a game of Chinese whispers (the derogatory name for a game of telephone), a sad reminder of how demonization of the other permeates everyday culture in the United States. Like the expression *Russian scandal*, *Chinese whispers* is said to be of European origin and meant to convey a prejudiced idea of the Chinese language and its unintelligibility. In other words, it is an old, very consecrated form of Orientalism—that is, using representations of the Orient to validate a particular idea of the West. In this way, the cartoon in itself is an ironic reenactment of prejudice rather than just a representation of the practice of prejudice. By invoking a practice that speaks of bigotry, Alcaraz effectively problematizes the roots behind the misunderstanding in Georgia. How can you blame people for being apprehensive when the fear of the other is built into monolingual culture, evident in the language itself? When, for lack of a better, less academic term, fear of the other is logocentric?

Once a monolingual culture begins to engage difference, things are bound to happen, such as when many immigrant employees were rounded up prior to the 2002 Salt Lake City Winter Olympics. In December 2001, preceding the Olympics and as part of an apparent effort to increase homeland security, federal and local authorities staged raids throughout the country. In Salt Lake City, sixty-nine people—the most in the entire country—were arrested; all worked at Salt Lake City International Airport.[41] To justify the operation, Salt Lake City authorities claimed their illegal status made the arrested vulnerable to blackmail by terrorists. One of the detainees, a manager at the Ben and Jerry's ice cream shop at the airport, had been working with a false Social Security card for ten years. Another detainee was allowed to remain in the United States until the baby his wife was expecting was born. Clearly, the circumstances behind the arrests seem baffling and escape almost any logic. Alcaraz, however, is particularly controversial in the imagery of his criticism. To communicate the sense of intimidation prompted by an international event in the heartland, he illustrates the Olympic symbol of five interconnected circles as cylindrical cells containing dejected Latinos. The image is highly illustrative, as a logo with international significance—theoretically embodying a celebration of difference, the meeting of all nations—turns into a repressive device used against a specific group. However, there is a certain deviation in the aim of this critique. A first impression could suggest the object of the cartoon is criticism of the Olympics rather than of authorities in Utah, who are detached from the international nature of the event. When security becomes the utmost concern and is viewed through the prism of a normative aspect of the local community, outsiders are easy to identify. In all likelihood, the prevalence in Utah of the Church of Jesus Christ of Latter-day Saints, a religious practice bent on homogeneity, if not in terms of race or ethnicity, certainly in terms of conformity to dogma, contributed to the event. So, when religion becomes a brand of homogeneity, it becomes easy to target those who, for historical reasons, happen to represent another faith, even if they do not practice it (although an increasing number of Latinos have converted to forms of Protestantism). Known as the preeminent Mormon enclave, Salt Lake City enjoys its fair share of international visitors. After all, Mormons are active travelers and practice missionary service worldwide. Brigham Young University, the largest religious university in the country, located in Provo, Utah, is particularly robust in its teaching of languages. However, this apparently vigorous engagement of difference is conflated into a single religious denomination, effectively diminishing the impact of a sensible assessment of difference. Conforming to the dictates of a single religious creed, all races and cultures blend into one, seeking a common denominator. Thus, the undocumented workers stood out like a sore thumb for their lack of cultural affinity amid a community thoroughly structured by religion. All these aspects add to Alcaraz's criticism of the absurdity of improperly managed security measures, yet they fail to be considered properly in a cartoon too reliant on the power of the Olympic logo, so unhinged from the likely circumstances engendering prejudice against a certain brand of difference, significantly more rooted in the context of the local culture.

It is hard not to see how the events of 9/11 have affected harshly the migratory landscape. To a large extent, 9/11 has influenced a particular variety of the US mind-set and has been embraced as justification by certain segments of national society to thwart further negotiation of immigration reform—most notably, the Tea Party, which discards any possibility of an amnesty or a path toward the eventual legalization of millions of undocumented workers. Rather than realize that resolution of this problem opens up a possibility of engagement for Republicans, the Tea Party has opted for further alienation among Latinos, who increasingly side with Democrats, despite their political ineffectiveness. Unlike Republicans, Democrats seem to welcome difference within their rank and file. Nevertheless, it is fairly obvious that the US immigration system is broken and in dire need of attention. Most applicants for immigration wait for years before being accepted into the country. Entrance to the United States is now a more protracted and cumbersome experience, be it on first instance (as a recent émigré) or as a regular traveler, and involves having to deal with a number of new measures (like a webcam snapshot or fingerprint reading). Given occasional paranoia and its impact on the appraisal of difference—until recently, Latinos were the proverbial incarnation for the other; with ISIS, Muslims have replaced them—the political will to implement immigration reform among many US representatives and senators has come to a halt.

In addition, when it comes to immigration, the number of people caught in limbo—like green-card soldiers enrolled in the US Armed Forces—has increased drastically, giving way to the questionable notion that people may be good enough to die for a country, but not to elect its government. In 2001, according to the press, more than 31,000 active-duty military personnel were legal residents but had not yet completed the naturalization process.[42] About a third of these people came from Mexico and other Spanish-speaking countries. For a while, during the Iraq war, George W. Bush tried to offer an expeditious way toward naturalization for these soldiers.[43] In 2003, to approach this aspect from a critical perspective, Alcaraz toyed mockingly with the idea that border militiamen, so adamant in their degree of animosity toward immigrants, should join Saddam Hussein's army, hoping to shoot more than a few among those enlisted in US forces. (The cartoonist does not contemplate the fact that, given the statistics on friendly fire—epitomized by the untimely death of NFL star Pat Tillman—joining Saddam's forces would not seem to be necessary.) Beyond the humor, the conflation of an archenemy of the country and a group of vigilantes does not seem practical because it promotes an understanding of prejudice in line with the demonization of certain Middle Eastern identities fostered by the Bush administration. To frame your object of critique in the same light—even as a joke—as parties that have been thoroughly vilified by the establishment is not a very felicitous strategy because even the ironic celebration of similarity will tend to undermine any argument.

On top of that, during the conflict, taking into consideration that the media—for example, the *New York Times* and PBS—started listing daily casualties, many immigrants gained heightened visibility, and many readers and viewers began to develop a better consciousness of the degree of diversity in the population. In spite of everything, the US Armed Forces represent a more candid microcosm—socially, racially, genderwise, and so on—of national society than perhaps many other, more privileged institutions in the country, such as the academe or the corporate sector, to name two obvious examples. In death, by appearing on the page of a newspaper or at the end of the daily news, these soldiers accomplished that which eluded them so persistently through their lifetime, an irony Alcaraz materializes through the image of a soldier on a TV screen while a flag-wearing militiaman proclaims his willingness to join the enemy and shoot down Latinos. While the cartoon's logic might be a stretch—sadly, as the shootings at a Sikh temple in Wisconsin in 2012, two Jewish centers in Kansas in 2014, the regional center in San Bernardino in 2015, and the gay nightclub in Orlando in 2016 show clearly, prejudice knows no bounds—it does convey well the extremes to which the failures of the current immigration system have affected the population, feeding paranoid responses that ultimately end in violence.

At the conclusion of his volume, Alcaraz tries to address the future, following Hollywood directives. And what better way to do this than to engage a man who has arrived from the future to become California's governor? In an image from 2003, he depicts Arnold Schwarzenegger, who, by this time, was beginning to serve his first term as governor. Alcaraz draws Schwarzenegger holding Pete Wilson (who served as cochairman of his gubernatorial campaign) by the hand and proclaiming his well-known line from *Terminator 2: Judgment Day*, only with a twist, "Hasta la vista, Latinos." In other words, even at this point, Alcaraz remains true to domestic cultural codes, validating criticism through the use of a consecrated piece of Americana. On Schwarzenegger's chest, he proudly wears a T-shirt that states, "I love 187." Like few others, Schwarzenegger personifies the fact that politicians tend to be very contradictory human beings. Ronald Reagan, the patron saint of Republicans, would write checks to a poor person as he cut the benefits of many.[44] An immigrant himself, Arnold Schwarzenegger embraced measures like Proposition 187 to his political benefit (given his more progressive position on topics like abortion, the immigration issue was one way to appeal to more conservative Republicans) while he committed adultery with his Guatemalan housekeeper, Mildred Patricia Baena. While Schwarzenegger was not instrumental in the passage of the anti-illegal immigration bill, he did vote for it. Many of Pete Wilson's aides—including one who had produced an incendiary 1994 TV commercial on immigrants—worked in Schwarzenegger's campaign.[45] And so, Alcaraz made a futile attempt to connect Schwarzenegger with the issue. The effort was fruitless. The Austrian-born politician was skillful at deflecting the connection of his name with explicit anti-immigration sentiments (despite his actions) and managed to bring down the vote to a matter of popularity detached from the implications of his political posturing. Thanks to his name recognition, which, as the result of his films, was higher among Latinos than that of Lieutenant Governor Cruz Bustamante, the Democratic candidate, Schwarzenegger went on to win the gubernatorial election, a feat that no other Republican candidate has accomplished since the passing of Proposition 187.

Alcaraz's work contemplates that which many US inhabitants imagine (and some fear): that in the future, Latinos will represent a greater percentage of the population than any other demographic. It is not ludicrous to contend that, if such a sizable portion of the population is neglected, it will necessarily bring forth the gradual decline of the country. Only if Latinos are given an opportunity—through better access to education and jobs—will the country move on, replicating the influence baby boomers had on the US economy. As early as 2000, Alcaraz was producing cartoons on this topic. To poke fun at the backlash that this development has engendered among certain groups, Alcaraz personifies them as an enraged child wielding a stick at a piñata party; in other words, a single Anglo bully amid a traditionally Latino celebration. The banner at the party makes reference to the dramatic growth among Latinos—60 percent—during the 2000 census, when they were officially identified as the largest minority population in the country, numbering between thirty-seven and forty million inhabitants. Less than a decade later, 2007 marked the first year that Latinos controlled more disposable personal income than any other minority group. According to the US Census Bureau, the projected purchasing power of the Latino community by 2017 is more than $1.5 trillion (or roughly 10 percent of the US total). Having become the largest minority, the number of Latinos keeps growing faster than the rest of the general population. Whereas the Latino population grew 43 percent from 2000 to 2010, non-Latinos expanded only 4.9 percent, which means the number of Latinos grew nearly ten times more rapidly.[46] In fact, they will still account for about 60 percent of the growth of the US population during the coming years.[47] According to 2010 census numbers, Latinos made up the largest, youngest, and fastest-growing racial/ethnic group in the United States, accounting for 16.3 percent (50.5 million) of the total population.[48] By 2035, when non-Hispanic whites will be outnumbered by minorities, Latinos are expected to reach 23 percent of the population, and one-third of all US children and youth will be Latino. If current trends remain unchanged, by 2050, Latinos will comprise one-third of the entire population.[49] As the number of Latinos increases, so will the corresponding rate of penetration of the market, so an enormous amount of capital will be at stake. Marketing research ratifies the notion that, when advertising matches cultural norms, it tends to be viewed more favorably and generate higher levels of purchase intent. As I have suggested previously, targeted marketing plays a key role in the interaction between mainstream US culture and Latinos. Most notably, targeted marketing can sometimes be perceived as offering legitimacy and validation rather than exploitation, an aspect that would contribute and hasten assimilation of Latinos into the mainstream.[50] In terms of Alcaraz's work, perhaps validation and legitimacy would be more effective than fostering a certain sense of infuriation and distrust, as his cartoon with the white aggressor at the piñata party may indicate. In the land of capitalism, consumerism sometimes offers a way to social integration. The lack of a path to legalization for millions offers very little in the way of access to this practice. In this context, Alcaraz's editorial cartoons, which range from the machinations of Disney to the mulishness of Republicans, serve well as a chronicle of perhaps the longest period in modern US history without significant immigration reform.

CHAPTER 4

LA CUCARACHA
An Alienated Bug's Struggle against a Hidden Norm

As Gregor Samsa awoke one morning from uneasy dreams he found himself transformed in his bed into a gigantic insect.
—Franz Kafka, *The Metamorphosis*

IN *LA CUCARACHA*, HIS NATIONALLY SYNDICATED COMIC STRIP, LALO ALCARAZ EMBRACES THAT most Kafkaesque of tropes: that of a man transformed into a bug.[1] While I have mentioned previously how this image of a cockroach is the product of many considerations pertaining to Mexican Americans and/or Latinos, to the extent that Alcaraz is also willing to portray Latino identity as belonging to a wider order, it is also pertinent to consider the influence of a twentieth-century literary classic. Within this context, I am willing to argue that the strongest point of *La Cucaracha* is Alcaraz's capability to denounce the normative nature of ethnocentrism, but only—as usual—with a twist. As Alcaraz proclaims in the introduction to the compilation published by Andrews McMeel, "Latinos are normal people. We are so mainstream it's ridiculous. I want to show how we speak Spanglish, how we relate to stuff on TV, how we feel alienated, and how we like watching *Friends*."[2] That is, Alcaraz is willing to encompass all aspects of Latinos in one fell swoop and to show how the community simultaneously stands inside and outside middle-of-the-road USA. This statement ratifies a germane aspect of Alcaraz's transition from editorial cartoons to comic strip: along the way, he seems to have developed a more personalized approach to deal effectively with the most vexing issue of his initial phase of work: an applicable critique of the veiled nature of normative culture. While in the early part of his career it seemed difficult to negotiate a critique of the Anglo mainstream from a peripheral perspective, given his occasional validation of the normative order (Alcaraz relied on prevailing codes, present in history and pop culture, for much of his criticism, thus playing into the system), in this latter phase, the figure of an anthropomorphized

129

cockroach provides a more suitable vehicle for the denunciation of a concealed cultural norm. (Not that the narrative device gets rid of certain setbacks.) And to this effect, the Kafkaesque device, which emphasizes the degree of alienation experienced by an individual in a particular context—in Kafka's account, it is his family life, led by an overbearing father; in Alcaraz's, it is daily existence as a Latino in Southern California in the 2000s—is concurrently peripheral and mainstream in nature. It provides one of the best-known examples of the consequences of affective isolation while having become a cornerstone of the most conventional canon of modern literature. From the beginning, the adoption of this model makes clear that Alcaraz is interested in the politics of the antihero, something that falls well within the bounds of most cultural production bent on a subversive, transformative message.

In fact, within the entire production compiled in the *La Cucaracha* volume, there is a particular strip that makes this very idea explicit, issuing a straightforward critique of the manner in which society implements exclusionary measures. Toward the middle of the volume, Alcaraz depicts an upset Cuco, the humanized cockroach, asking, "Why won't you let me in?!?" to the man guarding the door of the National Society of Inclusiveness, which is holding a big party that night, according to a sign posted on the entrance (95). The man's only response is, "Sorry, invite only." The vignette synthesizes everything about *La Cucaracha* in a single image: the feeling of being an outsider and the inability to gain access to a society bent on the implementation of a hidden norm; that is, the set of cultural imperatives that tend to benefit the interests of a privileged group. After all, this is how privilege works: it feigns naturalness, remaining invisible. From now on, Alcaraz's driving force will be to uncover the hidden cultural norm. As we have seen in the previous chapter, this latter notion is a key concept in his work. Standard cultural ideology—the notion that there is such a thing as a well-defined set of cultural constructs that, signifying benchmarks, are supported and disseminated throughout the nation as the consecrated knowledge for successful operation in society—is another one.

As I have suggested, Alcaraz's objective is to reveal the implicit dynamics of a cultural order that appears to be "natural," simultaneously offering acceptance and exclusion. Acceptance works only if you are willing to conform to the norms of the preferred cultural order; in one way or another, exclusion is the result of practically any other response. To make a case in point, the cover of the anthology features the entire *La Cucaracha* gang (Eddie, Alcaraz's alter ego; Cuco, the anthropomorphized bug; and Vero, loosely modeled on Alcaraz's wife) strolling past the neighborhood theater, which happens to be showing what appear to be newfangled Latino versions of a wide array of well-known motion pictures, distinctly representative of the wide spectrum

Why won't you let me in?!?, 2003. LA CUCARACHA © Lalo Alcaraz. Dist. by UNIVERSAL UCLICK. Reprinted with permission. All rights reserved.

of US culture: *My Big Fat Latino Movie* (echoing *My Big Fat Greek Wedding* [2002], an alternative hit gone mainstream), *Lord of the Rims* (a takeoff of *Lord of the Rings* [2001], a Hollywood blockbuster and franchise), *Burritoshop* (a play on *Barbershop* [2002], a comedy targeting a minority audience), *Maid in Malibu* (for *Maid in Manhattan* [2002], a romantic comedy seeking a crossover audience), and *Estar Wars* (*Star Wars* [1977], another Hollywood blockbuster and franchise). In short, Alcaraz renders the entire experience in a Latino milieu. By changing these titles and accentuating a common denominator—*latinidad*, or Latinness—Alcaraz highlights the role of an established cultural norm, responsible for the mediation of our everyday contact with society. When everything is translated into a Latino context, it appears "unnatural" because Latinness remains a departure from the norm. Yet Alcaraz's point is precisely this one: what everything would look like if, at some point, *latinidad* became the norm, rather than its white, Anglo-Saxon, Protestant, middle-class counterpart. By doing this, he brings the "natural" quality of the Waspy cultural norm to the forefront. At the end of the day, if population growth proceeds according to demographic estimates, Latinos will eventually achieve plurality status in the country. So, for Alcaraz, mainstream recognition might come in many ways. If it is not by way of appealing to a wider public as a crossover cartoonist, perhaps it will be when demographic conditions happen to catch up with him.

To make evident his critique of the fabricated nature of an established cultural order rooted in a particular construct of identity, the cartoonist translates everything into a "barrio" context, hoping to alert readers through the use of examples. If it were all in the conventional language of the cultural mainstream—partial to the hypothesized current cream of the crop (the 1 percent)—things would appear "normal" and blend into the background. Instead, Alcaraz Mexicanizes the norm. The hope is that, through the practice of cultural divergence, readers will be able to recognize the implicit partiality behind a mainstream cultural norm: the fact that the unspoken cultural order in any society tends to benefit the viewpoint of its elite, thus appearing to be "normal" or unconcealed. So make no mistake: everything that surrounds us—not just that which corresponds to the privileged—is determined by a cultural norm. Quite obviously, the practices of the subaltern are also determined by a cultural norm. The main difference is that the cultural norm of the subaltern is a lot more noticeable because it is not the prevailing one. Nonetheless, the question here is, does Alcaraz include this mode of representation out of critical acuity or is it mere ethnocentrism? For this reason, the neighborhood theater itself is called Cinespanglish, honoring the barrio's propensity for the mixing of languages. From this perspective, Spanglish, which starts as the peripheral contribution of the mixing of two cultures, gains widespread acceptance and is even celebrated in the form of sanctioned media production: through the film industry. On the corner there is a wrestling arena called Titans, hinting at the sport's significance in Mexican American settings. *Lucha libre*, a staple of Mexican culture, has made inroads in the United States and, in many ways, has been accepted by Anglos, who have recognized the significant role it plays south of the border. In part, this is one of the reasons behind Rafael Navarro's relative success with *Sonambulo*. To top it off, there is Jared Hess's *Nacho Libre* (2006), starring Jack Black; *¡Mucha Lucha!*, the animated television series broadcast by the Cartoon Network; and the Nashville rock band Los Straightjackets, which sports personalized wrestling masks. The coffee shop next door to the theater is called Barriobucks, with a *calavera* (reflecting the Mexican culture's fixation with these skulls, thanks to José Guadalupe Posada's artistic contribution via popularized lithography) as its logo. In this way, the ubiquitous Starbucks café, a fixture of many neighborhoods throughout the country, is Mexicanized. By translating an Anglocentric reality to the context of the barrio, Alcaraz shows how everything we seem to consume as "natural" is, in truth, heavily determined by an ethnocentric norm: that of a male, Anglo-Saxon, Protestant, upper-middle-class culture, a milieu that tends to favor sports like golf or tennis and a leisurely lifestyle centered on business networking in locales like fancy cafés and restaurants. Yet, to posit a critique of this order that excludes groups unwilling or unable to conform to its norms, it is also necessary to be extremely well versed on (and enjoy) its codes, to know it so well as to be able to put forward a competent scrutiny of its nature. In this sense, as member of a so-called minority, Alcaraz reproduces his alienation before an Anglo mainstream that only allows definitions of identities on its terms.[3] Cultural resistance is always an option but, to the extent that it is recognized as resistance, it stands outside the norm. That is, as a Latino cartoonist (rather than a non-Latino cartoonist), Alcaraz's options seem limited, and that is why he responds with a fierce critique of the normative nature of mainstream Anglo popular culture. His conjecture is as follows: from the blockbusters we consume to the beverages we drink to the clothing we wear, all cultural products (as well as many practices), regardless of their familiarity, are the result of an aesthetic and appreciation designed for an ideal consumer, theoretically representative of a certain generalized identity, thus universalizing a particular construct of social, racial, and gender centrism, so widespread that it appears to be conventional (particularly for anyone born and raised within such an order). People may play around and tweak this cultural production to make it fit their preferences, yet, in the end, even transformations wind up validating the hidden norm (as I discussed in the previous chapter). That is why, in neighborhoods around the United States that tend to lack diversity, uniformity appears evident to a somehow idiosyncratic level. And in those vicinities where diversity prevails, the norm is the embedded point of reference against which everything is measured. Mainstream culture is, by all definable measures, socio-, ethno-, and heteronormative.

By way of universalizing a Latino norm, Alcaraz's intent is to portray a world in which this bias comes to light. This is a world that intends to bring into the open and contest the causes for exclusion still prevalent in mainstream US culture, a set of practices ignored by a critical mass of people accustomed to and benefiting from them. After all, Alcaraz's work seems to suggest, people who are representative of the advantageous nature (to them) of this set of norms are seldom critical enough to keep them in mind or even to discuss them. It is very easy not to notice certain aspects of life if they happen not to affect you or if, for the most part, they manage to contribute to your sense of fulfillment. On the other hand, if you happen to depart by the slightest measure from this idealized construct, if these aspects exclude you or work against you, it is much easier to discern or to be troubled by them. Such is the plight of peripheral or marginal groups, who tend to perceive their cultural location outside the boundaries established by the normative discourse, particularly when this outreach embraces clumsy attempts to hegemonize. This is the point at which the differences in experiences in life acquire a more subtle nuance and beg to be recognized. In this sense, reminders are important. For example, during a recent exchange in the Supreme Court, Justice Sonia Sotomayor characterized the views on race of Chief Justice John G. Roberts Jr., who was raised in middle-class comfort in Indiana, as "out of touch with reality."[4] Most certainly, growing up middle class in the middle of a midwestern state to Anglo parents and growing up working class in the Bronx to Puerto Rican parents are two very dissimilar experiences. For this reason, it is highly likely that what appears immediately noticeable to Justice Sotomayor, as a result of her life experience, might totally elude Chief Justice Roberts's sense of awareness, never mind how acutely critical his skills may be on legal matters. No matter the extent of success of Lalo Alcaraz's attempt, his objective is to create a world that sheds light on the implications of these disparities.

This is the world of Cuco Rocha, the cockroach, who, as an outsider, comes into the picture destabilizing what appears to be natural. Just like Kafka's bug, which brings into the open the constrictions of a conformist society and the twisted dynamics of a repressive familial context in a German-speaking Prague that is torn between a variety of cultural norms (e.g., language, religion, national affiliation), Cuco brings into the open the contrast between a normative Anglo mainstream culture and the marginal nature of a peripheral alternative; for that matter, the disparity between humans and an insect, regardless of how humanized it is. Hence, his objective is to force this aspect and to translate everything into a Mex-centric order. In this way, through the description of how Latinos from the barrio manage to reproduce their cultural norm, creating a reality that is more comfortable to them (and thus reproducing the ethnocentrism of a more focalized mainstream—that of a Spanish-speaking district—though at a smaller scale and also mimicking the ethnocentrism of the ruling class), readers from other cultural contexts will gain cognizance and begin to problematize the artificial nature of their corresponding surroundings, however far they may be in a variety of ways (e.g., socially, racially, and/or sexually) from the idealized norm.

This reading is not far-fetched. Actually, it is substantiated by one of the early comic strips included in the compilatory volume, in which Alcaraz admits the influence of magical realism, a style of writing perhaps best epitomized by the work of Colombian author Gabriel García Márquez. Alcaraz defines *magical realism* as "the use of fantastical, dreamlike imagery found in some Latin American literature."[5] Taking into consideration García Márquez's success within US mainstream culture—his work has been accepted and celebrated by many, heightening the stature of Latin American cultural production—the measure by Alcaraz can be read as an effort to authenticate his work with a form that is proudly defined as autochthonous. García Márquez was quite outspoken about the impact of Kafka's *Metamorphosis* on his work, describing the reading of the book as a seminal moment in his life.[6] According to the Nobel Prize winner, the opening sentence of Kafka's book (which I have employed as this chapter's epigraph) showed him that a new way of writing was possible. García Márquez remained true to his word and almost outdid the Czech master with *One Hundred Years of Solitude*'s "Many years later, as he faced the firing squad, Colonel Aureliano Buendía was to remember that distant afternoon when his father took him to discover ice," an opening that has now been enshrined by world literature. Unfortunately, García Márquez's popularization of magical realism has also contributed largely to the stereotyping of Latin/o Americans as a group tinged by surrealism. I beg to differ: Latin/o Americans do not avoid reality; rather, we suffer from an excessive reality. In any case, what remains clear is the link between Alcaraz's admission of the influence of magical realism and the narrative device by the Czech author, which the cartoonist appropriates in a deft (and humorous) manner to symbolize the degree of alienation felt by the Latino community. In a very idiosyncratic way, the nature of *La Cucaracha* is a contemporary, Latino graphic equivalent to the spirit of the work of the novelist and literary critic Ralph Ellison, which chronicles so intensely the sense of estrangement within the African American community. From this viewpoint, given how it documents an individual's sense of isolation resulting from the omnipresence of a particular reading of ethnicity, *La Cucaracha*, the compilation volume, can be read not only as a more humorous and sarcastic take, like Ellison's *Invisible Man* (1952), but also as its more up-to-date and pictorial Latino equivalent.

COMICS STRIPS AND ALIENATION: REVEALING THE HIDDEN NORM

Nevertheless, for all the complexity of its narrative devices—or lack thereof; after all, we are talking about comic strips, a medium enthusiastically bent on the notion of lightness—reader reception may stand unaffected. In an ensuing comic strip, Alcaraz, true to his self-deprecating nature, laughs at the futility of his efforts when, despite his detailed admission of canonical influence, he depicts an exchange by a clueless pair of elderly Anglo-Saxon readers (*La Cucaracha* 8). The spectacled reader points out, "Look dear, a bug-eyed Latino has just gotten his own comic strip." To which his female companion retorts, "I'll write a complaint letter!" Before a readership unaware of the richness of cultural codes, the degree of thoughtfulness put into a proposal appears superfluous. Clearly, this couple's problem is not with the idea that a cockroach has been embraced to express dissension, but rather with the mere fact that a Latino has been given the opportunity to produce a nationally syndicated comic strip. This is a response at a very basic level. Alcaraz not only mocks a segment of the public that will not grasp the subtlety of his work; self-deprecatingly, he also mocks the uselessness behind the sophistication of the narrative device. Clearly, things are not that advanced when readers fail even to dwell on another, deeper level of reading. And so, to diagram a more constructive version of readers, Alcaraz identifies a hypothetically clueless couple, hoping to enlighten the audience about the nature of reception of a national syndicated Latino cultural object in certain corners of the country. This, he appears to suggest, speaks volumes about the degree of disengagement between ethnicities in the nation, which the cartoonist appropriates for comic relief.

In *La Cucaracha*, Alcaraz returns promptly to the topics covered in *Migra Mouse*, only now armed with what passes for a more hopeful and effective strategy. For instance, to discuss the ironies of the English-only movement, he describes an exchange between Cuco and Eddie, and a supporter of an English-only petition (*La Cucaracha* 9). When the man argues for the preservation of "the purity of the English language," Cuco answers, "Whoa, *déjà vu*." The French expression denotes the influence of other cultural traditions in the English language, perhaps embraced more extensively as the result of the attached cultural prestige. Also, in a more problematic way, it remits the reader to previous instances in which "purity" has been used as justification for actions. Given the not-so-distant memory of the invasion of Iraq, backlash against the French is still fresh in national memories, like when people started talking about "freedom fries." Furthermore, in a more expansive US context, it is not hard to think of greater equivalents: the purge of Native Americans, decimated and abandoned to their luck, and the even more questionable support of eugenics during the first half of the twentieth century, when it was used against European immigrants of working-class extraction, employing the excuse of supposedly inferior genetic stock. Once again, this is by no means an Anglo prerogative. In the Spanish context, *pureza de sangre* (blood purity), a concept of medieval origin brandished by conquistadors to justify all kinds of atrocities, according to which blood was equated with Christian lineage, immediately comes to mind. There are, most likely, many other examples of this train of thought. History is littered with a long trail of injustices. Nonetheless, within the general layout of experiences familiar to contemporary US readers, the machinations of Germany's Third Reich, with Hitler at the helm of a massive genocidal project and fixated on the purity of a theoretically untainted Aryan heritage, outdo them all, particularly for an older generation of readers. Alcaraz bears this keenly in mind. (That is why I have discussed his use of Hitler in the previous chapter.) Alcaraz's awareness of this fact contributes to his depiction of behavior of this nature as un-American, simultaneously inscribing his work within a US tradition of tolerance and acceptance of the other. Now, a potential problem with a critique of this kind is that, by claiming for himself the authority to delineate what stands within the bounds of acceptable national behavior—clearly, without a sense of irony—his response may comes across just as impulsive as those who attempt to discriminate against Latinos. To be exact, it is not practical to criticize a behavior by resorting to almost equal means.

On the following frame, to add contrast to humor, when the activist who claims "Too much diversity leads to conflict" is asked to describe the nature of conflict, he includes the phrase "*Mano a mano* type conflict." In other words, it is not only Cuco who embraces phrases from another language while using the English language, but also the activist, who, like most US residents, has already internalized a number of expressions of Spanish origin (perhaps through the work of Arriola). The illogicity behind the activist's efforts—the fact that he is vowing for unadulteration in a land that uses as its motto a distinct claim for the assimilation of difference—is colored by his complicity in the use of Spanish. The circumstance that this might be a position shared by many—people bent on purity, even though their lives are brimming with heterogeneity—stands as proof of a way of life concurrently based on the notion of acceptance and the mechanics of exclusion. Thus, Alcaraz addresses the issue by means of contradiction, hoping to highlight the paradoxical nature of many outcries within US politics.

Difference has many ways of being assessed in Alcaraz's work. Toward the end of the volume (*La Cucaracha* 121), to draw attention sarcastically to another contemporarily disruptive measure of difference—the degree of homophobia displayed by the media at some point or another—Alcaraz has Vero, Eddie, and Cuco watching an episode of a makeover show. When Cuco talks about the show, he does so in a rather clumsy, veiled fashion, describing the show's hosts as "fairly flamboyant fellas," a type of characterization that Vero describes flippantly as "a real non-controversial comics page way of putting it." Thus, in this case, Alcaraz is being self-critical and employing his strip to point out the limitations of the enactment of difference in his own medium. The best part of the joke, though, is that it allows the cartoonist to turn things around and use them for his own good, embracing some continuity in the topic, as in a subsequent strip featuring Cuco as the host of an imaginary TV show titled *Latin Eye for the Gringo Guy* (*La Cucaracha* 122). Like the 1950s show discussed in the previous chapter, the show assumes familiarity with US cultural codes, since the dynamics of the show mimic those of *Queer Eye for the Straight Guy* (2003–7). So, to some extent, Alcaraz is still playing with the same cards as during the initial part of his career. However, thanks to Cuco, Alcaraz now has a better way of standing within and outside the cultural mainstream; that's the beauty of narrative devices. The first guest of the show is a man sporting a crew cut and a T-shirt with a flag on it. Coincidentally, the man is called Red, as in a red state. The man's response to the show, though intended for Latinos, could easily personify the homophobia of certain viewers, "I got nothing against your 'Latino lifestyle.' I just don't get why you have to flaunt it in my face constantly! Like it's normal . . ." In this way, the assessment of difference combines the exclusionary perspectives wielded against gays and Latinos, demonstrating the parallels in the treatment of peripheral identities by way of mixing codes and shifting language. When handled with dexterity, difference allows the cartoonist to put forward a very sophisticated critique of the hidden norm, in spite of the fact that, at its core, the comic strip is structured in a similar way to his earlier production. All excluded groups can be treated analogously, the comic strip seems to claim.

Alcaraz's evolution also embodies thematic development. The commercialization of identity politics, a matter frequently discussed in *Baldo*, the other nationally syndicated Latino comic strip that is written and illustrated by Héctor Cantú and Carlos Castellanos, is another of Alcaraz's recurrent topics. In an early comic strip (*La Cucaracha* 10), the admission of the growth of the Latino population (as well as its economic coming of age), effectively becoming the largest minority identified by the federal government, is reflected in the offering of a credit card based on the image of Ricky Martin, an artist who embodies the initial crossover during the Latino boom at the end of the 1990s. In this sense, Alcaraz hints at familiar dynamics in the acceptance of difference in the United States. Money speaks louder than words and economic progressiveness customarily precedes social progressiveness. Plainly speaking, the market is more flexible than people. In simple terms, it is through the language of economic capability that groups gain a desirable spot within the overall context of US society. The fact that the credit card embraces Ricky Martin is particularly relevant because the Puerto Rican star came out as a homosexual in 2010, adding to his quality of difference. His presence adds to a string of vignettes in which Alcaraz deftly combines the exclusion of gays with the exclusion of Latinos. As a homosexual Latino star, Martin contributes to the greater acceptance of the gay community both in and outside Latin culture. Thus, with increased acceptance of Latinos comes increased protagonism in many of the measures of capitalism. This commercial side of acceptance is a matter to which the cartoonist will return repeatedly, as when he portrays Cuco and Eddie walking by a street plagued with billboards inviting them to drink beer (*La Cucaracha* 53)—in a very short stretch, the location has four huge signs. By the time Cuco and Eddie are walking back and commenting how much everything has changed since the Latino marketing boom hit, all the signs have been changed to Spanish. The message, though, remains the same: drink beer. The more things change, the more they remain the same, the cartoonist seems to be saying. In other instances, this newly gained acceptance results in paradoxical outcomes, like when Vero visits the mall and is convinced by a saleswoman to try on a line of clothing aimed at Latinas (*La Cucaracha* 96). The fact that at that point—2003—Latino purchasing power was $600 billion strong and growing might have something to do with this sudden surfacing of dressing options. Nonetheless, when Vero emerges from the dressing room, her outfit does not make her feel like J. Lo, Thalía, or Shakira, but rather like Chiquita Banana, judging from her Carmen Miranda–like

The Latino marketing boom, 2003. LA CUCARACHA © Lalo Alcaraz. Dist. by UNIVERSAL UCLICK. Reprinted with permission. All rights reserved.

attire, complete with fruits on her head and ruffles everywhere. In other words, economic acceptance is sometimes beneficial, but often it can also condone a stereotyped perception of peripheral groups, which only comes to reinforce the values and interests of identities benefited by the hidden norm, framing smaller collectivities as tangential or out of the mainstream. After all, an acceptance of the economic wherewithal of new groups comes along with concessions, many of which involve acquiescing to the priorities of the hegemon, including handling of identity. This is, most surely, the case with Vero's outfit.

And so, just to remind everyone that economic success does not necessarily imply social acceptance, the cartoonist follows immediately with a strip in which Cuco bursts Eddie's bubble. When Eddie is ecstatic about Latino acceptance, pointing out how salsa now outsells ketchup in the entire country, Cuco reminds him that, even if rap outsells rock, people do not see Gwyneth Paltrow dating Snoop Dogg. The mention of Paltrow—an actor who is equated with lily-white privilege; who attended Crossroads School (in Santa Monica), Spence (in New York), and UC Santa Barbara (alma mater of Michael Douglas, another actor equated with privilege); and who, a year later (the strip's copyright is from 2002), would wed Coldplay's lead vocalist, Chris Martin (although they divorced in 2015)—intends to bring to light how certain figures of US culture are construed as representative of the degree of separation between social, ethnic, and cultural realities, regardless of the degree of goodwill of the characters themselves. Just because people are fine consuming someone's culture—in fact, practicing transculturation and adapting it to their personal circumstances (in the case of Paltrow, Spanish cuisine, among others)—it does not mean that community contact will flow as freely, eventually fostering integration and renewed tolerance for alterity. Ethnic integration is a complex development and, in the corners of the nation where it has taken place organically, it has been a slow, gradual process, matured over the course of several generations. The reminder by Alcaraz hints at this fact.

Most of this humor is centered on the notion that it is necessary to make readers come to terms with the concept of a hidden norm. When a man confronts Cuco, Eddie, and Vero at a local café, he advocates for a "white entertainment industry" (*La Cucaracha* 12). It would be a fair equivalent for media like Telemundo, Univision, and BET, which cater to particular ethnicities, the man claims earnestly. To which Cuco simply responds, "There is." The brevity of his comeback clarifies the omnipresence of a hidden norm in mainstream media, despite Alcaraz's eventual clarification that the entire Hollywood industry champions a white norm (as made evident by the controversy about the Academy Awards and race). In this case, it is not about translating the overall context of life in the barrio to underscore the presence of a hidden norm, as in the neighborhood image from the volume's cover. In this case, it is about bringing into the open the fact that mainstream media tends to reproduce the viewpoints of the group in power or an elite group. And this practice tends to be very widespread and, in many cases, subconscious. In fact, it is so widespread, it appears to be "normal." Hence, it goes unnoticed and unrecognized. In other words, people reproduce the hidden norm because they have internalized it. To acknowledge in a succinct fashion the existence of a white entertainment industry is perhaps the more moderate approach, by way of humor and concision, to a critique of the implicit bias in media.

However, this is not the only way in which Alcaraz approaches this topic. In another instance, Eddie and Cuco are listening to the radio while riding in the car (*La Cucaracha* 58). Cuco suggests that he has just tuned in to the new liberal talk-radio network (Pacifica? NPR?), to which Eddie responds, "How can you tell?" Cuco quips, "Nothing but white people on it." In the course of the past decades, progressive radio in the United States—public and private—has made sizable strides in terms of diversity. It is not a matter of defending a medium as overconfident as progressive talk radio, but it is important to note that, in this sense, it has evolved, thus rendering Alcaraz's critique a tad futile. The problem with progressive radio, a listener could argue sarcastically, is not so much its explicit racial code, but its aurality: the fact that most of its personnel shares a common aural register and intonation, which tends to drift toward a white modulation. Another way to read this would be to claim that perhaps progressive radio has heeded his advice by reflecting the diversity of their listener base more accurately, yet still has failed aurally. Progressive radio stations now include a number of voices, ethnicities, and issues. One of the few explicit brands of difference they are lacking is quite probabably social diversity, given the barriers resulting from education. However, it is easy to see how in 2003, when this strip was published, many progressive networks lacked diversity of participants and topics within their programming. And beyond this, it is the nature of the discourse, fed on concerns that appear to be very judicious, that hints at a certain slant in the discussion of matters. It is the overall focus of programming—together with the cadence of language—that gives away a particular mind-set in coverage of the news. Then again, to strive for inclusiveness is in the best interest of any institution seeking community support—in a fashion akin to co-optation of the public, if you will. On the other hand, when people cannot make ends meet, they tend to care less about climate change, or rampant injustice and political conflict in faraway corners of the world, or any other topic regularly covered by progressive radio stations, for that matter. They might appreciate the reporting, but other things stand as priorities. It is this very kind of circumstance that fuels the suspicion of a hidden norm.

There are many ways to approach this topic. Some scholars have identified distinct traces of this slant in our use of language. In *English with an Accent: Language, Ideology, and Discrimination in the United States* (1997), linguist Rosina Lippi takes on the myth of the non-accent, so pertinent to many Latinos across the country. In the case of NPR, it is feasible to point out how its anchors reproduce a common register to the point of, on many occasions, eluding ethnic identification. In truth, what they are accomplishing is coming together behind a common register, which tends to be very "white." Lippi explains in detail how standard language (the well-shared, erroneous notion that there is such a thing as universal English) and non-accent are both abstractions and myths. Her research is well documented, but it describes an aspect of life in the United States that most immigrants learn through their daily experience. To this extent, she also speaks about a hidden norm, which people tend to assimilate as "natural." It is this norm that makes people think that there is such a thing as a universal, standard form of English (which in turn supports the notion of a hidden norm). Also, it is this train of thought that Alcaraz tends to rant against when he creates his comic strips. In a passage on the topic, Lippi clarifies, "In spite of all the hard evidence that language must be variable and must change, people steadfastly believe that a homogeneous, standardized, one-size-fits-all language is not only desirable, it is truly a possibility. This language does not exist in fact, but it certainly does exist as an ideal in the minds of the speakers" (44).

And so, it is this kind of approach, bent on homogeneity and on a certain sense of hypothetical uniformity, that hinders the pragmatic acceptance of disparate identities in a larger society. The very same thing happens with widespread culture. After all, the culture of any country tends to express and ratify the interests of groups in power. So, for the most part, these interests are portrayed as "natural," as part of the unquestionable cultural location of a greater collectivity, whereas those of new groups are always perceived as different and, occasionally, as threatening. And so, when Alcaraz has Cuco answer succinctly, what he is putting forward is the idea that national media simply express and ratify the viewpoints of groups in power, which, in the case of the United States—not necessarily so in other locations—coincides more often than not with what currently stands as the most sizable ethnicity, never mind differences of class, gender, or sexual orientation. The point with Alcaraz is precisely this one: the country is headed in the opposite direction and the culture needs to be updated to reflect this fact. It is this idea that Alcaraz toys with in the course of the strip on progressive talk radio.

The manner in which these ideas happen to make it to the reader varies according to readership and content. No matter the context of any individual, a properly functioning cultural industry is usually quite adept at circulating and upholding the viewpoints and values of a hegemonic group, as Gramsci judiciously observed in his writings.[7] To draw attention to this point, Alcaraz created a strip that poses a critique of the role of the *New York Times* as a benchmark of good journalism (*La Cucaracha* 89). When Cuco asks Eddie about a rough day at work, Eddie complains about how his boss is asking for more sensationalized fictional stories. Cuco then suggests the press should try to emulate the *Times* a bit more. Then, contrarily, reading from the *Times*, he points out that Bat Boy and the *chupacabra* are teaming up to tackle the Middle East situation, precisely the kind of technique Eddie is complaining about at work. It follows that, even if the *Times* were adopting strategies of this nature, it would most likely be because the practice of journalism is changing in accordance with the preferences of its readers. And, as a result, the degree of penetration of information upholding a hidden norm will, in all likelihood—never mind the unconventionality of the methods—be more effective. By referencing Bat Boy (a creature from *Weekly World News*) and the *chupacabra* (a figure from Latino folklore, originally from Puerto Rico), Alcaraz is adding his very own bit to the mix, fully aware of their tongue-in-cheek part within the narrative of the comic strip. However, as always, there is more than one way to read the strip. By including Bat Boy and the *chupacabra* in a medium as prestigious as the *Times*, the cartoonist could be showing how even the most outlandish version of peripheral identity is susceptible to co-optation. The remaining question would be whether this was what Alcaraz had in mind beyond his critique of the contemporary practice of journalism.

It is in contrast to this hidden norm that constructs for other identities are developed. In an earlier strip (*La Cucaracha* 15), Alcaraz chronicles the trip of an illegal immigrant to the north. The frames show the man waving good-bye to his family, crossing the desert, hiding by the border, waiting for an opportunity to cross into the United States, eluding the lights of an immigration helicopter, arriving in an almost empty city (unlike Mexican cities, which tend to overflow with city life), looking for work and finding it (by

Lazy immigrant!, 2002. LA CUCARACHA © Lalo Alcaraz. Dist. by UNIVERSAL UCLICK. Reprinted with permission. All rights reserved.

standing on the neighborhood corner, as in many places around the country), and working arduously under the sun; finally, as he is laying exhausted on the sidewalk, a white, middle-class US citizen walks by and, derisively, calls him "lazy immigrant." Then again, in this particular case, though I understand and appreciate Alcaraz's viewpoint, I tend to disagree. Nowadays, in most of the United States, when people see humble immigrants of Mexican and/or Latino descent, they tend to recognize that they are hard workers. And I do not say this lightly. People might not even agree with their presence, but the fact that they are hard workers—hence, stealing jobs from US citizens, in the eyes of some—appears undeniable. As a result, it is pretty apparent to many US inhabitants, regardless of their location—a metropolitan area or the countryside—that Mexican and/or Latino/a immigrants are hard workers. After all, they are everywhere: cooking, cleaning, landscaping, building, renovating, educating, caring for children, and so on—even in the academe. Now, quite obviously, I will not pretend to equate myself with undocumented workers. Clearly, their plight is superior to any of my circumstances. Then again, the nature of their occupation, which might render them socially invisible, is still relevant enough to be aware of their economic impact; without the heavy subsidy to the national economy that workers of Mexican, Central American, and South American origin represent, the US economy would find itself in even more challenging circumstances. While the white pedestrian conforms to generalized prejudice, which seems to be Alcaraz's point, the version of Mexican and/or Latino/a identity posited by the undocumented immigrant manages to remind us of the travails of many workers in US society.

In other instances, Alcaraz's critique is way more conventional, as when he writes about the absence of Latinos on television (*La Cucaracha* 16). In truth,

TV networks, 2002. LA CUCARACHA © Lalo Alcaraz. Dist. by UNIVERSAL UCLICK. Reprinted with permission. All rights reserved.

this is the same subject, only treated from the opposite viewpoint, criticizing the mechanics of omission. If, on the one hand, the hidden norm operates in terms of its implicitness, on the other, it operates by way of omission, sometimes subtracting presence, intentionally or not, from other groups. In this respect, following along these lines, Alcaraz creates a comic strip in which he develops an alternative meaning for the acronyms of all the broadcast networks: ABC stands for "Anything But Color"; CBS is "Can't Beat Segregation"; NBC is "No Brown Characters"; and FOX is "Full-On Xclusion" (*La Cucaracha* 20). This is a way of framing national media along the notion of a hidden norm, so the mechanics of omission are interpreted in accordance with a palpable degree of support of the interests of certain groups.

That is why in Alcaraz's work the politics of difference burst in at any moment. Even during the Christmas holidays, a time usually reserved for harmony and reconciliation, the conversation between his characters jumps into the terrain of race (*La Cucaracha* 18). In a whimsical manner, Cuco and Eddie toy with the notion of a "white" Christmas, with the bias implicit in the twist of the cultural expression, which, according to them, happens to embody the preferences or interests of the majority. Instead, half-mockingly, with some irony and sarcasm, they suggest the possibility of a "brown" Christmas. Then again, critical as he is, Alcaraz does not claim anything about how the upholding of a Christian tradition is, in itself, a substantiation of a hidden norm: the idea that Christianity is synonymous with US identity (which it is not; in fact, some of the founding fathers—chiefly, Jefferson, Franklin, and Paine—were remarkably distrustful of institutionalized religion). Along the same lines, by criticizing Alcaraz on the basis of the construct of a state, I am legitimating the notion of the government of the United States of America as a faithful representative of a construct of nation—so there you go. I do not blame Alcaraz; sometimes it is very hard to escape the grasp of the hidden cultural norm.

To address some more incongruous topics, the Mexican American cartoonist even takes the opportunity to be self-referential. On page 23 of the *La Cucaracha* volume, there is a strip that addresses the problem with assimilation when it comes to a hidden norm. Having heard a conversation in which Eddie and Vero discuss common "American" sayings (the quotation marks are from the comic strip), Cuco tries to come to the couple's assistance. Eddie immediately fires back at him, asking whether it is the fact that he is Latino that poses an obstacle to his understanding of sayings in English. Just to prove the point, he employs a maxim that highlights double standards, only he changes it a bit. Whereas the original saying is "People who live in glass houses shouldn't throw stones," meaning people should not criticize others for flaws that they share, Eddie's version is, "Those who live in glass houses shouldn't get stoned," which comes across as complacent or lenient, at the very least. In this manner, Eddie is at the same time clueless and ironic. The thing is, regardless of how anyone muddles the message of a saying, in order to get acquainted with a culture's repertoire of aphorisms, said to embody some of its most common values and mores, any individual has to interact with the target culture and, to a certain extent, allow it to penetrate a personal domain of identity. That is, for Eddie to twist a saying in English—and to twist it he would most likely have to have been familiar with its correct version, never mind how ill-informed—he must have internalized aspects of a US-centered perception of culture and society. Thus, he is in an enviable position to point out the contradictions behind double standards evident in a US context, such as those arising from the lack of critique of a hidden norm. In this sense, thanks to the figure of Cuco, this critical exercise differs from Alcaraz's legitimation of a cultural norm during the first stage of his production. In this case, it is not just a matter of sharing a product of the established norm to criticize it; it also entails a degree of self-criticism, revealing an awareness of a twist in the politics of identity. From this perspective, if anybody is willing to criticize the production of Latino/a-based cultural production, such as *La Cucaracha*, they should first realize how everything else disseminated by media also happens to offer a point of view, setting aside how covered up it might be.

At some other points, Alcaraz has to identify customarily employed mechanisms in his own production to sustain the notion of a hidden norm—in particular, notions like tokenism, which pay lip service to the requisites of society. That is why he includes Mike, a self-referential African American who discusses the notion of tokenism, only to stare at the reader and ask, "What's everybody looking at?" (*La Cucaracha* 100). By addressing the reader directly—by breaking the fourth wall, to use a theater term—Alcaraz is acknowledging his awareness of the mechanics of cultural politics. Thus, as a critic of tokenism, Mike himself is uncomfortable with the notion that he incarnates a token. (Just as Lalo Alcaraz may be uncomfortable with the notion that his success may be perceived, to some extent, as an outcome of tokenism.) Also, he may include characters of this nature because they allow him to call attention to points that are especially relevant to the troubles of Latinos as a group, as when they migrate and many times carry along prejudice from their original countries. By placing judgments in someone else's voice, Alcaraz attempts to deal with self-criticism. For example, Mike questions Cuco about how he can say that Latinos are the largest minority group when many Latinos identify themselves as "white." To which Cuco replies that Latinos are the largest group, not the smartest (*La Cucaracha* 106). This exchange is quite important because it deals with the difference between race and ethnicity, a matter seldom discussed among Latinos. Since race is an issue that tends to be less problematized in Latin America, the strip's dialogue embodies latent contradictions. Traditionally, Latin Americans favor a prism of class. Upon embracing US culture (and thus becoming "Latinos"), there is a pragmatic shift toward race, as this is the paradigm favored by US society. However, while siding with Latino/a viewpoints, some Latin Americans of mostly European descent occasionally fail to relinquish classist attitudes founded on an internalization of racial prejudice—that is, the notion that fair skin should dictate a better social status. So, the exchange between Mike and Cuco points out how many Latinos will swiftly identify themselves with an Anglo culture they perceive as friendly, yet fail to grasp that, even if they are Caucasians, they will not be accepted or treated as full-blown equivalents of Anglo-Saxons for the simple reason that, culturally speaking, they are not (which spells out their rather superficial understanding of race). In other words, this haphazard attempt to identify differently is sometimes a way to look for a nonexistent shortcut on the way to greater acceptance in US society, underlining pervasive estrangement. And yet, the contradictions emanating from a relationship with the hidden norm are constant. Alluding to Afro-Latinos, Mike takes exactly the opposite standpoint, arguing they count double (*La Cucaracha* 107). When groups identify themselves with a paradigm, conscious of where they stand in terms of ethnicity, class, gender, or race, it tends to be because they have already assimilated the notion of a hidden norm and thus define themselves in opposition to it, be it for purposes of resistance or co-optation. Thus, it is feasible for Mike to view white Latinos as turncoats and Afro-Latinos as allies. And all this comes from a character who is not Latino, so, in a sense, Alcaraz is playing it safe. Just as the cultural industry is supportive of the hidden norm, Alcaraz is liable to manipulate another group's identity for the sake of his own judgment.

The hidden norm is a universal notion. As I have suggested earlier, every culture has one. In some instances, the norm being supported can even result

Not the smartest, 2003. LA CUCARACHA © Lalo Alcaraz. Dist. by UNIVERSAL UCLICK. Reprinted with permission. All rights reserved.

from an elite's internalization of some other culture's values. To underscore this point, Alcaraz offers stabs at Spanish-language networks, habitually criticized for their whitened representations of Latin American society. As a result, in terms of ethnicity and class, some enactments pertaining to these networks do not conform well to the representation of a world characteristic of Latin American reality. It is a common criticism against Latino/a television networks—particularly in the case of soap operas, known as *telenovelas*, which generally seem to offer an embellished version of events—that many of its actors do not represent well the average population of Latin American countries, or even of Latino/a communities in the United States, which tend to be mostly mestizo or Afro-descendant. Traditionally the staple of the lower and middle classes, soap opera programming is populated regularly by individuals emerging from the upper echelons of national society, as is the case with the star system of Mexican television giant Televisa, which produces much of the material broadcast by the Univision network in the United States. As a result, blonde, blue-eyed, and fair-skinned actors tend to abound in its stories. On its *telenovelas*, even the actors with some mestizo descent appear whitened through a veneer of class. A common case in point concerns Mexican superstar Thalía Sodi, who, during her early TV career, played the part of blue-collar heroines, a role for which she was preposterously ill-suited, considering the degree to which her personal class background and the Televisa star system had managed to polish her ways. When playing the part of the humble country girl, Sodi had to be trained to reproduce the appropriate linguistic register, and even then, her working-class accent came across as affected. To address this issue, Alcaraz shows Eddie asking Vero about blondes supposedly going extinct by 2208, to which she responds by singling out Spanish-language television as a suitable refuge for blondes as species (*La Cucaracha* 26).

Yet, Latin American media are not the sole object of criticism. In the United States, things are not all that different when it comes to denial. To continue with his critique of representation and visibility in media (and make things more evenhanded, opting for a target north of the border), Alcaraz targets director Ron Howard as a classic representative of the Hollywood studio system (*La Cucaracha* 28). After all, Howard has been a staple of US media since the age of eight, first playing Opie Taylor in *The Andy Griffith Show* (1960–68) and then the part of Richie Cunningham in *Happy Days* (1974–84). In this particular case, what concerns the Mexican American cartoonist the most is the fact that Howard cast actress Jennifer Connelly to play the role of Alicia Nash (née Lardé) in *A Beautiful Mind* (2001), a motion picture for which he earned an Oscar for Best Director and Connelly the Academy Award for Best Supporting Actress (she mentioned Lardé during her acceptance speech). The film tells the story of Nobel laureate John Nash, who endured years of struggle with schizophrenia. Alicia Lardé was Nash's wife, an upper-class Salvadoran woman who migrated when her father, a medical doctor, left for the United States in 1944. To Alcaraz, the actual details of Nash's story are irrelevant, although, according to many, Lardé was especially responsible for Nash's success because she took him in as a boarder during his most acute time of crisis and, thirty-eight years after their initial divorce (which took place only three years into their first marriage), remarried him. What the cartoonist wants to point out is how, in the very uncommon case of a Latina accepted as a physics major by a prestigious institution like MIT in 1955, an account of a person who could stand as an important role model for many Latina adolescents, Hollywood chooses to whitewash the story and obscure the character's descent. The omission is compounded by the fact that the person responsible for this change is the epitome of the all-American boy (Opie, Richie), thus ratifying the prevalence of the hidden norm. When Vero ventures all of this information, Eddie shares that Howard has dropped out of a remake of the 1960 film *The Alamo*. Howard was probably upset that Mexicans won at the Alamo, Vero states emphatically. Therefore, the relationship between Howard's work and an implicit level of support for a hidden norm comes to light. It is a tragedy that, following *A Beautiful Mind*'s success and their remarriage, John and Alicia Nash perished in a car accident on the New Jersey Turnpike on May 23, 2015.

The media industry is not the only institution Alcaraz criticizes regularly. The armed forces, which tend to target Latino/a communities heavily in their recruitment efforts, are also a favorite subject. To call attention to this fact, Alcaraz plays around with the slogan of a popular army advertising campaign. In his comic strip, the phrase "An Army of One" turns into "An Army of Juan," denouncing the hypothetically disproportionate number of Latinos in the ranks (*La Cucaracha* 32). The problem is, according to general statistics published by the government, the percentage of enlisted personnel of Latino descent in the armed forces is said to still rank far below the actual level of

Latinos within the general population. According to these data, whereas Latinos represented 18 percent of the population in 2010, enlisted personnel only represented 12 percent of the institution. In 2015, Latinos accounted for 17 percent of enlisted personnel.[8] One could agree with Mark Twain, who famously said, "There are lies, damn lies, and statistics," arguing that numbers are whatever you make of them. However, the fact is the Latino population is growing at such a rate that it is almost impossible for armed forces enrollment to keep up with it. At another point in this text, I have ventured an alternative reading: there is a fair number of enlisted men in the armed forces pursuing naturalization; that is, they do not figure statistically as US citizens, and a sizable portion of them tend to be Latinos. It could be that when the Department of Defense puts out its information, it does not include this group among its data in terms of race or ethnicity, since, officially speaking, they do not yet count. So, with this information in mind, the actual point of view supported by the cartoonist—that the number of Latinos in the armed forces is disproportionate—may be a matter better left open for discussion. In any case, what would certainly turn to be more interesting would be an indictment of the overall progress of Latinos within the institution, given the general dearth of higher-ranking Latino/a officers. According to official information, officers of Latino descent only represented 6 percent of the forces.[9] This is the government actually sharing information that calls attention to a scarcity of Latino/a officers in its ranks. In this way, the so-called glass ceiling, which is evident to many immigrants as the result of national-origin discrimination and is a practice amply documented by some scholars, becomes painfully apparent.

In "The Invisible Minority: Revisiting the Debate on Foreign-accented Speakers and Upward Mobility in the Workplace," the political science scholar Soji Akomolafe documents the travails of what he calls the "invisible minority," victims of accent discrimination, a group that he describes in painstaking detail as being underrepresented in terms of legal action (8). In his work, Akomolafe clarifies how, according to the 2002 US Equal Employment Opportunity Commission (EEOC) manual, an employment decision based on foreign accent does not necessarily violate Title VII (which bans national-origin discrimination against any individual) if an individual's accent materially interferes with the ability to perform his or her job duties. It is clearly stipulated in this manual that an employer may only base an employment decision on accent if effective oral communication in English is required to perform job duties and the individual's foreign accent materially interferes with his or her ability to do so. Although Akomolafe states that, in the eyes of the law, a violation of accent discrimination is technically also a violation of national origin, he also explains that proving national origin or accent discrimination in the workplace is perhaps one of the hardest things to do in a court of law

(10). The implications of Akomolafe's work on the scant number of higher-ranking Latinos are rather stark, which is not to say that accent is the only reason for the lack of promotion. So, given that Latinos do not represent a high percentage of the enlisted forces, it could prove more practical instead to focus on how they, be it through their accent or other characteristics, fail to be promoted at a satisfactory rate. Needless to say, the bias behind this practice of exclusion is just another materialization of the hidden norm.

There are other forms of exclusion that are even less fair. On page 74 of the compilation, Alcaraz depicts Cuco at a bar, sitting next to a typical working stiff overflowing with nationalism, a rabid white guy (his T-shirt reads "So Damn Insane") who tells him to be quiet and support the troops. In response, Cuco claims that his (Cuco's) support for the troops is even stronger than his. When the man questions this, Cuco asks why the government doesn't grant immediate citizenship to every immigrant soldier. The man appears perplexed, to which Cuco retorts, "Finally, some real 'shock and awe,'" alluding to the "shock and awe" campaign during the initial phase of the invasion of Iraq by the Bush administration. In truth, the term was coined as an attempt to develop a post–Cold War military doctrine.[10] Nevertheless, what Alcaraz manages to suggest is an additional practice in which the present order within an institution like the armed forces operates against immigrants. Although changes have been implemented recently, reducing the time for naturalization for immigrant soldiers from three years to one, these efforts have been, for the most part, the result of the Obama administration, which, despite its mixed record in terms of immigration, is a tad friendlier to legal aliens than previous Republican administrations, particularly when it comes to the armed forces.[11] In any case, what remains clear is that the glass ceiling has many ways of operating, effectively shutting people off from a well-deserved recognition of years of hard work.

The topic of Latinos in the US Armed Forces is expanded greatly through Alcaraz's account of Eddie's cousin, Chava, who is stationed in a military base somewhere in the Middle East. Thanks to the conflict in the region, Alcaraz is able to turn this subject on its head. In fact, Chava's experience speaks volumes more about life in the barrio rather than life in the war, as readers would tend to expect. For instance, his military base has fewer weapons than his neighborhood back home, and his life is in peril, not because of the conflict, but because his mates may discover he has been hoarding the canned tortillas his mother sent him (*La Cucaracha* 44). Such is the yearning for something that evokes the flavor from home. In fact, when a Saddam-like Iraqi sentry (this is the cartoonist's way of mocking the idea that all Iraqis look alike; all Iraqis look similar in his cartoons) observes the US troops from a distance with his binoculars, he is perplexed: rather than a US army, he reports that

Propaganda, 2003. LA CUCARACHA © Lalo Alcaraz. Dist. by UNIVERSAL UCLICK. Reprinted with permission. All rights reserved.

the country is about to be invaded by the combined armies of Mexico and Puerto Rico (assuming the humorous notion that an Iraqi national is able to apply a stereotype of Mexican or Puerto Rican appearance), alluding once again to the high numbers of ground troops of Latino/a descent. In other words, in Alcaraz's comic strip, aside from stereotyping the Iraqis, a stereotype of Mexicans or Puerto Ricans is also circulated and validated. As we have seen in the work of Arriola and Cantú and Castellanos, stereotypes are almost unavoidable. Therefore, why not use them to our advantage, hoping to foster some critical insight? Although the official numbers do not seem to support the cartoonist's viewpoint, Alcaraz's use of the war experience may be ideal to put forward his point: how things are usually relative. When the state fails to assist you or to even recognize your presence as an element of society, it is appropriate to seek opportunities that will increase your profile in the eyes of government. Unfortunately for some segments of society, this shift involves the risk of death in an armed conflict, a circumstance that seldom seems to affect the children of the privileged. Yet, Chava's experience in the army is not only helpful to criticize the institution he belongs to. It also works in terms of things he comes into contact with during the war, like when he writes to Eddie complaining about the Iraqis getting their news from Al Jazeera, an obvious source of propaganda, according to Chava (*La Cucaracha* 67). Instead, he argues, US soldiers get their news from FOX. Eddie's perplexed expression when he reaches this line gives away his thoughts: FOX is no different from Al Jazeera—or any other media, for that matter. Concealed within the supposedly objective stance of any communication outlet is the implicit idea of a prescient subjectivity, in addition to any inadvertent underwriting of the hidden norm. Reproduction of viewpoints is either a manner of complicity or internalization. Thus, Chava's naïveté should come to many unsuspecting readers as a hint of the dynamics of the hidden norm and the way in which its enactment might be at work in many of their preferred media, including, most judiciously, *La Cucaracha* itself.

Another institution that Alcaraz addresses within his critique of a standard cultural ideology—that is, a system of ideas through which the values and mores of a particular group in power are disseminated as a norm, in a way that their legitimacy appears natural and unquestionable—is the educational system. In the United States, as in many other places, the educational system plays a key role in the integration of individuals into the greater fabric of society by way of providing the necessary codes and information to perform successfully in a variety of contexts. Like many other institutions in US society, it is a machine of identity. Admittedly, in *La Cucaracha*, Vero's character is based on Alcaraz's wife, who works as a schoolteacher. And, of all places, the classroom environment is the ideal scenario to expose how a common cultural ideology, bent on the preservation of privileges for a chosen few, is enacted and reproduced in a familiar setting. The cartoonist shows Vero with a colleague, Mrs. Ramos, who is going to teach the children about "the glorious discovery of America," which Vero describes as a fairy tale (*La Cucaracha* 34). History, with all its fabrications and versions of events sanctioned by victors, becomes a viable vehicle for a notion that is vexing to many Latin Americans and Latinos: the idea that the Americas were "discovered" by Europeans, a version that appears very problematic to many people south of the border, given the greater percentage of racial mixing in populations from this part of the hemisphere in comparison to the United States. Thus, these days, many people refer instead to "the arrival of Europeans" rather than to "the discovery," arguing conventionally that these lands were inhabited and well known by many; they only were "new" to the Europeans and their descendants, the Euro-Americans. So, when Alcaraz strives to make the point, aside from the humor and pointing out the relationship between a version of history pregnant with Euro-American bias and a hidden norm, his strategy is to allude to the shared fictional nature of fairy tales, which also stand as another way of promoting a mind-set dear to Anglo-Saxon values. As an abbreviated version of a desired order, fairy tales familiarize the population from an early age with notions compatible with normative aspirations (most reproachingly, in terms of gender). With this consideration in mind, Alcaraz promotes a partially critical outlook, not only of the educational system and history as a discipline, but also of the early mechanics of proselytization through folkloric mythology. While he is quite outspoken about the implications for Latinos, he fails to state anything about gender. Many of these accounts, whether historical or mythological, are founded on a patriarchal order. The fact that he uses a female character to criticize should, if nothing else, also allow for the opportunity to advance a critique of gender normativity. This omission does not work in his best interest. If Alcaraz is to transcend his Latino condition as cultural actor, a more comprehensive mode of criticism on this aspect would be key.

Fairy tale, 2003. LA CUCARACHA © Lalo Alcaraz. Dist. by UNIVERSAL UCLICK. Reprinted with permission. All rights reserved.

At times, his critiques are more effective. On another occasion (*La Cucaracha* 76), Mrs. Ramos is preparing to administer an exam to her students and Vero asks whether she thinks standardized tests can be a bit culturally biased against inner-city students. The matron replies that this is nonsense and that they should get busy with the exam on the history of Amish buggy making. Alcaraz has obviously included this topic to call attention to how detached this subject matter on this type of examination may be from the everyday life of residing in a city. Standardized examination is designed with ideal examinees in mind—this topic has been researched extensively, pinpointing multiple biases, even regionalisms—and these characters tend to differ greatly in terms of social standing, views on gender, and ethnicity from Latino students in urban environments, not to mention multiple other aspects of life. And this idealization of an examinee is, on the whole, an integral part of the institutionalization of a hidden norm. The ideal examinee is conceived as thoroughly acquainted with the interests and policies behind the hidden norm. Consequently, by demanding students to perform well in these exams, aside from asking them to be well versed on particular forms of knowledge, what the educational system is actually accomplishing is the sanctioning of a view of certain collectivities with respect to ideal performers, who, in all likelihood, must be more proficient on the ways of standard cultural ideology.

The world of alienation of Cuco Rocha is intimately tied to the implementation of the hidden norm. And standard cultural ideology has many ways of rearing its ugly head. On page 40, Alcaraz deals with what, and not just in jest, he could call "a repressive arm of the state": the police. When a police officer stops Cuco and Eddie and asks rhetorically whether they know why he stopped them, Cuco retorts, "Actually, yes, officer. A recent nationwide flurry of statistical studies and reports indicates motorists of color are stopped by police in greater percentages than their numbers in the population." By quoting this information, Alcaraz is merely posing a critique of racial profiling, which is another way in which the hidden norm seems to operate. There is little need to go far to encounter evidence of racial profiling in the country. Institutions like the American Civil Liberties Union (ACLU) and the Center on Juvenile and Criminal Justice circulate ample substantiation on this topic. For example, in "Racial Disparities and the Drug War," Esona and Shelden make a cogent case against racial profiling. Among the ample proof they provide, they cite the following information related to the war on drugs: in May 2000, according to the Drug Litigation Project, blacks constituted 13 percent of drug users in the United States, 37 percent of those arrested on drug charges, 55 percent of those convicted, and 74 percent of all drug offenders sentenced to prison.[12] Many other charts and tables in Esona and Shelden's article corroborate the point of view argued by Alcaraz in his comic strip. And events like Trayvon Martin's death, which remains a tragic parameter of comparison for multiple questionable events throughout the country, and the debacles in Ferguson, Missouri, resulting from the violent demise of Michael Brown; in Staten Island, New York, resulting from the unexcusable death of Eric Garner; and in Baltimore, Maryland, from Freddie Gray's, reiterate the fact that, as a cultural practice, racial profiling has been internalized by a fair percentage of the population, from store clerks to police officers, independent of institutional affiliation.

To posit his criticism on the multiples ways in which society enables a hidden order, the cartoonists employs a great variety of mechanisms. Among them, there is the presence of a mustachioed Latino cowboy who has turned Republican—in Alcaraz's eyes, a bit of a blasphemy and a renegade (*La Cucaracha* 41). When Cuco and Eddie meet him at a bar, he is singing the praises of President (George W.) Bush. But the real point of Alcaraz's criticism is an opportunity to question the United States' validity as a meritocracy. According to the Latino Republican cowboy, the United States is a great land of opportunity and, therefore, affirmative action is needless. When he suggests that the concept of a meritocracy still applies, Cuco expands, "Yes, you are judged solely on the merits of your connections," a notion that seems remarkably similar to what works in many other societies throughout the world. In other words, according to the cartoonist, the United States does operate as a meritocracy, except that, within this scheme, any individual's level of progress pertains to the quality of personal networking, which involves measures of class, race, and gender, among other considerations. In this way, Alcaraz suggests the level of interweaving of the hidden norm in the social and cultural fabric of daily life in the United States. According to this perspective, people with regular access to channels of power and political visibility—the 1 percent, so to speak—hold a definite edge over the rest of the population. And because Alcaraz is targeting a larger nationwide audience instead of appearing so

Pulled over, 2003. LA CUCARACHA © Lalo Alcaraz. Dist. by UNIVERSAL UCLICK. Reprinted with permission. All rights reserved.

identified with one political group—his mocking of the Latino Republican may be misunderstood as support for Democrats—it is more convenient to personify political views and interests in a character that may serve a purpose within his community by pointing out the implicit fallacies of Latinos who have gone conservative, tending to dismiss a time when things were not so rose-colored and forsaking fellow Latinos. On the other hand, to criticize the failures of a hypothetical meritocratic model on the basis of ethnicity and class only highlights the cartoonist's failure to contemplate other factors (like gender, age, and so on) as part of an overall critique.

Another way to see this is when Cuco, Vero, and Eddie go to the movies to watch something called "The History of Affirmative Action: The Movie" (*La Cucaracha* 59). Once they walk out of the theater, Cuco complains in a mystified manner that "I got the part about how affirmative action existed for over 200 years for the privileged class . . ." Quite clearly, this history is limited to the US context; in other latitudes, this has been the norm for centuries. Then Vero grumbles, "Yeah, but they lost me at the surprise twist ending, when they kill it as soon as people of color need it." In turn, Eddie is just plain upset and oblivious: he thought he was going to watch an action flick. By following established cinematographic conventions—the surprise twist ending, the movie claiming a reliable account—Alcaraz is able to address the evolution of partiality in US society through jokes. While the characters pretend to be discussing a film, like most people do when they come out of the movies, what they are really dissecting through their conversation is the way in which US society has favored the interests of a few during most of its official history as a nation and has failed to implement progressive measures to address this level of inequity.[13] Thus, in one ingenious move, the cartoonist combines a set of cultural codes related to cinematography and criticism of implicit bias in national society from its very inception as a body politic. While this may be interpreted as a validation of the established cultural order—after all, Alcaraz is alluding to notions emanating from the cinematographic tradition—the degree of cluelessness of the characters as spectators serves as an antidote for complacency.

And yet another way to address the significance of connections or networking, denouncing how the United States is not as meritocratic as it pretends to be, shows up on page 70 of the *La Cucaracha* volume. Vero is reading a newspaper that has published a list of the one hundred most powerful people in Hollywood. Unsurprisingly, Steven Spielberg appears at the top of the list. She then starts reading the list of the one hundred most powerful Latinos in Hollywood and, to Eddie's befuddlement, finds out that Steven Spielberg's gardener occupies the number-one spot. Half in jest, the finding points out two key notions: for one, the United States' sense of meritocracy does have a lot to do with good connections, and second, within this scope, Latinos' access to the upper echelons of society is still very limited, given the restricted assortment of occupations available. Within this scheme, Latino/a social ascent is strongly limited by its level of acquaintance with other, more prestigious individuals. In the same spirit, Alcaraz has a joke about a Newport Beach city councilman opposing adding grassy areas to the local state beach. With grass, the man argues, Mexicans will come and claim it as theirs. To which Alcaraz adds a punch, hinting at the way stereotypes limit communities, just as in the previous joke: Mexicans will only be allowed on the grass if they are accompanied by a mower or a leaf blower (*La Cucaracha* 103)—that is, Mexicans will only be allowed at the beach if they come as landscapers, ready to service the property of a privileged community, never as true beachgoers.

Then again, affirmative action becomes a concept that transcends this manner of critique. In another strip, Vero is speaking to José, one of two precocious, fiercely opinionated elementary kids (recurring characters in the strip), and the boy inquires about the president's wish to hinder affirmative action (*La Cucaracha* 73)—quite evidently, he's talking about George W. Bush. Vero answers him, explaining that the president believes all US inhabitants should have an "even playing field." Staring at the rough terrain of the Pioneer Elementary playground, marked "Watch your Step" and littered with rocks and detritus, the child replies, "The president's never seen *our* playing field." In another instance, in a closely related illustration, the radio in Eddie's car broadcasts a story about the Bush White House warning educational institutions not to actively recruit minority students to increase diversity (*La Cucaracha* 91). According to Bush, many institutions of higher education achieved diversity without affirmative action. The remarks, the strip promptly adds, were made by a commencement speaker at McDonald's University. In fact, there is no such thing as McDonald's University; McDonald's does sponsor a learning institution, but calls it Hamburger University. But that is not the point. The idea is that a Republican president advises against affirmative action in spite of the fact that he fails to imagine better circumstances for successful "minority" students. Along the way, what becomes blatantly clear is that, regardless of the conjectural levelness of conditions in US society, there remains much disparity, especially in terms of disenfranchised communities. The playing field is not even simply because the level of opportunities—influenced by class, race, gender, and many other factors, never mind the specificity of certain backgrounds—has never been the same. So much so that, in point of fact, even a child can notice it.

It is hard not to notice that, regardless of Alcaraz's level of identification with any ideology, Republicans do not fare very well in his production, be it by way of a particular incarnation or through a general comment. For instance, when Eddie and Cuco listen to the radio while riding the car, they hear a news report about Republican leaders stating that "Americans should strive for a color-blind society by ignoring a person's race or ethnicity" (*La Cucaracha* 88). This message repeats the usual refrain from conservative sectors of the Supreme Court, which argue that "the way to stop discrimination on the basis of race is to stop discriminating on the basis of race," a contradictory contention at best, as government mandates can hinder the implementation of race-related policies, yet do little to counteract extensive racial discrimination across society. All well in theory, but the truth in reality is somewhat harsher. When the Jayson Blair scandal came to light—Blair is a former journalist with the *New York Times* who resigned from the paper in 2003 as a result of a plagiarism scandal (among others, he plagiarized a Latina journalist)—the strip reminds us, Republicans immediately launched a tirade consistently alluding to Blair's African American ethnicity as a marker in the incident. Hence, the political party comes across as hypocritical and two-faced, perhaps more so than Democrats, who tend to embrace race as a winning card rather than an obstacle. And just to clarify that he has no hard-core allegiances, the cartoonist has strips like the one in which the car's radio plays the story about Democrats accusing Republicans of ignoring Latino voters and only being capable of superficial, empty gestures when courting the vote (*La Cucaracha* 116). The statement, it turns out—and Alcaraz embellishes the story with unapologetic humor—was made by "Ricardo" Gephardt, "Juan" Kerry, and Howard "Refried" Dean, alluding to politicians' habitual tendency to embrace the linguistic tradition of certain constituencies to ingratiate themselves—*Hispandering*, I believe it is called. From this viewpoint, the Democrats are as superficial in their approach to Latinos as Republicans are, an aspect manifest in their failure to achieve immigration reform despite President Obama's repeated promises during the electoral campaign and, most troubling, in the numbers of people deported in the past few years, exceeding by far the statistics for deportees in previous Republican administrations.

Perhaps for this reason, the conservative Latino character is not just about backlash or renegade politics. Like anything else in *La Cucaracha*, he's an opportunity for old-fashioned misunderstanding. When the man complains about the lack of support for Estrada's judicial nomination, amazingly, Cuco agrees with him (*La Cucaracha* 62). Something must be amiss, readers will surmise. Cuco then draws attention to the importance of Estrada's work in law enforcement and traffic regulation, which should have been reason enough to approve him to the high court, he argues. Finally, Cuco openly expresses his support for *Erik* Estrada, the Puerto Rican actor from the 1970s TV show *CHiPs*, for a position as head of Homeland Security. It is only then that the conservative character clarifies he was talking about Latino judicial nominee Miguel Estrada, who did not receive approval for a post in the United States Court of Appeals. An unintended virtue of Alcaraz's work is how, upon touching on a number of sensitive issues, it serves as a historical record of the day. Estrada is an attorney who became embroiled in a controversy when President George W. Bush nominated him for the United States Court of Appeals in the Washington, DC, circuit. A native of Honduras, Estrada is well known for his conservative record. As a result, Democrats blocked his nomination with a filibuster, setting a precedent for Court of Appeals nominations. To Alcaraz, however, aside from an opportunity for humor, the incident embodies a chance to clarify how social views trump ethnicity. The fact that Miguel Estrada is Latino matters little if his views are contrary to the interests of the community, according to the cartoonist. I may agree with Alcaraz, but what is at stake here is the nature of the critique. While Alcaraz justifies this strategy as part of his attempt to draw a line, it also delineates clearly the binary, almost reductive, propensity of his politics, occasionally bent on reaction rather than resolution. The problem behind criticizing a binary order is that, sooner or later, criticism is also likely to reproduce a binary order. Alcaraz embraces narrative mechanisms like the conservative Latino to try to deflect responsibility, yet the result is not always felicitous.

Another relevant, recurring character in Alcaraz's production is the Taco Cart Guy. As suggested, Alcaraz employs him to ventilate many double standards implicit in the culture and society at large. When Eddie and Cuco order six tacos of *asada*, they notice Taco Cart Guy is selling FTC T-shirts, so they inquire about the Federal Trade Commission (*La Cucaracha* 86). The vendor clarifies that this is not the case. He is selling them for a higher cause. When Cuco and Eddie wave back, we see that FTC stands for "Free Tommy Chong." And so, as on other occasions, Alcaraz uses the comic strip to make a personal point. This departure from the seriousness of his editorial production familiarizes us with an Alcaraz who seems more comfortable in his own skin, taking the liberty to embrace lighter, less all-encompassing issues. In 2003, the Canadian comedian Tommy Chong, famous for his years of work with Latino funnyman Cheech Marín, became involved in two police operations related to the trade of drug paraphernalia. In the end, after being tried, Chong served nine months in federal prison. The case may appear unrelated, since it does not necessarily deal with ethnicity or a handicap of the Latino/a community, but, given the impact of the war on drugs on various disenfranchised populations—Esona and Shelden make a clear case for this, with pie charts illustrating how African Americans and Latinos have borne the brunt of drug enforcement[14]—it is a way to frame the partiality of these measures from another perspective. Nevertheless, Chong personifies a fringe figure for two reasons: first, he is from Canada, a country that, during the Bush years, epitomized the preservation of many things dear to US progressives, and, second, he makes no apologies for his support of the right to consume marijuana. Following the scandal, Chong was apprehended and prosecuted, serving time in prison next to Jordan Belfort, of *The Wolf of Wall Street* fame. Nonetheless, Alcaraz could say, under the same circumstances, privileged, better-connected individuals could face an entirely different fate.

To expand further on the inner workings of the hidden norm, Alcaraz puts forward a number of amusing ideas. For instance, he portrays Cuco at a drafting table designing new currency for the country (*La Cucaracha* 42). Amazingly, despite the fact that the US government repeatedly changes and complexifies its designs, hoping to make things harder for counterfeiters, current US currency remains remarkably traditional in terms of iconography when compared to its equivalents from other latitudes, which tend to be much more colorful and inclusive in their representation. The Euro, for example, has a wide assortment of designs corresponding to each of the nations of its union. In this respect, European states have been far more effective in their co-optation, promoting the illusion of inclusion. To draw light on this aspect, Cuco designs bills with Dolores Huerta, Geronimo, Malcolm X, MLK Jr., and Cesar Chavez at the center, rather than the traditional parade of founding fathers from the colonial period. The measure explains how history and politics contribute to collective and individual identification within a society. In other words, it is through our interaction with artifacts of this nature—such as currency, an anthem, a flag, a passport; the unmistakable signs of a state, the material expression of the idea of nation—that individuals gradually interpret and internalize their location within an order. Quite understandably, within this exercise, what the cartoonist hints at is that, contained by this arrangement, certain ethnicities fare much worse than others. As on other occasions, Alcaraz has once again foretold events: on April 20, 2016, treasury secretary

New US currency, 2003. LA CUCARACHA © Lalo Alcaraz. Dist. by UNIVERSAL UCLICK. Reprinted with permission. All rights reserved.

Jacob Lew announced that former slave and abolitionist Harriet Tubman will replace the seventh president of the United States, white slave owner Andrew Jackson, on the new twenty-dollar bill. In addition, although Abraham Lincoln and Alexander Hamilton will continue to grace the fronts of the five- and ten-dollar-bill notes, respectively, the backs will feature women and civil rights leaders, including Lucretia Mott, Sojourner Truth, Elizabeth Cady Stanton, Alice Paul, Susan B. Anthony, Marian Anderson, and the Reverend Martin Luther King Jr.

However, with a twist of humor, Alcaraz is always generous enough to concede some limitations on behalf of Latinos, like when he portrays Eddie rushing out of his home (*La Cucaracha* 47) and explaining to Vero that he is late for his Latino time-management seminar. Time and space are, most definitely, two central cultural constructs of any society. Compared with their perception in the United States, they embody very distinctive constructs within the Latino/a community. In the United States, thanks to changing seasonal weather, time tends to feature in a more precise fashion than south of the border. Also, the realm of privacy tends to supersede the public sphere, as compared to Latin America. Hence, as a way to admit a characteristic of Latinos that may contrast sharply with its versions in the Anglo-Saxon world, Alcaraz uses a concept in itself instituted by Anglo culture: the management seminar, establishing clearly the difference between each culture's approach toward the resolution of its problems. While the cartoon strip pretends to be talking about time and how it is handled by each culture, in truth, it also posits an ironic critique of the way in which Anglo culture prefers to deal with issues, by way of thoroughly planned initiatives. Once again, by mocking

Latino/a culture, Alcaraz is able to indict Anglo culture for its imposition of a norm, which it pretends to come across as "natural."

Such an approach doesn't always work well. That's why Alcaraz portrays Charles Schulz's Lucy with her customary kiosk for advice next to an almost identical kiosk served by a Latino worker (*La Cucaracha* 51). Instead of Lucy's ever-present "The doctor is in" sign, the booth operated by the Latino laborer has one that says, "The cheap immigrant labor is in." In this way, the cartoonist is addressing the concept of mental hygiene as a middle-class habit, so typical of US society (rather than as an upper-middle-class, Latin American privilege [except in locations like Argentina]), and using it to highlight the myriad ways in which Latino/a labor impacts the national economy, down to the services offered by children throughout the summer. The joke is more meaningful than it appears, as Lucy is transported from her very homogeneous midwestern context to a street in Southern California, in which the line of customers does not include the bunch of suburban white kids from the *Peanuts* crew but a white man, a white woman, an African American, and Cuco and Eddie. The shift is indicative of the wide contrast in demographics between California and the Midwest. According to the Racial Dot Map generated by the University of Virginia's Cooper Center for Public Service, Milwaukee, Detroit, Saint Louis, Cleveland, and Chicago—all midwestern enclaves—are the most segregated cities in the country.[15] This does not imply this is Alcaraz's personal inquest on segregation. Rather, his criticism of a middle-class social habit conforms to patterns of demographic exclusion. The message, the cartoon strip seems to say, is that the United States is changing: its population is older and more urban and diverse, so the service sector is going to have to adapt. And if the population is changing, so should societal order, hopefully attenuating the consequences of an outdated cultural ideology, willing to privilege a segment of the population that now appears even less representative than before.

Alcaraz also discusses how a new generation of fully assimilated Latinos is interacting with mainstream US culture and sometimes coming up with innovative ways to negotiate identity issues, occasionally circumventing the hidden norm. Neto, Eddie's younger brother, seems to enjoy *rock en español*, which Alcaraz labels "roc en español." The kid's name, Neto, has multiple readings: in colloquial Spanish, it may mean something is well defined (as in "net weight"), although it can also allude to the fact that Neto is very technologically savvy (as in "Internet"). When he tries to write a *rock en español* song even though he knows little Spanish—bear in mind that Neto is fully assimilated, so his Spanish-language skills are limited—he writes the lyrics in English and then translates them phonetically, totally oblivious as to whether the words actually make any sense in Spanish (*La Cucaracha* 55). It is this way of negotiation that might represent an obstacle to standard cultural ideology, as this new generation of Latinos applies a different logic to issues and prefers instead to embrace detours and ignore the customary channels of access to information, managed by cultural gatekeepers and thoroughly influenced by the hidden norm. Neto's attitude is typical of his generation, which, although it has embraced English, still resorts to improvised means, in most cases giving way to Spanglish. From the perspective of standard cultural ideology or a hidden norm, though, Spanglish is viewed as a disruption because it ignores the regular modes of communication in accepted language and creates a new norm, which cannot be regulated by a monolingual precept. In short, to deal with Spanglish, aside from criticizing it from an English point of view—and in the United States, English has seldom thrived as purism—cultural gatekeepers would have to include a Spanish perspective—since Spanish does tend to be a more regulated tongue. In due time, this admission of Spanish would eventually come to mitigate English's stature as the single arbiter of cultural ideology, impacting its weight and stature. So, whether it is celebrated or criticized, Spanglish enhances the presence of Latinos by way of language.

This is not the only way that Neto, as a millennial, brings an introspective view to the culture. In one of Neto's few inward-looking moments (as long as it does not happen to involve his generation), Alcaraz employs him as a sounding board so he can question some cultural practices among Latinos. When Tío Toño and Tía Chela come to talk to Neto, which he immediately interprets as lecturing, they claim Neto's style of clothing—the turned-around baseball cap, a hoodie, sweatpants, and sneakers—is bringing shame to the family (*La Cucaracha* 57). Most definitely, the ironic twist is that Tío Toño and Tía Chela's way of dressing is not especially edifying. In an unrivaled display of kitsch, Tío Toño wears an oversize chain pendant proclaiming his astrological sign, which is visible thanks to a patterned, open-chest shirt. His belt buckle is huge, as is his cowboy hat, and his fringed pants give way to cowboy boots. Not to be outdone, Tía Chela wears a skimpy outfit—a miniskirt with a top—exposing her middle-aged belly. She wears a headband, a necklace with a heart, and fringed cowboy boots. Once again, the strip follows the usual dynamics. While at first glance the strip is about Neto's way of dressing, in truth, the critique centers on the lack of moderation on the part of previous generations. In light of being chastised by people who dress like this, Alcaraz seems to suggest, it is almost gratifying that Neto sticks to comfortable, sensible clothing appropriate to his age group. Alcaraz's humor seems to miss the fact that, from Tío Toño and Tía Chela to Neto, the process of assimilation to US culture is reflected in the way each generation embraces a different aesthetic, including clothing. It could be argued that one reason for the cartoonist's sense of relief for Neto's departure from his relatives' tackiness is his

Mexican versions, 2003. LA CUCARACHA © Lalo Alcaraz. Dist. by UNIVERSAL UCLICK. Reprinted with permission. All rights reserved.

further internalization of US cultural codes. Thus, while he rejects the style of elders, he finds Neto's outfits less outrageous.

A key insight in the work of Alcaraz is that there are almost endless approaches to point out the way in which the hidden norm is enacted. One of the most perceptive examples is his adaptation of African American narratives. On page 66 of the *La Cucaracha* volume, there is a strip that takes two popular African American motion pictures, *Barbershop* (2002) and *How Stella Got Her Groove Back* (1998), and transforms them into Mexican American versions: *Burritoshop* and *How Consuelo Got Her Groove Back*. In the first case, the story has been shifted to a San Francisco neighborhood *taquería*; in the second, "an uptight Latina travels to Acapulco and falls for a *muy guapo* cliff diver/cumbia instructor." Both narratives have been adapted to a Latino context, yet one could argue that this is not what is really at stake in this example. If the comic strip were to be interpreted in a self-conscious manner, its main point could be to highlight how, by emulating and adapting an African American narrative, the cartoonist is concretely aware of a precedent in the struggle against a hidden norm. In other words, cultural products like the two African American narratives are their community's way of engaging and debunking standard cultural ideology and therefore dealing with the hidden norm. In this sense, to pay attention to and mimic the dynamics of two successful African American narratives is, in a way, to pay heed to the lessons of a struggle within mainstream US culture. After all, the stature of African American culture has only increased since the time of the civil rights era, at moments surpassing Anglo-Saxon culture in popularity and thus influencing the hidden norm. Hence, it is only understandable that, half in jest, Alcaraz will rephrase some of its efforts, hoping to have at least a fraction of the influence that African American narratives have attained, redefining the very nature of US identity.

In another strip, Alcaraz tries to center on the idiosyncrasies of cultural determination, which tend to have an impact on how a particular group may assimilate and deal with standard cultural ideology. In other words, the cultural baggage of any community may impact the group's ability to integrate successfully into US society. To call attention to this aspect, Alcaraz focuses on something that may border the concept of the stereotype: how Latinos tend to talk with their hands (*La Cucaracha* 69). As an explanation, Cuco claims, "It's called *gesticulation*. I think many 'Latin' cultures talk with their hands." By *Latin*, Alcaraz may not even be alluding exclusively to Latin America. Rather, Cuco may refer to cultures influenced by the linguistic legacy of the Roman Empire; that is, cultures with a Romance-language linguistic background, preferably located around the Mediterranean and along the Western Hemisphere. For instance, the description could apply equally well to the stereotype of working-class Italian Americans from the Northeast. Yet, for the most part, this group arrived during the late nineteenth and early twentieth centuries and has been assimilated almost completely by US culture. As any group becomes more and more assimilated, it tends to abandon its earlier ways and replace them with an established cultural norm from its place of adoption, a product of the prevailing elite and a more pragmatic choice in terms of daily life. One hundred years later, Latinos are traveling along the same path, except that today's communication infrastructure allows immigrants to preserve their home culture in a more viable manner. And so, gesticulation, which has remained an important feature in the definition of certain groups of the past, is alive and well in present-day immigrants. Whether the comic strip's superficial delineation of identity is factual or self-deprecating is left for the reader to decide.

Yet another way to approach this subject is through the lens of negotiation between ethnic preferences and US influence. On page 70, Alcaraz shows Cuco making faces of pain. When Eddie comes to him, alarmed by the expressions, Cuco explains that he is just trying to support free speech but finds it very painful. He then holds out a CD of the Dixie Chicks. It is important to remember the widespread condemnation of the Dixie Chicks on the eve of the Iraq invasion in 2003, when they said at a concert in the United Kingdom that they were ashamed that George W. Bush was from Texas, as they were (although raised in Texas, Bush comes from old New England stock, like John Kerry, his ninth cousin twice removed). In response, country music fans crushed their CDs and boycotted them, and their sponsors dropped them. The anecdote shows how Cuco, who views himself as a US inhabitant, tries to relate to free speech, a notion that would appear foreign or quaint in many corners of Latin America. However, he also comes to terms with the reality that, aesthetically speaking, country music is not very appealing to many Latinos. Although country music shares many musical elements with other folkloric traditions in Latin America, its narratives fail to speak to or to generate a sense of identification with immigrant urban youth. This might have something to do with the fact that, even in its more contemporary incarnations, country music is a strongly culturally determined product, with a very fixed construct in terms of audience (and it seems not to be willing to make any efforts to diversify its base). Additionally, one could argue, it may also be because, by and large, this audience does not seem especially concerned by the lack of cultural malleability of its practice in a country with a rapidly shifting population. (In other words, we are speaking of a potentially shrinking cultural practice.) However, just like anything else, it is important to keep in mind that cultural determination works both ways. Alcaraz uses Mother's Day to highlight this aspect (*La Cucaracha* 78). Eddie calls his mom twice, on Mexican Mother's Day and during its US version (a day later, according to the strip). The humor arises from the fact that a day afterward, once both holidays have passed, Mom calls Eddie complaining about his lack of communication. Nevertheless, what comes out loud and clear in the strip is the notion of how each culture, perhaps with more practical commercial imperatives in mind, determines a date for its convenience. This is but another way of pointing out that all cultures have a hidden norm, because all cultures work on the basis of idealized, model individuals as their constituents, supposedly good children who will call to congratulate their mothers on the corresponding day. And the more anyone departs from this ideal constituent, the greater the necessary effort will be to overcome any potential cultural hindrance.

Mixed in with commercial imperatives, nationalism also brings troublesome implications. The Cinco de Mayo holiday is a typical example (*La Cucaracha* 75). Even so, Alcaraz situates it in the context of backlash against the French as the result of their opposition to the invasion of Iraq, just as the holiday echoes backlash against the French in Mexico. Just as the perception of certain nationalities shift according to historic circumstances, so does the political location of beholders. In a strip set on the day of the celebration, Eddie, Vero, and Cuco are reveling at a street festival. When a protester arrives, claiming the holiday is un-American, Cuco asks what's wrong with "too much partying, too much spending, and lots of corporate sponsorships?" When the man ventures that Cinco de Mayo is an obscure foreign holiday, Cuco informs him that the date commemorates the Mexican defeat of the French in 1862. At this point, it is important to recall the backlash against the French during the time of the invasion of Iraq (the French government was staunchly against it). Otherwise, the final vignette of the strip makes little sense. This aspect again reminds us how Alcaraz's production eventually becomes a matter of historic record, highlighting comics' fixedness in a contemporary context. Once he learns that the holiday commemorates a snub to the French, the man, who had sported a T-shirt with a sizable image of the US flag on it, has changed his outfit: he now wears a huge Mexican hat and bandoliers and carries a sign stating "Mexico #1, France is el stinko!" In other words, when sharing enemies, allegiances shift rapidly. In this sense, support for initiatives promoting Latino/a interests is circumstantial rather than reliable and trustworthy. Based on a nationalist mentality, supporters of a hidden norm, whether they are aware of it or not, may back efforts of Latino integration merely with short-term interests in mind. And, at even more critical times, like when one celebrates a rite of passage condoning belonging—like the Fourth of July—the defense of an order against the constant encroachment of criticism passes for jolly humor, like when Cuco tries to persuade Neto to follow his partisan views and Eddie begs him to drop politics for one day (*La Cucaracha* 102). Yet the truth is that, at times, nation trumps everything. Nationalism, in fact, can condone behaviors that enhance the degree of isolation of a community or country, feeding a lack of intellectual curiosity that is extremely complacent—so content that, in effect, it can occasionally drive a country into trouble or circumstances with unprecedented consequences, as in the case of Iraq, now fragmented to the point of ridicule despite trillions of taxpayer dollars. To put forward this idea with a less alarming approach, the cartoonist portrays Chato and José, the two clever elementary kids, doing something rather silly: once summer comes, they complain about having nothing to do and nowhere to go. In the last frame of the strip, where the words "And nowhere to go" appear, Alcaraz illustrates the entire planet (*La Cucaracha* 118), as if saying, "If your lack of adventurous spirit takes you nowhere, if you fail to contemplate lands beyond national borders as feasible destinations, it is because you are unwilling to see the myriad possibilities before you." After all, even though *La Cucaracha* is about the Latino/a experience, it is also about the US experience and, as such, its sense of criticism must extend to a more enlightened way of enacting identity, most definitely beyond the confines of the hidden norm and standard cultural ideology. Not only does the vignette chastise Chato and José; it also criticizes the generally isolationist mind-set of US culture.

When all is said and done, despite its flaws, *La Cucaracha* manages not only to be a chronicle of an age, but also to document how the Latino/a community—particularly, Chicanos and Mexican Americans—have to negotiate differences in order to conquer a spot within US society. The struggle of many contemporary Latinos might not be comparable to those of the civil rights era or even to those led by Cesar Chavez and Dolores Huerta, but they are still far from negligible. In fact, it is in the subtlety of a response and a resistance—well, in comparison to tactics from the past, not that political resistance is frequently subtle—that we can recognize the extent of the road to travel. With this outlook in mind, it is safe to admit that, perhaps more so than any other Latino/a product of the period, perhaps because of its longevity and the variety of topics it manages to cover, *La Cucaracha* documents well the predicaments of Latinos during the longest period in US modern history without substantial immigration reform and right before the onset of a paradigmatic shift in terms of demographics. In the course of writing this text, Latinos have overtaken non-Hispanic whites as the largest demographic group in California.[16] And that, in itself, makes it worthy of study for scholars of popular culture, and Latino/a and US culture in particular. Cuco Rocha may embody present-day alientation but, in the course of assimilation, Latinos, like previous groups before them, will play a meaningful part in the future of this country. And along with this will come, we hope, a shift in the cultural expectations of the average citizen, signifying a redefinition of US identity.

CHAPTER 5

A Q&A WITH LALO ALCARAZ

THE FOLLOWING ARE SOME QUESTIONS THAT TRY TO SHED LIGHT ON LALO ALCARAZ'S EVOLUtion as cartoonist and provide context for part of his work, so readers are better able to grasp the circumstances surrounding his cultural production. They come from an interview with the cartoonist during the fall of 2014.

HFL: Lalo Alcaraz, the ability to live and perform satisfactorily in two cultures contributes to a comparative view of the world and enhances your critical skills. When did you first become aware of your biculturalism? What role did being bilingual and bicultural play in your childhood?

LA: I grew up as a Mexican kid in Southern California, Lemon Grove, California, to be exact, near San Diego. I grew up like most border kids, going back and forth across the border to Tijuana. I knew I was Mexican, and white San Diego always reminded me that I was Mexican, and supposed to be from a lower, unfavorable class, but it didn't really sink in that I was truly bicultural until one day in front of the Aztec Calendar stone in the Museo de Antropología in Mexico City. I can remember being in awe of its scale and the intricate artwork. It made me realize I was part of an ancient and grand culture. I wasn't just a "dirty Mexican," like I had been told by American culture.

HFL: What is your earliest recollection of a relationship with some form of graphic narrative? You have mentioned *MAD Magazine* and *Gordo* by Gus Arriola, among your early influences, but what other kinds of comics or cartoons were you exposed to as a child?

LA: I love those comics, *MAD* taught me the language of satire, and of course the value of caricature and political snickery! And *Gordo*'s artwork was stunning, and of course, the only representation of any sort of Mexican or Latino for that matter, in comics and almost in anything. (I have to brag that I just finally acquired my first Gus Arriola original Sunday artwork from a dealer at Comic-Con. It's just beautiful, and published the day before I turned six months old in 1964.)

Other comics I was exposed to as a kid were the Mexican pulp comics like *Kalimán*, westerns, and *lucha libre* comics. I loved the *lucha libre* movies of the '70s and my mom would take me to see them in Tijuana every few weeks for the big matinee of Santo and Blue Demon movies. I also consumed all newspaper comics and, as a teen and in college, read *Doonesbury* and *Bloom County* religiously.

HFL: At what point did you become aware of your Latino identity—that, to an Anglo mainstream, you embodied difference? Also, you have been vocal about witnessing the unfair treatment given to your parents. Did this have anything to do with the development of a Latino consciousness?

LA: I grew up as the typical first-generation child of immigrants, the translator. So I had to deal with adults at doctors' offices, social service agencies, and school, in English, and I saw firsthand how people talked to my mom and my dad. And what little rights they had. They were exploited by employers, and just kept grinding through. This is why it sickens me to see how immigrants are still treated, especially poor brown immigrants from Mexico and Latin America. It's my life work to fight back against this injustice. So, yes, it was direct. Foremost, even before I witnessed the cultural whitewashing of American history and nonwhite culture, my conscience was stirred by the immigrant worker's struggle of my own parents.

HFL: Many people argue the US education system is failing to serve Latinos well. However, you have talked about the importance of a school instructor and a counselor in your development as an illustrator during your high school years and an eventual transition into college, respectively speaking. Could you please share more about these people? Do you still keep in touch with them?

LA: I had a few very special people in my educational experience from elementary school on, numerous teachers who paid attention to my artistic ability. I was that kid, the "best drawer" in school, and that always drew attention to me, and some teachers knew to cultivate that in me. One teacher in particular was Ms. Nichols, my high school art teacher. She made me the teaching assistant for the art classes, and always encouraged me to look at the art school art catalogs for the private art schools like Cal Arts and Otis Parsons. I didn't know that a poor *cholo* couldn't afford to go to these schools, but I dreamt anyway. Fittingly, I ended up teaching at Otis recently, and I'm sure that would give Ms. Nichols a feeling of satisfaction. Also, I had a high school counselor, Coach Edge. I did get to speak with him and thank him for giving me the kick in the pants I needed to push myself towards a higher education. He was the only African American faculty member at my high school, and really was pivotal in making me take the right courses to be able to even apply to college.

HFL: Your college years seem to have been marked by your participation in MEChA and Latino activism. How did this experience affect your worldview?

Is there a particular moment in your time with MEChA in college that you recall as especially significant for your career?

LA: Uh, we call it Chicano activism. I often brag I was in two of the baddest MEChA chapters, at San Diego State *and* at UC Berkeley. I still stay in touch with Mechistas nationwide, and support their efforts when I can. MEChA was a primary reason we had an audience at UC Berkeley when I started a Chicano comedy group, the Chicano Secret Service. It was our built-in audience, and helped us grow confidence in our stage skills. Our first show was at a MEChA meeting, and we went on to tour the nation and even work with Chicano playwright Luis Valdez's Teatro Campesino. At both settings we learned the value of protesting against injustice—and a healthy fear of the cops!

HFL: Undergraduate education marks some of the most formative years in our lives. In this respect, your time at San Diego State must have been seminal. What was it like working for the university's newspaper at San Diego State? What did you learn about a lifelong career as cartoonist?

LA: I believe 99 percent of editorial cartoonists work as their college paper cartoonist, I'm no exception. Even back then my reputation was that of being the biggest hate-mail receiver. Some say getting hate mail and angry reactions must be why cartoonists do what they do, but it's not true. We just have something to say, and it disturbs idiots. The other valuable lesson I learned was how to crank work out day after day. There's nothing like a daily deadline to force you to polish and streamline your process.

HFL: By the time you attended college, your taste in graphic narratives had changed a bit. You have mentioned *Doonesbury* and *Bloom County*, in particular, as influences from this period. How did exposure to new forms of graphic narrative change you? Nowadays, what are your greatest influences?

LA: The Internet as a whole, really. And memes. And the speed of it all. I still do what I do, can't unlearn old tricks, especially if they still work. What I like is the instant distribution and short reaction time I can work with when a major news story happens. People get shocked when I post a cartoon drawn in the hour or so after a news tragedy happens, like the daily school shooting, or a plane crash. Some don't take it well, and aren't used to my sometimes quick reaction time. I also like graphic novels a lot, and buy comic books all the time, too numerous to mention here.

HFL: During your time at Berkeley, you cofounded a comedy group and met future work colleagues like Esteban Zul, from Aztlan Nation. How did Berkeley, as an institution with a long tradition of social activism and political militancy, affect your view of national reality and mark your cultural production? Are there any big differences in Lalo Alcaraz before and after Berkeley? I mean, aside from the MA in architecture.

LA: Esteban and I created *POCHO* magazine while I was up at Berkeley, which became a cult hit and taught me to love self-publishing. Zines were huge at the time, before the proliferation of blogs, so it was as instant gratification as you could get. We became the premier proponents of *pochismo*, and spearheaded the revival of Pocho Pride. Also *POCHO* magazine made me a better and funnier writer.

HFL: After grad school, once you returned to LA, you worked for *LA Weekly* from 1992 to 2010. In a sense, this period marks some of your most fruitful years as a cultural actor. How would you describe these years as an editorial cartoonist and what did you learn from the experience? Are there any fond memories?

LA: The LA riots was the incident that shook LA's political and cultural landscape, so much so that I was offered a cartoon in the pages of the *LA Weekly*, and I took full advantage of the new platform. It exposed me to many people, and led to me self-syndicating my content, and then it led to me becoming a syndicated editorial cartoonist, so I am very grateful for the time I spent there. Again, nothing can refine a mind like a deadline, even if it's weekly. People still come up to me and say they read me in the *LA Weekly* every week, even though I haven't been in there for four years, after the wholesale comics apocalypse in its pages. Even Matt Groening's *Life in Hell* was axed!

HFL: How would you describe Daniel D. Portado? Thanks to this character, you first gained some wide name recognition among Latinos. Did it get you into trouble? And, given Stephen Colbert's success with an analogous type, have you ever considered creating a new, updated version of this character?

LA: Daniel D. Portado is the *vendido* that lives inside all of us. He is the ultimate caricature of a sellout "Hispanic" (which is what Chicanos call them) who would side with the majority Anglo culture in the form of the Republican Party, and sell out his own people—and encourage them to "self-deport." This is the concept we originated in this political context, of immigrants so fed up with the continuing anti-immigrant sentiment in the US, who would rather deport themselves rather than deal with the barrage of irrational racist laws that they keep throwing at them. I think it never really got me into trouble, but it was a great use of my sense of satire, and the fake group "HISPANICS FOR WILSON" really presented a great vehicle to push the limits of Chicano satire, which I try to keep pushing.

HFL: Where did the idea for *La Cucaracha* come from?

LA: I wanted to support my habit of drawing comics, so I angled for a syndicated comic strip. After a couple of attempts, they picked the wrong guy—*me*—a non-mainstream, non–willing to draw watered-down "Hispanic" friendly maraca-shaking characters, and I instead drew *La Cucaracha*, which was my version of *Doonesbury* and *Bloom County* set in the barrio. [It is] basically a hyper version of East LA.

HFL: Aside from Vero, there is a dearth of female characters in your production, an aspect that contrasts sharply with the production of other Latino cartoonists, like the Bros. Hernandez, whose world is very rich in terms of female identity. How do you account for this aspect of your production?

LA: Well, Eddie's mom Maria exists in the strip, and she is based partly on my mother, who recently passed away and was very influential in my artistic life. So, your question is very hurtful.

Just kidding, nothing hurts me!

Vero, who is based on my wife, who is a very strong Chicana, doesn't have to carry the load of all womanhood on her back. I'm not gonna pretend I'm some kind of feminist cartoonist, so I'm not that overconfident on writing for a universe of female characters. Instead, I try to support Vero's situation in the strip, in which she's a teacher, and I try to cover issues that affect women in the strip, like the Supreme Court Hobby Lobby decision, which limits birth-control coverage in their employee health-care plan.

HFL: Despite its controversial nature, *La Cucaracha* has managed to endure. How would you describe your experience with the comic strip during its many years of publication? Which one do you think is your most memorable comic strip in *La Cucaracha*?

LA: *La Cucaracha* is a classic name, which I was searching for. I was hoping to mark my strip with a classic Mexican reference, and the old folk song "La Cucaracha" (which has origins in Europe, I hear), which was a political satire vehicle, fit the bill perfectly. I have a few memorable strips in *La Cucaracha*, but I can't remember any of them.

HFL: When the comic strip got canceled in some papers as the result of backlash, what kind of feedback did you receive, if any? What has been the most extreme response you have ever received for your work?

LA: I don't care about the feedback; they are wrong every time, I can guarantee it. It's the same old extreme response I've gotten all my life. I've been told not to speak my mind, not to have an opinion, and to be happy with my lot in life and stop complaining about it, or else I'm a treasonous traitor. Oh well.

HFL: What was it like working with Ilan Stavans? After all, despite both being Mexican, your backgrounds are very dissimilar. You come from a working-class background, more symbolic of a wider spectrum of Latinos, whereas, regardless of his goodwill and degree of empathy, Stavans is the product of a privileged upbringing, representative of a very small segment of the Mexican population.

LA: I think he listens to me because he realizes I am a street *cholo*. We balance each other out somehow; it's still funny and weird that we ever hooked up to make books. But it works.

HFL: During your career, you have been featured and interviewed in a variety of media. Do you feel that the media's perception of your work has evolved? What have been your best and worst experiences with the media?

LA: My bad experiences with the media is limited to typos.

HFL: A key part of your work is your strong connection to the Latino community. Yet the Latino community you worked with as student is perhaps somewhat different from the one you engage nowadays—if only because it is larger and more varied. What kind of changes have you seen in the community in the course of the past two decades and how would you account for these changes?

LA: I have tried to keep cognizant [of] the changing Latino demographic while realizing still that the vast majority is of Mexican descent. Of course there are many Latinos from Central America who are experiencing the "*pocho*" phenomena in their own way, and I try to realize that they are out there too. What we have in common, besides language and our love for *pupusas*, is immigration. This is the never-ending battle we have to fight.

HFL: During your time as a cartoonist, we have witnessed a political shift in the nation. Not only have we turned into a nation of blue and red states, but also people seem increasingly comfortable in settings that confirm, rather than question, their political views, furthering cultural and ideological isolation. From your point of view, what is the origin of this shift and how do you think the situation will evolve?

LA: It's because fascist right-wing corporate assholes want it this way, instead of the boring, but effective, "pay your taxes and vote" model. They want rich people to run everything openly, and that's not the American way. At least pretend.

HFL: When it comes to politics, the Republican Party lags far behind in its appeal to Latinos. However, the Obama administration has deported an inordinate amount of Latinos, betraying the spirit of its promises during the election campaign. In this sense, both parties fail to grasp their responsibility toward the fastest-growing demographic in the country. What is your advice for politicians?

LA: Jesus, I want to be Obama all the way, but I can't support his deportation policy, which is basically, CALL GUINNESS WORLD RECORDS!

HFL: What is your opinion of Pete Wilson and Arnold Schwarzenegger? Of President Obama and Hillary Clinton?

LA: Pete and Arnold suck, they can kiss my brown ass. Obama is good, bad on deportations, but great on lots of other stuff, just held down by GOP haters. Hillary, she can call me and ask me herself.

HFL: From your production, what is your favorite editorial cartoon? And which one of your cartoons has generated the widest response?

LA: The Twin Teepees [for the anniversary of 9/11, two burning teepees with a US flag and the words "Never forget" on the background] is the one cartoon people often say, damn Lalo, that's the best thing I've ever seen, you can quit cartooning now.

HFL: What does Lalo Alcaraz think about the lack of a political will in the government regarding immigration reform? Do you view it as symptomatic of our times, given the Republican Party's unwillingness to negotiate a path toward the legalization of millions of undocumented workers?

LA: Yes.

HFL: At present, there is a great variety of quality work in the illustrated medium in the United States. Thanks to graphic novels, comics and cartoons are experiencing a boom. Which authors appeal to you the most and what new cartoonists do you find promising? Are there any Latinos among them?

LA: Sure.

HFL: Has Lalo Alcaraz contemplated the possibility of authoring a graphic novel?

LA: Dude, I've done two. You call them history books. [NOTE: Alcaraz is correct. His two books with Stavans *are* graphic novels. However, I was asking about production in this format illustrated and scripted by Alcaraz himself, like *La Cucaracha*.]

HFL: What are your expectations for the future, given your continued collaboration with Stavans and the coming series with FOX?

LA: Three-book deal. Ten seasons.

HFL: Finally, as a prominent Latino cultural actor, what advice would you have for young Latinos interested in the comics medium?

LA: Wait till I'm dead, then you can have it all! [*Laughs*]

CONCLUSION

AS I HAVE STATED, THIS TEXT IS NOT ROOTED IN HAGIOGRAPHIC SPIRIT. TRUTH BE TOLD, PART of the attraction of Lalo Alcaraz as a subject for study emerges from his flawed nature, intense demeanor, and recalcitrant temperament, and not from any personal disposition to adulate. It is precisely for these traits that the work of Alcaraz signifies an appealing object of study, considering the close relationship between his cultural production and the circumstances affecting the national debate on immigration reform. It is plain that Alcaraz's personality is influenced by the travails of the Latino experience in Southern California, which, on the whole, do not represent an easy life. Just as the South bears a long history as the site of prolonged discrimination of the African American community, culminating with the struggle for civil rights, Southern California, since well before the days of the Zoot Suit Riots of 1943, has borne the dubious honor of being the primary setting for many of the disparaging constructs of Mexican American identity, given its foundational role in the formation of Chicano communities—although dutifully shared with Texas, it must be admitted. This much is reflected in many of Alcaraz's cartoons and comic strips, which, despite their extensive use of humor and parody, document far-reaching disenfranchisement and alienation. And these two latter aspects should not stand as obstacles for the further dissemination of the cartoonist's work. On the contrary, to the extent that Latinos are rapidly attaining plurality in a number of states, these conditions need to be addressed, with the hope of facilitating social integration and class mobility. Hence, as a Latino cultural actor who has chosen to concentrate on topics related to immigration, Alcaraz has had to figure out a way to engage his audience while at the same time accomplishing a challenging transition: the shift from a production method based on the validation of previously existing cultural paradigms that constitute the status quo and hoping to be perceived as one more concerned citizen, to a more sensitive phase in which his work implements strategies to question the validity of a hidden cultural norm. Like many previous cartoonists—this is a common account in the history of US cartooning—his graphic production tells the story of someone who has had to adjust her or his style and art to achieve the objects benefiting her or his community. Along the way, the main risk for Alcaraz is to accomplish this transition without pigeonholing himself in the role of a cartoonist with an almost exclusively Latino/a audience. Alcaraz has also had to figure out an effective way to deal with and criticize the events surrounding the current immigration crisis, mostly centered on Latinos and a handful of other peripheral identities, and yet remain appealing to the sizable English-speaking public, an audience that frequently responds to these events with more than a degree of detachedness. This is, for the most part, a hard act to balance.

While Alcaraz makes much of the fact that he is *pocho*—a descendant of Mexicans who has embraced Anglophone culture—it is plain that to take his work to a greater public, regardless of the present dynamics of demographic growth in the country, he must try to appeal to and engage with a wider public composed of multiple ethnicities and backgrounds. Either that, or he must embody the cultural crossover. Otherwise he would just be riding a wave empowered by numbers, which does not happen to be a winning bet. Reliable cultural legitimation happens best when it is the result of cross-cultural appeal, attaining an almost universal character—such as, for example, that found in Gabriel García Márquez's fiction, which is said to connect with people from all over the world. As a cultural actor, it is always better to be legitimated by the relevance of what you produce rather than by the sheer weight of statistical supremacy in the target audience. As a Latino cartoonist, as a cultural actor materializing from a group with a still-tangential effect on national reality, it is crucial that the validation of his work results from its measure of cultural bearing rather than from the weight furnished by a greater demographic presence. This would certainly not be the case for an Anglo cartoonist in the contemporary US comics industry because any viewpoints or opinions on the workings of other groups are generally legitimated on the basis of hegemonic precedent. After all, the situation of many contemporary US cartoonists, generally representative of the ethnic and racial bias of participants at events having to do with comics and cartoons across the nation, is a direct consequence of the extent of the applicability of a cultural norm. However, when any judgments or critiques arise from the practice of a Latino/a cartoonist, it is quite predictable that many of these are influenced or take strongly into account the multiple ways in which Latino/a identity is imagined by the prevailing ethnic mind-set—just as would be the case for any other ethnicity. It is for this very reason that his being known solely as a Latino cartoonist might backfire. Like any cultural actor, Alcaraz should be interested in being consumed by white kids in the heart of Indiana, by Mexican Americans in Arizona, by African Americans in Alabama, and by Asian Americans in California—by *all* readers, regardless of race and ethnicity—given what this might imply for the circulation of his viewpoints and overall cultural acceptance. In other words, the ideal is to produce critical material on race and ethnicity that appeals to a base interested in the subject yet not limited by a specific construct of race and ethnicity. The problem of living in a ghetto, mentally or physically, is that, ultimately, you are limited to a ghetto. It is not only important to base your cultural production on that which you know and inform others about yourself, but it is also equally important to generate a message that transcends and surpasses social, racial, and gender boundaries—particularly when this message pertains strongly to a certain social, racial, and gender construct. And, as the United States advances toward becoming a more diverse society in the course of the present century, one in which no group possesses a clear majority, it is imperative that identities previously viewed and interpreted as peripheral manage to be interpreted and consumed as more mainstream.

The current century will witness the growth of Latinos from being the largest "minority" at the national level to attaining plurality within the overall population. This is already the situation in three states, two of which happen to be the two most populated ones: California, New Mexico, and Texas. In this sense, they lead an overall demographic trend. Thus, as Alcaraz's work gains circulation—be it through his graphic art or his writing for an animated TV series—it is possible that it will reach a wider audience or at least embrace a greater variety of subjects. Euro-American privilege will be around for a while, yet it is very likely that, as a logical consequence of the thematic and methodological evolution of his production, Alcaraz will step out of his comfort zone, a feat that has not been accomplished by many established cartoonists, who have usually labored and produced within the preeminence of their ethnic group during their entire lifetime. If an artist happens to be born and mature contentedly within the prevailing cultural norm, it is quite unlikely that she or he will venture beyond her or his comfort zone. For someone like Lalo Alcaraz, bent on disseminating accounts of life experiences of Latinos, this move might be unavoidable. It is the commonsensical consequence of the inner dynamics of his work. In addition, any event that significantly affects the situation of millions of Latinos—undocumented or otherwise (it is important to consider the many legal immigrants who have petitioned for access for their loved ones)—will serve as a springboard for his characters, so concerned about social and ethnic inequity. In the end, once politicians and the government have stopped toying with the future of many families, in effect exploiting them as a negotiating device, Alcaraz should welcome the opportunity to have one last say.

NOTES

INTRODUCTION

1. Rob Keyes, "Over 40 DC and Marvel Movies Will Hit Theaters in the Next 6 Years," *Screen Rant*, 17 November 2014. Available at http://screenrant.com/dc-marvel-movie-schedule-2015-2020/. Accessed 29 June 2015.

CHAPTER 1

1. Sonia M. Sotomayor, dissenting, *Schuette v. Bamn*, 572 US ___ (2014), 22 April 2014, p. 46. Available at http://www.supremecourt.gov/opinions/13pdf/12-682_8759.pdf. Accessed 29 June 2015.

2. According to Erin Meyer's *The Culture Map: Breaking through the Invisible Boundaries of Global Business* (New York: Public Affairs, 2014), the United States is the lowest-context culture in the world, making simple, clear, and effective communication a must.

3. Available at http://www.internationalcomicartsforum.org/past-icaf-programs.html.

4. See Wikipedia's entry for the "List of Highest-Grossing Films" at https://en.wikipedia.org/wiki/List_of_highest-grossing_films. Accessed 21 June 2016.

5. See Wikipedia's constantly evolving entry for the "List of Films Based on Comics" at http://en.wikipedia.org/wiki/List_of_films_based_on_comics. Accessed 10 April 2015.

6. A brief look at Leguizamo's stab at the comics medium, his 2015 autobiographic novel *Ghetto Klown*, illustrated by Christa Cassano and Shamus Beyale, can clarify a lot in this sense. See John Leguizamo, *Ghetto Klown* (New York: Abrams ComicArts, 2015).

7. See both entries at the online version of *The American Heritage Dictionary of the English Language*: https://www.ahdictionary.com/word/search.html?q=Latino; https://www.ahdictionary.com/word/search.html?q=Hispanic. Accessed 17 January 2016.jokingly things can sometimes get I am citing sources such as the Census Bureau, which tends to use it repeatedly.eau fails to d

8. US Census Bureau, "About Hispanic Origin," 25 July 2013. Available at http://www.census.gov/topics/population/hispanic-origin/about.html. Accessed 17 January 2016.

9. US Census Bureau, *Statistical Abstract of the United States: 2012*, 131th ed. Available at http://www.census.gov/library/publications/2011/compendia/statab/131ed.html/. Accessed 25 June 2016. Also see US Census Bureau, *New Census Bureau Analyzes U.S. Population Projections*. Available at http://www.census.gov/newsroom/press-releases/2015/cb15-tps16.html. Accessed 25 June 2016.

10. David Leonhardt, "In Climbing Income Ladder, Location Matters," *New York Times*, 22 July 2013. Available at http://www.nytimes.com/2013/07/22/business/in-climbing-income-ladder-location-matters.html?pagewanted=all&_r=0. Accessed 29 June 2015.

11. "Mexican Leader Criticized for Comment on Blacks," *CNN*, 15 May 2005. Available at http://www.cnn.com/2005/US/05/14/fox.jackson/. Accessed 29 June 2015.

12. "News Release. The Employment Situation—January 2016," US Bureau of Labor Statistics, US Department of Labor, 5 February 2016. Available at http://www.bls.gov/news.release/pdf/empsit.pdf. Accessed 20 February 2016.

13. Emma Lazarus, *Selected Poems and Other Writings* (Peterborough, ON/Orchard Park, NY: Broadview Press, 2002).

14. Raisa Camargo, "Chicano Cartoonist Lalo Alcaraz Weighs In on the Election," *VOXII News*, 27 September 2012. Available at http://voxxi.com/2012/09/27/lalo-alcaraz-weighs-election/. Accessed 29 June 2015.

15. Lalo Alcaraz, *Migra Mouse: Political Cartoons on Immigration* (New York: RDV Books/Akashic, 2004), 15.

16. Ibid., 16.

17. Robert Mackey, "The Deep Comic Roots of 'Self-Deportation,'" *New York Times*, 1 February 2012. Available at http://thelede.blogs.nytimes.com/2012/02/01/the-deep-comic-roots-of-self-deportation/?_php=true&_type=blogs&_r=0. Accessed 29 June 2015.

18. John Rogers, "Comic Strip Returns after Protests," Associated Press, 8 March 2007. Available at http://www.boston.com/business/articles/2007/03/08/comic_strip_returns_after_protest/. Accessed 29 June 2015.

19. You can find most of this information on his website, http://laloalcaraz.com/bio; he also shared additional biographical details by personal e-mail correspondence.

20. Dennis Romero, "Lalo Alcaraz: Most Mexcellent," *LA Weekly*, 22 May 2012. Available at http://blogs.laweekly.com/informer/2012/05/lalo_alcaraz_people_2012.php. Accessed 29 June 2015.

21. Al Carlos Hernandez, "Legendary Cartoonist Lalo Alcaraz," *La Prensa San Diego*, 4 November 2011. Available at http://laprensa-sandiego.org/stories/legendary-cartoonist-lalo-alcaraz/. Accessed 25 June 2016.

22. See www.pocho.com.

23. Kim Geiger, "Herman Cain: 'How Do You Say "Delicious" in Cuban?,'" *Los Angeles Times*, 17 November 2011. Available at http://articles.latimes.com/2011/nov/17/news/la-pn-cain-cuban-20111117. Accessed 21 June 2016; CollectiveCheckup, "Newt Gingrich: Spanish Is Language of the Ghetto," YouTube, 25 January 2012. Available at https://www.youtube.com/watch?v=_rF694NzjPU. Accessed 21 June 2016.

24. Andrew Rosenthal, "Bush Encounters the Supermarket, Amazed." *New York Times*, 5 February 1992. Available at http://www.nytimes.com/1992/02/05/us/bush-encounters-the-supermarket-amazed.html. Accessed 29 June 2015.

25. Sara Inés Calderón, "6 Tech Questions with Cartoonist Lalo Alcaraz," *Más Wired*, 8 August 2012. Available at http://www.maswired.com/6-tech-questions-with-cartoonist-lalo-alcaraz/. Accessed 29 June 2015.

26. Camargo, "Chicano Cartoonist Lalo Alcaraz Weighs In."

27. Nina Terrero, "How Cartoonist Lalo Alcaraz Made It to 'Bordertown,'" *NBC Latino*, 15 November 2013. Available at http://nbclatino.com/2013/11/15/how-cartoonist-lalo-alcaraz-made-it-to-bordertown/. Accessed 29 June 2015.

CHAPTER 2

1. Chris Wilson, "Find Out If Your State Is America's Past or Future," *TIME Labs*, 13 July 2015. Available at http://labs.time.com/story/census-demographic-projections-interactive/. Accessed 10 April 2015.

2. For more information on the history of Latino/a participation in the world of superheroes, be it as villains or do-gooders, see Héctor Fernández L'Hoeste, "Superhero for a New Age: Latino Identity in the US Comics Industry," in *Ages of Heroes, Eras of Men: Superheroes and the American Experiencd*, ed. Julian Chambliss, William Svitavsky, and Thomas Donaldson (Newcastle upon Tyne, UK: Cambridge Scholars, 2013), 196–213. The fact that, in the beginning, Latinos only represented villains or disposable superheroes should not be discounted. It tells the story of a rising ethnicity for which there was not much cultural space at the start.

3. For more on Arriola and his comic strip *Gordo*, see Robert Harvey's *Accidental Ambassador Gordo: The Comic Strip Art of Gus Arriola* (Jackson: University Press of Mississippi, 2000).

4. Hector Cantú, "Gordo Creator Took Accent off Stereotype," *Dallas Morning News*, 11 December 2000. https://www.highbeam.com/doc/1G1-68869368.html. Accessed 10 July 2016.

5. Robert Reich, "The Truth about the American Economy," RobertReich.org, 30 May 2011. Available at http://robertreich.org/post/5993482080. Accessed 21 June 2016.

6. Ana Merino, "The Bros. Hernandez: A Latin Presence in Alternative U.S. Comics," in *Redrawing the Nation: National Identity in Latin/o American Comics*, ed. Héctor Fernández L'Hoeste and Juan Poblete (New York: Palgrave Macmillan, 2009), 251.

7. Gilbert Hernandez, *Love and Rockets X* (Seattle, WA: Fantagraphics, 1999).

8. Merino, "Bros. Hernandez," 256.

9. Frederick Luis Aldama, *Your Brain on Latino Comics: From Gus Arriola to Los Bros. Hernandez* (Austin: University of Texas Press, 2009), 154.

10. Ibid.

11. Rafael Navarro, "About the Author," Sonambulo.com, 2005. Available at http://www.sonambulo.com/About_Rafael.html. Accessed 21 June 2016.

12. Dorothea Fischer-Hornung and Monika Mueller, eds., *Sleuthing Ethnicity: The Detective in Multiethnic Crime Fiction* (Madison, WI: Farleigh Dickinson University Press, 2003).

13. Anne Rubenstein, "El Santo's Strange Career," in *The Mexico Reader*, ed. Gilbert Joseph and Timothy Henderson (Durham, NC: Duke University Press, 2002), 570–78.

14. Jesús Martín-Barbero, "The Processes: From Nationalisms to Transnationalisms," in *Media and Cultural Studies: Keywords*, 2nd ed., ed. Meenakshi Gigi Durham and Douglas Kellner (Malden, MA: Blackwell, 2012), 555.

15. Ibid., 640.

16. Aldama, *Your Brain on Latino Comics*, interviews on 128–43.

17. According to John Horrigan of the Pew Research Center, Internet access through a mobile device is highest among Latinos, at 89 percent versus 83 percent for African Americans and 84 percent for whites; John Horrigan, *America Unwired*, Pew Research Center, Wireless Internet Use—Pew Internet andAmerican Life Project. Available at http://pewresearch.org/pubs/1287/wireless-internet-use-mobile-access. Accessed 1 November 2013. In addition, according to Pieraccini et al., online usage among young Latinos is growing at a faster rate than the general market. Online usage in Spanish is also increasing as both Latinos who prefer Spanish increasingly go online and the number and quality of Spanish online media options increases; Cristina Pieraccini, Leonardo Hernandez, and Douglass Alligood, "The Growing Hispanic Market," *International Journal of Integrated Marketing Communications* 2.1 (Spring 2010): 29–39.

18. *Spanish USA, 1984 (840000) Summary*, Bates no. 504616837/6839. Available at https://industrydocuments.library.ucsf.edu/tobacco/docs/#id=spljo095. Accessed 29 June 2015; Yasmin M. Jones, *Previous Hispanic Research*, 16 December 1987, *Mangini v. RJ Reynolds Tobacco Company*. Bates no. 507129143/9151. Available at https://www.industrydocumentslibrary.ucsf.edu/tobacco/docs/#id=grcv0095. Accessed 1 November 2013.

19. "Exploratory Market of Hispanic Smokers," *Mangini v. RJ Reynolds Tobacco Company.* Bates no. 507132498/2425. Available at https://www.industrydocumentslibrary.ucsf.edu/tobacco/docs/#id=hmyg0097. Accessed 1 November 2013.

20. "Acculturation." *Merriam-Webster's Collegiate Dictionary*, 11th ed. (Springfield, MA: Merriam-Webster, 2003).

21. Franz Boas, *The Central Eskimo* (Washington, DC: Bureau of American Ethnology Annual Report, Smithsonian Institution, 1888; repr. University of Nebraska Press, 1964), 631–32.

22. Michel Laroche, Chankon Kim, Michael Hui, and Marc A. Tomiuk, "Test of a Nonlinear Relationship between Linguistic Acculturation and Ethnic Identification," *Journal of Cross Cultural Psychology* 29.3 (1998): 418–33.

23. Frederick A. Palumbo and Ira Teich, "Marketing Segmentation Based on the Level of Acculturation," *Marketing Intelligence and Planning*. ABI/INFORM Global 22.4 (2004): 472.

24. Liria Barbosa and Angelina Villarreal, "Acculturation Levels Play Role in Marketing Strategy," *Marketing News* 42.3 (15 February 2008): 26–28.

25. Kelly McDonald, "Relating, Not Translating: Why and How to Market to US Latinos," *Illinois Banker* 1.3 (March 2006): 12–13.

26. See, for example, Ramón Corona and Mary Beth McCabe, "Acculturation in Marketing to Latinos in the US," *Journal of Business and Economic Research* 9.9 (September 2011): 67–70.

27. Barbosa and Villarreal, "Acculturation Levels Play Role," 26–28.

28. See "BBDO Special Reports on Hispanic Viewing" (unpublished 2007 BBDO manuscript), cited in Pieraccini, Hernandez, and Alligood, "Growing Hispanic Market," 29–39.

29. Pieraccini, Hernandez, and Alligood, "Growing Hispanic Market," 29–39.

30. Julie Liesse, "The Latino Identity Project: Understanding a Market," *Advertising Age* 78.8 (19 February 2007): A5–A8.

31. Ibid., A7.

32. For detailed account of the growth of the Mexican population in New York City, see Francisco L. Rivera-Batiz, "Newyorktitlan: A Socioeconomic Profile of Mexican New Yorkers," *Regional Labor Review* 6.2 (Spring/Summer 2004): 32–43. According to census figures, Mexican population in New York increased from 61,722 in 1990 to 186,872 in April 2000. By 2005, it had risen to 227,842, still far below Puerto Ricans (790,609) or Dominicans (570,641), according to the Public Use Microdata Series (PUMS) issued by the US Census Bureau. Undocumented estimates give the possible number as 451,149 Mexicans living in New York City in 2005. If present trends persist, Mexicans will become the largest Latino nationality in the city in 2035. A more contemporary source is Laird Bergad's "Mexicans in New York: 1990–2010," a data report for CUNY's Center for Latin American, Caribbean, and Latino Studies, available at http://clacls.gc.cuny.edu/latino-data-projects-reports-national-origin-groups/.

CHAPTER 3

1. Germán Arciniegas, *El continente de siete colores* (Buenos Aires: Editorial Sudamericana, 1965), 110.

2. Mark Hugo Lopez, "In 2014, Latinos Will Surpass Whites as Largest Racial/Ethnic Group in California," *Fact-Tank/Pew Research Center*, 24 January 2014. Available at http://www.pewresearch.org/fact-tank/2014/01/24/in-2014-latinos-will-surpass-whites-as-largest-racialethnic-group-in-california/. Accessed 10 April 2015.

3. Artistide R. Zolberg, "Reforming the Back Door: The Immigration Reform and Control Act of 1986 in Historical Perspective," in *Immigration Reconsidered: History, Sociology, and Politics*, ed. Virginia Yans-McLaughlin (New York: Oxford University Press, 1990), 315–39.

4. Ginger Thompson and Sarah Cohen, "More Deportations Follow Minor Crimes, Records Show," *New York Times*, 6 April 2014. Available at http://www.nytimes.com/2014/04/07/us/more-deportations-follow-minor-crimes-data-shows.html?_r=0. Accessed 10 April 2015.

5. For a more detailed account of Obama's vicissitudes, see Jeffrey Toobin's article "American Limbo: While Politicians Block Reform, What Is Happening to Immigrant Families?," *New Yorker*, 27 July 2015, 30–35.

6. Kit Johnson, "The Wonderful World of Disney Visas," *Florida Law Review* 63 (1 April 2011): 915. Available at http://papers.ssrn.com/sol3/papers.cfm?abstract_id=1839544. Accessed 10 April 2015.

7. Ibid., 956; see also Britta Conroy-Randall, "Critics Accuse J Visa Program of Exploiting Foreign Students," *PRI's The World*, 6 October 2011, which quotes a figure of 18.2 million. Available at http://www.pri.org/stories/2011-10-06/critics-accuse-j-visa-program-exploiting-foreign-students. Accessed 10 April 2015.

8. Jean Beaudrillard, *America* (New York: Verso, 2010).

9. Greg Miller and Brad Lotterman, "Disassociating Myth and Practice: Pete Wilson's Campaign against Immigration," *Argumentation and Values: Proceedings of the Ninth SCA/AFA Conference on Argumentation* (Annandale, VA: Speech Communication Association/American Forensic Association, 1995), 196–203.

10. Adalberto Aguirre Jr., Edgar Rodriguez, and Jennifer K. Simmers, "The Cultural Production of Mexican Identity in the United States: An Examination of the Mexican Threat Narrative," *Social Identities* 17.5 (September 2011): 695–707.

11. Redacción, "Las peligrosas rutas de migración el el Mediterráneo," *BBC Mundo*, 24 October 2013. Available at http://www.bbc.com/mundo/noticias/2013/10/131015_internacional_migracion_europa_africa_mapas_amv. Accessed 22 June 2016. See also "The Mediterranean's Deadly Migrant Routes," *BBC.com*, 22 April 2015. Available at http://www.bbc.com/news/world-europe-32387224. Accessed 22 June 2016.

12. "Migrants Die in Italy Shipwreck off Catania," *BBC News Europe*, 10 August 2013. Available at http://www.bbc.com/news/world-europe-23645112. Accessed 10 April 2015.

13. Wladimir Pantaleone, "Hundreds Dead, Missing as Migrant Boat Sinks off Italy," *Reuters*, 3 October 2013. Available at http://www.reuters.com/article/2013/10/03/us-italy-migrants-idUSBRE9920AX20131003. Accessed 10 April 2015.

14. "The Mediterranean's Deadly Migrant Routes," *BBC.com*, 22 April 2015. Available at http://www.bbc.com/news/world-europe-32387224. Accessed 22 June 2016.

15. "IOM Counts 3,771 Migrant Fatalities in Mediterranean in 2015," *Iom.int*, 5 January 2016. Available at http://www.iom.int/news/iom-counts-3771-migrant-fatalities-mediterranean-2015. Accessed 22 June 2016.

16. See data.unhcr.org/Mediterranean/regional.php. Accessed 22 June 2016.

17. Pam Fessler, "Trauma Plagues Many Immigrant Kids in US Illegally," *NPR Morning Edition*, 8 August 2014. Available at http://www.npr.org/2014/08/08/338606412/trauma-plagues-many-immigrant-kids-in-u-s-illegally. Accessed 10 April 2015. While some Central American nations operate successful programs for the care of youth and children—Costa Rica's Patronato Nacional de la Infancia is a clear example—others, such as Honduras, lack the means for the protection of minors, intensifying the exodus of youth besieged by gangs like the Mara Salvatrucha and the Barrio 18, both of which thrive in the region as the result of the Clinton administration's deportation policy. Born in Los Angeles, these gangs experienced accelerated growth when many of its members were deported to Central America, a location with less resources for law enforcement; thus, they were set free to prey on children.

18. Niall Ferguson, *Civilization: The West and the Rest* (New York: Penguin, 2011).

19. Scott Gold, "The Artist behind the Iconic 'Running Immigrants' Image," *Los Angeles Times*, 4 April 2008. Available at http://www.latimes.com/local/la-me-outthere4apr04,0,3591780 .story#axzz2x4msQuuT. Accessed 10 April 2015.

20. Ibid.

21. "Farrakhan Again Describes Hitler as a 'Very Great Man,'" *New York Times*, 17 July 1984. Available at http://www.nytimes.com/1984/07/17/us/farrakhan-again-describes-hitler-as-a -very-great-man.html. Accessed 21 April 2015.

22. Jorge Mariscal, "The Far Right and Anti-Mexican Racism," *Counterpunch*, 29–31 August 2003. Available at http://www.counterpunch.org/2003/08/29/the-far-right-and-anti-mexican -racism/.

23. Paul Farhi, "Elephants Are Red, Donkeys Are Blue: Color Is Sweet, So Their States We Hue," *Washington Post*, 2 November 2004. Available at http://www.washingtonpost.com/wp-dyn /articles/A17079-2004Nov1.html. Accessed 10 April 2015.

24. Kathy Escamilla et al., "Breaking the Code: Colorado's Defeat of the Anti-Bilingual Education Initiative (Ammendment 31)," *Bilingual Research Journal* 27.4 (Fall 2003): 357–82.

25. "Mexico Seeks Charges Against Alleged Arizona Vigilantes," Associated Press, *Los Angeles Times*, 18 May 2000. Available at http://articles.latimes.com/2000/may/18/news/mn-31390. Accessed 10 April 2015.

26. Tim McGirk and Ronald Buchanan, "Border Clash," *TIME* 155.26 (26 May 2000): 24.

27. Pauline Arrillaga, "'Climate of Violence' Leads to Death in Texas Desert," *Los Angeles Times*, 20 August 2000. Available at http://articles.latimes.com/2000/aug/20/news/mn-7448. Accessed 10 April 2015.

28. Anne-Marie O'Connor, "Border Sniper Incidents Making Agents Wary," *Los Angeles Times*, 14 July 1997. Available at http://articles.latimes.com/1997/jul/14/news/mn-12527. Accessed 10 April 2015.

29. Fernanda Santos, "Shootings by Agents Increase Border Tensions," *New York Times*, 10 June 2013. Available at http://www.nytimes.com/2013/06/11/us/shootings-by-agents-increase -border-tensions.html. Accessed 10 April 2015.

30. Todd Miller, "War on the Border," *New York Times*, 17 August 2013. Available at http:// www.nytimes.com/2013/08/18/opinion/sunday/war-on-the-border.html?_r=0.

31. Camille J. Bosworth, "Guest Worker Policy: A Critical Analysis of President Bush's Proposed Reform," *Hastings Law Journal* 56 (2004): 1095–1120.

32. Kirk Siegler, "Watchdog's New Target: Embattled LA Sheriff's Department," *NPR News*, 21 April 2014. Available at http://www.npr.org/2014/04/21/304558213/la-countys-new-watchdog -may-not-have-much-bite. Accessed 10 April 2015.

33. For more information, see the *Los Angeles Times* collections on Riverside County police brutality, available at http://articles.latimes.com/keyword/police-brutality-riverside-county. Accessed 10 April 2015.

34. Mireya Navarro, "On California's Urban Border, Praise for Immigration Curbs," *New York Times*, 21 August 2001. Available at http://www.nytimes.com/2001/08/21/us/on-california -s-urban-border-praise-for-immigration-curbs.html?src=pm&pagewanted=1. Accessed 10 April 2015.

35. Aguirre, Rodriguez, and Simmers, "Cultural Production of Mexican Identity."

36. Navarro, "On California's Urban Border."

37. Deborah Sontag, "Calls to Restrict Immigration Come from Many Corners," *New York Times*, 13 December 1992. Available at http://www.nytimes.com/1992/12/13/weekinreview/the -nation-calls-to-restrict-immigration-come-from-many-quarters.html. Accessed 10 April 2015.

38. See the website for Zero Air Pollution Los Angeles at http://www.zapla.org/.

39. Jonathan Eig, "Sounding the Alarm Takes Heavy Toll on Eunice Stone," *Wall Street Journal*, 17 June 2003. Available at http://online.wsj.com/news/articles/SB105581300717867000. Accessed 10 April 2015.

40. Lisa Huriash et al., "Terror Scare Shuts Alligator Alley," *Sun-Sentinel*, 14 September 2002. Available at http://articles.sun-sentinel.com/2002-09-14/news/0209140264_1_law-enforcement-three-men-eunice-stone. Accessed 10 April 2015.

41. "Indictments in Operation Safe Travel," *CBSNews.com*, 11 December 2001. Available at http://www.cbsnews.com/news/indictments-in-operation-safe-travel/. Accessed 10 April 2015.

42. Valerie Alvord, "Non-Citizens Fight and Die for Adopted Country," *USA Today*, 8 April 2003. Available at http://usatoday30.usatoday.com/news/world/iraq/2003-04-08-noncitizen-usat_x.htm. Accessed 10 April 2015.

43. Mark Krikorian, "Green-Card Soldiers Don't Pass Muster," *Los Angeles Times*, 6 May 2003. Available at http://articles.latimes.com/2003/may/06/opinion/oe-krikorian6. Accessed 10 April 2015.

44. See the transcript of PBS's *The American Experience* episode "Reagan" at http://www.pbs.org/wgbh/americanexperience/features/transcript/reagan-transcript/, in which Michael K. Deaver, his deputy chief of staff, describes how Reagan would mail checks to people just as he cut the benefits of many. Accessed 10 April 2015.

45. Greg Krikorian, "Schwarzenegger's Prop. 187 Support Could Hinder Him," *Los Angeles Times*, 12 August 2003. Available at http://articles.latimes.com/2003/aug/12/local/me-race12/2. Accessed 10 April 2015.

46. US Census Bureau, *Statistical Abstract of the United States: 2012*, 131th ed. Available at http://www.census.gov/library/publications/2011/compendia/statab/131ed.html/. Accessed 25 June 2016.

47. Felipe Korzenny and Betty Ann Korzenny, "The Composition of the Hispanic/Latino Market," in *Hispanic Marketing: Connecting with the New Latino Consumer* (New York: Routledge, 2011), 39–79.

48. US Census Bureau, "2010 Census Shows America's Diversity." Available at http://www.census.gov/newsroom/releases/archives/2010_census/cb11-cn125.html. Accessed 1 November 2013.

49. US Census Bureau, *Statistical Abstract of the United States: 2012*, 131th ed. Available at http://www.census.gov/library/publications/2011/compendia/statab/131ed.html. Accessed 25 June 2016.

50. Harriet A. Washington, "Burning Love: Big Tobacco Takes Aim at LGBT Youths," *American Journal of Public Health* 92.7 (2002): 1086–95; Elizabeth A. Smith and Ruth E. Malone, "The Outing of Philip Morris: Advertising Tobacco to Gay Men," *American Journal of Public Health* 93.6 (2003): 988–93.

CHAPTER 4

1. The language of *The Metamorphosis*, Kafka's seminal text, does not allude specifically to an insect, but rather to a bug (an unclean animal unfit for sacrifice), as noted by Susan Bernofsky in her afterword for a new translation. See Susan Bernofsky, "On Translating Kafka's 'The Metamorphosis,'" *New Yorker*, 14 January 2014. Available at http://www.newyorker.com/online/blogs/books/2014/01/on-translating-kafkas-the-metamorphosis.html. Accessed 25 June 2016.

2. Lalo Alcaraz, *La Cucaracha* (Kansas City, MO: Andrews McMeel, 2004), 6.

3. For a relevant analysis of Mexican American unwillingness to conform to Anglo-American cultural codes, see pp. 96–102 of Ray Suarez's *Latino Americans: The 500-Year Legacy That*

Shaped a Nation, in which he discusses the importance of cultural practices such as the adoption of the zoot suit in 1940s Los Angeles.

4. Adam Liptak, "Sotomayor Finds Her Voice among Justices," *New York Times*, 6 May 2014. Available at http://www.nytimes.com/2014/05/07/us/politics/sotomayor-finds-her-voice-among-the-justices.html?_r=0. Accessed 10 April 2015.

5. Alcaraz, *La Cucaracha*, 7.

6. Gabriel García Márquez, *Living to Tell the Tale* (New York: Vintage, 2003), 272.

7. See p. 380 of Antonio Gramsci's *The Gramsci Reader: Selected Writings, 1916–1935* (New York: New York University Press, 2000), in which the Italian theoretician comments on the role of media and the Church in the promotion of ideology.

8. "Hispanics in the U.S. Army," https://www.army.mil/hispanics/. Accessed 10 July 2016.

9. Ibid.

10. See Harlan K. Ullman and James P. Wade, *Shock and Awe: Achieving Rapid Dominance* (Washington, DC: Center for Advanced Concepts and Technology, 1996).

11. Mizanur Rahman, "Immigrant Soldiers Get Fast Track to Citizenship," *Houston Chronicle*, 15 January 2010. Available at blog.chron.com/immigration/2010/01/immigrant-soldiers-get-fast-track-to-citizenship/. Accessed 25 June 2016.

12. Destani Esona and Randall G. Shelden, "Racial Disparities and the Drug War" (San Francisco: Center on Juvenile and Criminal Justice, 2009); and Fatema Gunja, "Position Paper: Race and the War on Drugs," American Civil Liberties Union, *Drug Policy Litigation Project*. May 2003; statistics on p. 1. Available at https://www.aclu.org/files/FilesPDFs/ACF4F34.pdf. Accessed 1 August 2015.

13. To this respect, see Michael Kimmel's renowned TED Talk on "Why Gender Equality Is Good for Everyone—Men Included," available at TED.com, http://www.ted.com/talks/michael_kimmel_why_gender_equality_is_good_for_everyone_men_included?language=en, which clarifies the mechanics of affirmative action; Kimmel notes that "white men [have been] the single greatest beneficiaries of an affirmative-action program in the history of the world—it's called the history of the world."

14. Esona and Shelden, "Racial Disparities and the Drug War."

15. Redacción, "Los mapas que muestran los lugares con mayor segregación racial de EE.UU," *BBC Mundo*, 1 August 2015. Available at http://www.bbc.com/mundo/noticias/2015/08/150728_eeuu_mapas_segregacion_racial_bd. Accessed 1 August 2015. While the Racial Dot Map offers the information, only some media have highlighted its results, thus emphasizing specific readings of the information.

16. Javier Panzar, "It's Official: Latinos Now Outnumber Whites in California," *Los Angeles Times*, 8 July 2015. Available at http://www.latimes.com/local/california/la-me-census-latinos-20150708-story.html. Accessed 1 August 2015.

WORKS CITED

Akomolafe, Soji. "The Invisible Minority: Revisiting the Debate on Foreign-Accented Speakers and Upward Mobility in the Workplace." *Journal of Cultural Diversity* 20.1 (Spring 2013): 7–14.
Alcaraz, Lalo. *La Cucaracha*. Kansas City, MO: Andrews McMeel, 2004.
———. *Migra Mouse: Political Cartoons on Immigration*. New York: RDV Books/Akashic, 2004.
Aldama, Frederick Louis. *Your Brain on Latino Comics: From Gus Arriola to Los Bros Hernandez*. Austin: University of Texas Press, 2009.
American Dad! FOX. Fuzzy Door Productions, Underdog Productions, Fox Television Animation, and 20th Century Fox Television, 2005– .
The Andy Griffith Show. CBS. Danny Thomas Enterprises, Mayberry Enterprises, and CBS Television Network, 1960–68. Television.
Ant-Man. Dir. Peyton Reed. Perf. Paul Rudd, Michael Douglas, Evangeline Lilly, Corey Stoll, Michael Peña, and Bobby Cannavale. Marvel Studios, 2015. Film.
The Avengers. Dir. Joss Whedon. Perf. Robert Downey Jr., Chris Evans, Mark Ruffalo, Chris Hemsworth, Scarlett Johansson, and Jeremy Renner. Marvel Studios, 2012. Film.
Barbosa, Liria, and Angelina Villarreal. "Acculturation Levels Play Role in Marketing Strategy." *Marketing News* 42.3 (15 February 2008): 26–28.
Belfort, Jordan. *The Wolf of Wall Street*. New York: Bantam Books, 2007.
Birdman; or, The Unexpected Virtue of Ignorance. Dir. Alejandro González Iñárritu. Perf. Michael Keaton, Zach Galifianakis, Edward Norton, Naomi Watts, and Emma Stone. Fox Searchlight Pictures, 2014. Film.
Boas, Franz. *The Central Eskimo*. Washington, DC: Bureau of American Ethnology Annual Report, Smithsonian Institution, 1888. Repr. University of Nebraska Press, 1964.
Breathed, Berkeley. *The Bloom County Library*. San Diego, CA: IDW, 2009.
Buchanan, Patrick. *The Death of the West: How Dying Populations and Immigrant Invasions Imperil Our Country and Civilization*. New York: Thomas Dunne Books/St. Martin's Press, 2002.
Cantú, Héctor, and Carlos Castellanos. *The Lower You Ride, the Cooler You Are: A Baldo Collection*. Kansas City, MO: Andrews McMeel, 2001.
———. Night of the Bilingual Telemarketers: Baldo Collection No. 2. Kansas City, MO: Andrews McMeel, 2002.
Chandler, Raymond. *The Big Sleep*. New York: Vintage Books, 1992.
Chua, Amy, and Jed Rubenfeld. *The Triple Package: How Three Unlikely Traits Explain the Rise and Fall of Cultural Groups in America*. New York: Penguin Press, 2014.
Corona, Ramón, and Mary Beth McCabe. "Acculturation in Marketing to Latinos in the US." *Journal of Business and Economic Research* 9.9 (September 2011): 67–70.
CSI: Crime Scene Investigation. CBS. Jerry Bruckheimer Television, Alliance Atlantis, CBS Productions, CBS Paramount, and CBS Television Studios, 2000– . Television.

CSI: Miami. CBS. Jerry Bruckheimer Television, Alliance Atlantis, CBS Productions, CBS Paramount, and CBS Television Studios, 2002–12. Television.
A Day without a Mexican. Dir. Sergio Arau. Perf. Caroline Aaron, Tony Abatemarco, Melinda Allen, Frankie J. Allison, and Maria Beck. Eye on the Ball Films, IMCINE, Jose and Friends, Plural Entertainment, and RTG Productions, 2004. Film.
De Cervantes Saavedra, Miguel. *Don Quixote de la Mancha.* Oxford: Oxford University Press, 2008.
Deadpool. Dir. Tim Miller. Perf. Ryan Reynolds, Morena Baccarin, Ed Skrein, T. J. Miller, Gina Carano, Leslie Uggams, and Brianna Hildebrand. Marvel Studios, 2016. Film.
Delisle, Guy. *Pyongyang: A Journey in North Korea.* Montréal, QC: Drawn and Quarterly, 2005.
———. *Shenzhen: A Travelogue from China.* Montréal, QC: Drawn and Quarterly, 2006.
Eisner, Will. *A Contract with God and Other Tenement Stories.* New York: DC Comics, 1996.
El Inmigrante. Dir. Dave Eckenrode, John Eckenrode, and John Sheedy. 6512 Productions, Impala Roja, and Ouzel Motion Pictures, 2005. Film.
Ellison, Ralph. *Invisible Man.* New York: Vintage International, 1995.
Espinosa, Frank. *Rocketo.* Berkeley, CA: Image Comics, 2006.
"Exploratory Market of Hispanic Smokers." *Mangini v. RJ Reynolds Tobacco Company.* University of California San Francisco Library, Truth Tobacco Industry Documents. Bates no. 507132498/2425. Available at https://www.industrydocumentslibrary.ucsf.edu/tobacco/docs/#id=hmyg0097. Accessed 1 November 2013.
Family Guy. FOX. Fuzzy Door Productions, FOX Television Animation, and 20th Century Fox Television, 1999–2003; 2005– . Television.
Ferguson, Niall. *Civilization: The West and the Rest.* New York: Penguin, 2011.
García Márquez, Gabriel. *One Hundred Years of Solitude.* New York: HarperCollins, 2003.
Guardians of the Galaxy. Dir. James Gunn. Perf. Chris Pratt, Zoe Saldana, Vin Diesel, Bradley Cooper, Lee Pace, Djimon Honsou, Glenn Close, and Benicio del Toro. Marvel Studios, 2014. Film.
Happy Days. ABC. Miller-Milkis Productions, Henderson Productions, Miller-Milkis-Boyett Productions, and Paramount Network Television, 1974–84. Television.
Hernandez, Gilbert, Jaime Hernandez, and Mario Hernandez. *Love and Rockets.* Agoura, CA: Fantagraphics Books, 1986.
Horrigan, John. *America Unwired.* Pew Research Center. Wireless Internet Use—Pew Internet and American Life Project. Available at http://pewresearch.org/pubs/1287/wireless-internet-use-mobile-access. Accessed 1 November 2013.
Huntington, Samuel P. *Who Are We? The Challenges to America's National Identity.* New York: Simon and Schuster, 2004.
Jones, Yasmin M. *Previous Hispanic Research.* 16 December 1987. *Mangini v. RJ Reynolds Tobacco Company.* University of California San Francisco Library, Truth Tobacco Industry Documents. Bates no. 507129143/9151. Available at https://www.industrydocumentslibrary.ucsf.edu/tobacco/docs/#id=grcv0095. Accessed 1 November 2013.
Kafka, Franz. *The Metamorphosis.* New York: W. W. Norton, 2015.
Korzenny, Felipe, and Betty Ann Korzenny. "The Composition of the Hispanic/Latino Market." *Hispanic Marketing: Connecting with the New Latino Consumer.* New York: Routledge, 2011. 39–79.
Lamerica. Dir. Gianni Amelio. Perf. Enrico Lo Verso, Michele Placido, Piro Milkani, and Carmelo Di Mazzarelli. Alia Film, Cecchi Gori Group Tiger Cinematografica, Arena Films, RAI 1, Canal Plus, Vega Film, CNC, 1994. Film.

Laroche, Michel, Chankon Kim, Michael Hui, and Marc A. Tomiuk. "Test of a Nonlinear Relationship between Linguistic Acculturation and Ethnic Identification." *Journal of Cross Cultural Psychology* 29.3 (1998): 418–33.
Lazarus, Emma. *The Poems of Emma Lazarus*. Boston: Houghton, Mifflin, 1889.
Leave It to Beaver. Writ. Joe Connelly, Bob Mosher, and Dick Conway. Dir. Norman Tokar, David Butler, Norman Abbott, and Hugh Beaumont. Gomalco/Kayro-Vue Productions, 1957–63. Television.
Liesse, Julie. "The Latino Identity Project: Understanding a Market." *Advertising Age* 78.8 (19 February 2007): A5–A8.
Lippi, Rosina. *English with an Accent: Language, Ideology, and Discrimination in the United States*. New York: Routledge, 1997.
Man with a Million. Dir. Ronald Neame. Perf. Gregory Peck, Jane Griffiths, and Ronald Squire. J. Arthur Rank Organisation and Group Film Productions, 1954. Film.
Martín-Barbero, Jesús. "The Processes: From Nationalisms to Transnationalisms." *Media and Cultural Studies: Keyworks*, 2nd ed. Ed. Meenakshi Gigi Durham and Douglas Kellner. Malden, MA: Blackwell, 2012. 545–67.
McDonald, Kelly. "Relating, Not Translating: Why and How to Market to US Latinos." *Illinois Banker* 1.3 (March 2006): 12–13.
Merriam-Webster's Collegiate Dictionary. 11th ed. Springfield, MA: Merriam-Webster, 2003.
Miami Vice. NBC. Michael Mann Productions, 1984–89. Television.
Miller, Frank. *The Dark Knight Returns*. New York: DC Comics, 2002.
———. *Sin City*. Milwaukie, OR: Dark Horse Comics, 1991–2000.
———. *300*. Milwaukie, OR: Dark Horse Comics, 1999.
A Million to Juan. Dir. Paul Rodriguez. Perf. Paul Rodriguez, Tony Plana, Bert Rosario, and Polly Draper. Crystal Sky Worldwide, Prism Entertainment Corporation, and Trimark Pictures, 1994. Film.
Modern Family. ABC. Lloyd-Levitan Productions, Picador Productions, Steven Levitan Productions, and 20th Century Fox Productions, 2009– . Television.
Moore, Alan, and Dave Gibbons. *Watchmen*. New York: DC Comics, 1987.
Navarro, Rafael. *Masks of Sonambulo*. La Habra, CA: Ninth Circle Studios, 2003.
Palumbo, Frederick A., and Ira Teich. "Marketing Segmentation Based on the Level of Acculturation." *Marketing Intelligence and Planning*. ABI/INFORM Global 22.4 (2004): 472.
Pieraccini, Cristina, Leonardo Hernandez, and Douglass Alligood. "The Growing Hispanic Market." *International Journal of Integrated Marketing Communications* 2.1 (Spring 2010): 29–39.
Reich, Robert. "The Truth about the American Economy." RobertReich.org. 30 May 2011. Available at http://robertreich.org/post/5993482080. Accessed 21 June 2016.
Rodríguez de Montalvo, Garci. *Amadís de Gaula*. Madrid: Consejo Superior de Investigaciones Científicas, Instituto Miguel de Cervantes, 1959–69.
Rubenstein, Anne. "El Santo's Strange Career." *The Mexico Reader*. Ed. Gilbert Joseph and Timothy Henderson. Durham, NC: Duke University Press, 2002. 570–78.
Sacco, Joe. *Journalism*. New York: Metropolitan Books/Henry Holt, 2012.
———. *Palestine*. Seattle, WA: Fantagraphics Books, 2001.
———. *Safe Area Goražde*. Seattle, WA: Fantagraphics Books, 2000.
Satrapi, Marjane. *Embroideries*. New York: Pantheon Books, 2005.
———. *Persepolis*. New York: Pantheon Books, 2003.
Scarface. Dir. Brian De Palma. Perf. Al Pacino, Steven Bauer, and Michelle Pfeiffer. Universal Pictures, 1983. Film.
Schulz, Charles M. *Peanuts*. New York: Rhinehart, 1952.

The Simpsons. FOX. Gracie Films, 20th Century Fox Television, Klasky Csupo, Film Roman, and the Curiosity Company, 1989– . Television.

Smith, Elizabeth A., and Ruth E. Malone. "The Outing of Philip Morris: Advertising Tobacco to Gay Men." *American Journal of Public Health* 93.6 (2003): 988–93.

Spanish USA, 1984 (840000) Summary. RJ Reynolds Tobacco Company. University of California San Francisco Library, Truth Tobacco Industry Documents. Bates no. 504616837/6839. Available at https://www.industrydocumentslibrary.ucsf.edu/tobacco/docs/#id=spljo095. Accessed 29 June 2015.

Spiegelman, Art. *Maus: A Survivor's Tale*. New York: Pantheon Books, 1986.

Stand and Deliver. Dir. Ramón Menéndez. Perf. Edward James Olmos, Estelle Harris, Mark Phelan, Daniel Villarreal, and Lou Diamond Phillips. American Playhouse, Olmos Productions, and Warner Bros., 1988. Film.

Stavans, Ilan, and Lalo Alcaraz. *Latino USA: A Cartoon History*. New York: Basic Books, 2000.

———. *A Most Imperfect Union: A Contrarian History of the United States*. New York: Basic Books, 2014.

The Terminator. Dir. James Cameron. Perf. Arnold Schwarzenegger, Linda Hamilton, and Michael Biehn. Hemdale Film, Pacific Western, Euro Film Funding, and Cinema 84, 1984. Film.

Trudeau, Gary B. *Doonesbury*. New York: American Heritage Press, 1971.

Twain, Mark. *The £1,000,000 Bank-Note and Other New Stories*. New York: Oxford University Press, 1996.

US Census Bureau. "2010 Census Shows America's Diversity." Available at http://www.census.gov/newsroom/releases/archives/2010_census/cb11-cn125.html. Accessed 1 November 2013.

Waid, Mark, and Alex Ross. *Kingdom Come*. New York: DC Comics, 1997.

Washington, Harriet A. "Burning Love: Big Tobacco Takes Aim at LGBT Youths." *American Journal of Public Health* 92.7 (2002): 1086–95.

Wilson, Chris. "Find Out If Your State Is America's Past or Future." *TIME Labs*. 13 July 2015. Available at http://labs.time.com/story/census-demographic-projections-interactive/. Accessed 10 April 2015.

INDEX

ABC, 29, 64, 144
acculturation, 8, 39, 41, 57, 59, 61–65, 181n20
affirmative action, 107, 154–57
Aldama, Fred, 5, 48–49, 57, 59, 180n9
Alonzo, Cristela, 15
Amendment 31, 109, 183n24
amnesty, 32, 72–73, 113–14, 125
armed forces, 33, 42, 73, 106, 125–26, 148–50
Arnaz, Desi, 16
Arriola, Gustavo "Gus," 8, 26, 39–45, 47–48, 57, 69, 137, 151, 168, 180n3, 180n9
assimilation, 32, 57, 59, 63, 72, 103, 107, 137, 167
Atlanta, x–xi, 4, 18–21
Atlanta Journal-Constitution, 4, 18–19
Atlas, Charles, 115–17

Baca, Lee, 114
Baldo (Baldomero Bermúdez), 8, 15, 48, 56–60, 64–65, 138
Bat Boy, 142
Bermúdez, Baldomero, 8, 15, 48, 56–60, 64–65, 138
Birdman, 7
Bloom County, 27, 169–70, 172
Boogie El Aceitoso, 15
Boondocks, The, 28
Border Patrol, 23, 80, 90, 111–12, 116–17
Bracero, 67, 112
Bros. Hernandez, 8, 39–40, 44–48, 172, 180n6
Buchanan, Pat, 6, 32, 100, 108
Bush, George H. W., 33, 179n24
Bush, George W., 19, 23, 32, 72, 75, 95, 113–14, 125–26, 150, 154, 156, 158–59, 164

California, x, 3, 18, 20, 24, 27, 30, 37–38, 42, 45–46, 48, 52, 54, 71–72, 75, 85, 90–91, 93, 95, 98–100, 103, 106, 108–9, 111, 114–15, 118, 122, 126, 161, 167, 175–77, 181n2, 183n34, 185n16; origin of, 70–71; Southern, 4, 30, 47, 72, 89, 91, 101, 115, 117, 130, 161, 168
Caltrans, 89–91, 93, 110
Cantú, Héctor, 8, 15, 39–40, 48, 56, 58–59, 61, 64, 69, 138, 151, 180n4
Castellanos, Carlos, 8, 15, 39–40, 48, 56, 58–59, 61, 64, 69, 138, 151
CBS, 16, 29, 144
Charlie Hebdo, 3
Chascarrillo, Maggie, 46–47
Chavez, Linda, 107
Chicanos, 25, 27–28, 30, 32, 53, 66–67, 108, 170–71, 175, 179
Chicano Secret Service, 27, 170
Chupacabra, 142
Clinton, Bill, 74, 100, 116, 182n17
Clinton, Hillary, 173
Colonias, 24
Creature Entertainment, 5
Creepy, ix
Cucaracha, La, 9, 15, 18–19, 27–29, 33, 81, 129–67, 171–74
Cuco, 28, 130, 134, 136–42, 144–46, 150, 153–55, 157–59, 161, 164–67
cultural norm, 36, 38, 40–41, 45, 47–48, 56–57, 81–82, 89, 130–32, 134, 144–45, 164, 175–77

DAPA (Deferred Action for Parents of Americans and Lawful Permanent Residents), 4
Dark Horse, 13, 152
Day without a Mexican, A, 122
DC Comics, 5, 7, 41, 52
Delisle, Guy, 14
Democrats, 20, 32, 75, 125, 155, 157–58
difference, 11, 17, 19–20, 33, 40–42, 44–45, 48–49, 59–60, 63, 78, 95, 98, 103–4, 107, 111, 117–18, 123–25, 132, 137–38, 140, 144, 146, 160, 169

Disneyland, 77, 122
dissociation, 79
Dobbs, Lou, 6
Doonesbury, 27–28, 169–70, 172
Drawn and Quarterly, 13

Eddie, 130, 136–40, 142, 144–45, 147–48, 150–51, 153–58, 160–61, 164–66, 172
Ellison, Ralph, 135
English-only movement, 102, 104, 106–7, 109, 136
Escalante, Jaime, 106
Espinosa, Eusebio de Haro, 110
Espinosa, Frank, 8, 15, 36, 39, 48–53, 57, 69
established cultural norm, 36, 47, 57, 131, 164
Estrada, Miguel, 158

Feggo (Felipe Galindo), 66
Ferguson, Niall, 85
First Second, 13
Flores, Enrique Funes, 114–15
Fontanarrosa, Roberto, x, 15
FOX, 10, 26, 30, 34, 144, 151, 174
FOX News, 6, 26, 31, 107–8
Fox, Vicente, 21, 113–14
Franquin, André, 11

gesticulation, 164
Glass, Hopey, 46
Gordo, 8, 26, 42–45, 47, 168, 180n3
Goscinny, René, 11
Green Lantern, ix

Hart-Cellar Act, 72–73
Hergé, 11
Hernandez brothers, 8, 39–40, 44–48, 172, 180n6
hidden norm, 9, 129–67
Hispandering, 157
Hispanics, 16–17, 23, 29, 34, 58, 128, 167, 171, 178nn7–8, 180n17, 181n19, 184n47
Hitler, Adolf, 94–95, 98, 136, 183n21
Hood, John, 89, 93, 110
Howard, Ron, 148

ICAF (International Comics Art Festival), xi, 11–12, 14–15, 18–19
ICAF (International Comics Art Forum), 12, 178n3
IIRIRA (Illegal Immigration Reform and Immigrant Responsibility Act of 1996), 74

IJOCA (International Journal of Comic Art), 12
immigration, x, 3–4, 6–7, 9, 18, 21–25, 29, 31–32, 35, 38–41, 43, 48, 50–51, 59, 64, 66, 69–128, 150, 157, 167, 173–76, 179n15, 181n3, 182n9, 183n34, 183n37, 185n11
Imperial Beach, 116–18
INS (Immigration and Naturalization Service), 73, 75
Invisible Man, 135

Johnson, Kit, 77, 182n6
José, 156, 166

Ketcham, Hank, 36, 98
King, Rodney, 114–15

Lardé, Alicia, 148
Latinidad, 42, 67, 131
Lavado, Joaquín Salvador, ix–x, 15
leaf blowers, 119–20
Leguizamo, John, 15, 178n6
Limbaugh, Rush, 6
Lippi, Rosina, 141, 188
Lopez, George, 15–16
Los Angeles County Sheriff's Department, 114, 183n32
Love and Rockets, 8, 45–47, 180n7
Luba, 46–47

MAD Magazine, 26, 168
Mafalda, 15
Marvel Comics, 5, 7, 13, 41, 52, 178n1
Marvel Romance Redux, 116
MEChA, 27, 108, 169–70
meritocracy, 108, 154, 156
Mexican Americans, 8, 16, 28, 37, 45, 54, 65–66, 98, 132, 145, 148, 163, 175, 184n3
Mexican threat, 80, 117
Mickey Mouse, 75
Migra Mouse, 29, 70–128, 136, 179n15
migration, 8, 14, 38–40, 42, 45, 48–53, 56–57, 60–62, 65–66, 74, 79–85, 100, 125
Mike, 145–46
Miller, Frank, 13
Miller, Todd, 112
Million to Juan, A, 121
Modern Family, 5
monocultural norm, 8, 55, 64, 69
monolingualism, 107
Mundo Hispánico, 4

NAFTA (North American Free Trade Agreement), 83
Nash, John, 148
national-origin discrimination, 149
Navarro, Rafael, 8, 39, 48, 52–54, 56, 58, 69, 132, 180n11
NBC, 29, 144
Neto, 28, 161–63, 166
New York Times, 20, 74, 112, 116–17, 142
Nixon, Richard M., 16, 93
NOI (Nation of Islam), 96
noir, 8, 48, 52–54
normative cultural order, 8
normative culture, 82
NPR, 29, 140–41
Nuevo Georgia, El, 4

Obama, Barack, 3–4, 23, 74–75, 114, 150, 157, 173–74, 182n5
Olmos, Edward James, 16, 106
Operation Gatekeeper, 116–18
O'Reilly, Bill, 6, 32, 108
Orientalism, 123

Pilgrims, 85, 87–88
Pocho, 26–27, 29, 32, 121, 171, 176
Portado, Daniel D., 27–28, 171
Posada, José Guadalupe, 121, 132
Proposition 187, 27, 75, 78–81, 113, 122, 127
Proposition 203, 103
Proposition 227, 106

Question 2, 109
Quino (Joaquín Salvador Lavado), ix–x, 15

Ramirez, Peter, 40
Reagan, Ronald, 44, 46, 72, 74–75, 79, 100, 107, 126, 184n44
Republican Party, 32, 100, 107–8, 173–74
Republicans, x, 24–25, 28, 32, 74, 79, 93, 95, 100–101, 106–9, 113, 127, 150, 154–55, 157–58, 173–74
Risso, Eduardo, 8, 39, 41, 65, 67–68
Rius (Eduardo del Río), 36
Roberts, John G., Jr., 133
Rocha, Cuco, 28, 130, 134, 136–42, 144–46, 150, 153–55, 157–59, 161, 164–67
Rocketo, 8, 15, 48–51
Rodriguez, Paul, 15–16, 121
Rodriguez, Richard, 107
Ross, Alex, 13

Sacco, Joe, 14, 82–83
Sánchez, Felix, 34
San Diego Convention, 100–102
Satrapi, Marjane, 14, 55
Schulz, Charles, 36, 44, 88, 161
Schwarzenegger, Arnold, 24, 32, 126–27, 173, 184n45
self-deportation, 28, 179n17
Sierra Club, 119
Simpson-Mazzoli Act, 72–73
Simpson-Rodino Act (Immigration Reform and Control Act of 1986), 44, 72–73
Sodi, Thalía, 147
Sonambulo, 8, 48, 52–57, 59, 132, 180n11
Sotomayor, Sonia, 11, 133, 185n4
Spanglish, 27, 105, 129, 132, 162
Spiegelman, Art, 13, 55
Stand and Deliver, 106
standard cultural ideology, 130, 152–53, 162–64, 166
style of drawing, 88
superheroes, 6–7, 13, 40, 180n2

Telemundo, 28–29, 140
Televisa, 147
terrorists, 122, 124
Thalía, 147
Top Shelf, 13
Trillo, Carlos, 8, 39, 65–68

Uderzo, Albert, 11
universal English, 141
Univision, 64, 140, 147
Unz, Ron, 81, 106, 109

Vampirella, ix
Vásquez, Alicia Sotero, 114–15
Vergara, Sofía, 5, 16
Vero, 28, 130, 137–40, 145, 147–48, 152–53, 155–56, 160, 165, 172
Vertigo, 13

Walt Disney Company, 75, 77
Wilson, Pete, 24, 28, 32, 75, 79, 81, 94–96, 98–100, 122, 126–27, 171, 173, 182n9

Your Brain on Latino Comics, 5, 180n9

www.ingramcontent.com/pod-product-compliance
Lightning Source LLC
Chambersburg PA
CBHW030624230426
43661CB00053B/2127